THE NOBILITY AND EXCELLENCE OF WOMEN, AND THE DEFECTS AND VICES OF MEN

THE
OTHER VOICE
IN
EARLY MODERN
EUROPE

A Series Edited by Margaret L. King and Albert Rabil Jr.

OTHER BOOKS IN THE SERIES

HENRICUS CORNELIUS AGRIPPA

*Declamation on the Nobility and
Preeminence of the Female Sex*

Edited and translated by Albert Rabil Jr.

LAURA CERETA

Collected Letters

Edited and translated by Diana Robin

TULLIA D'ARAGONA

Dialogue on the Infinity of Love

Edited and Translated by Rinaldina Russell
and Bruce Merry

CECILIA FERRAZZI

Autobiography of an Aspiring Saint

Edited and Translated by
Anne Jacobson Schutte

MODERATA FONTE

The Worth of Women

Edited and Translated by Virginia Cox

VERONICA FRANCO

Poems and Selected Letters

Edited and Translated by Ann Rosalind Jones
and Margaret F. Rosenthal

ANTONIA PULCI

*Florentine Drama for Convent
and Festival*

Translated by James Wyatt Cook
Edited by James Wyatt Cook and Barbara
Collier Cook

ANNA MARIA VAN SCHURMAN

*Whether a Christian Woman Should
Be Educated and Other Writings
from Her Intellectual Circle*

Edited and Translated by Joyce L. Irwin

Lucrezia Marinella

THE NOBILITY AND EXCELLENCE OF WOMEN, AND THE DEFECTS AND VICES OF MEN

✌

Edited and Translated by
Anne Dunhill

Introduction by
Letizia Panizza

THE UNIVERSITY OF CHICAGO PRESS
Chicago & London

Anne Dunhill is a novelist and translator who lives in London.
Letizia Panizza is a senior lecturer in Italian at Royal Holloway
College, University of London.

The University of Chicago Press, Chicago 60637
The University of Chicago Press, Ltd., London
© 1999 by The University of Chicago
All rights reserved. Published 1999
Printed in the United States of America
08 07 06 05 04 03 02 01 00 99   1 2 3 4 5

ISBN 0-226-50545-6 (cloth)
ISBN 0-226-50546-4 (paper)

This translation was supported by a generous grant
from the National Endowment for the Humanities.

Library of Congress Cataloging-in-Publication Data

Marinella, Lucrezia, d. 1653.
    [Nobiltà et l'eccellenza delle donne, co' difetti et mancamenti
degli uomoni. English]
    The nobility and excellence of women, and the defects and vices of
men
        p.   cm.—(Other voice in early modern Europe)
    Includes bibliographical references and index.
    ISBN 0-226-50545-6 (cloth : alk. paper).—ISBN 0-226-50546-4
(pbk. : alk. paper)
    1. Women—Early works to 1800.   2. Women—History—Renaissance,
1450–1600.   3. Women—Italy—History—Renaissance, 1450–1600.
I. Dunhill, Anne.   II. Panizza, Letizia.   III. Title.   IV. Series.
HQ1148.M2713   1999
305.4—dc21   99-39095
                                                                              CIP

CONTENTS

THE OTHER VOICE IN
EARLY MODERN EUROPE:
INTRODUCTION TO THE SERIES

Margaret L. King and Albert Rabil Jr.

THE OLD VOICE AND THE OTHER VOICE

In western Europe and the United States women are nearing equality in the professions, in business, and in politics. Most enjoy access to education, reproductive rights, and autonomy in financial affairs. Issues vital to women are on the public agenda: equal pay, child care, domestic abuse, breast cancer research, and curricular revision with an eye to the inclusion of women.

These recent achievements have their origins in things women (and some male supporters) said for the first time about six hundred years ago. Theirs is the "other voice," in contradistinction to the "first voice," the voice of the educated men who created Western culture. Coincident with a general reshaping of European culture in the period 1300 to 1700 (called the Renaissance or early modern period), questions of female equality and opportunity were raised that still resound and are still unresolved.

The "other voice" emerged against the backdrop of a three-thousand-year history of misogyny—the hatred of women—rooted in the civilizations related to Western culture: Hebrew, Greek, Roman, and Christian. Misogyny inherited from these traditions pervaded the intellectual, medical, legal, religious, and social systems that developed during the European Middle Ages.

The following pages describe the misogynistic tradition inherited by early modern Europeans, and the new tradition which the "other voice" called into being to challenge reigning assumptions. This review should serve as a framework for the understanding of the texts published in the series "The Other Voice in Early Modern Europe." Introductions specific to each text and author follow this essay in all the volumes of the series.

THE MISOGYNIST TRADITION, 500 B.C.E.–1500 C.E.

Embedded in the philosophical and medical theories of the ancient Greeks were perceptions of the female as inferior to the male in both mind and body. Similarly, the structure of civil legislation inherited from the ancient Romans was biased against women, and the views on women developed by Christian thinkers out of the Hebrew Bible and the Christian New Testament were negative and disabling. Literary works composed in the vernacular language of ordinary people, and widely recited or read, conveyed these negative assumptions. The social networks within which most women lived—those of the family and the institutions of the Roman Catholic church—were shaped by this misogynist tradition and sharply limited the areas in which women might act in and upon the world.

GREEK PHILOSOPHY AND FEMALE NATURE. Greek biology assumed that women were inferior to men and defined them merely as childbearers and housekeepers. This view was authoritatively expressed in the works of the philosopher Aristotle.

Aristotle thought in dualities. He considered action superior to inaction, form (the inner design or structure of any object) superior to matter, completion to incompletion, possession to deprivation. In each of these dualities, he associated the male principle with the superior quality and the female with the inferior. "The male principle in nature," he argued, "is associated with active, formative and perfected characteristics, while the female is passive, material and deprived, desiring the male in order to become complete.[1] Men are always identified with virile qualities, such as judgment, courage, and stamina; women with their opposites—irrationality, cowardice, and weakness.

The masculine principle was considered to be superior even in the womb. Man's semen, Aristotle believed, created the form of a new human creature, while the female body contributed only matter. (The existence of the ovum, and the other facts of human embryology, were not established until the seventeenth century.) Although the later Greek physician Galen believed that there was a female component in generation, contributed by "female semen," the followers of both Aristotle and Galen saw the male role in human generation as more active and more important.

In the Aristotelian view, the male principle sought always to reproduce itself. The creation of a female was always a mistake, therefore, resulting from an imperfect act of generation. Every female born was considered a

---

1. Aristotle, Physics, 1.9 192a20–24, in *The Complete Works of Aristotle*, ed. Jonathan Barnes, rev. Oxford translation, 2 vols. (Princeton, 1984), 1:328.

"defective" or "mutilated" male (as Aristotle's terminology has variously been translated), a "monstrosity" of nature.[2]

For Greek theorists, the biology of males and females was the key to their psychology. The female was softer and more docile, more apt to be despondent, querulous, and deceitful. Being incomplete, moreover, she craved sexual fulfillment in intercourse with a male. The male was intellectual, active, and in control of his passions.

These psychological polarities derived from the theory that the universe consisted of four elements (earth, fire, air, and water), expressed in human bodies as four "humors" (black bile, yellow bile, blood, and phlegm) considered respectively dry, hot, damp, and cold, and corresponding to mental states ("melancholic," "choleric," "sanguine," "phlegmatic"). In this schematization, the male, sharing the principles of earth and fire, was dry and hot; the female, sharing the principles of air and water, was cold and damp.

Female psychology was further affected by her dominant organ, the uterus (womb), *hystera* in Greek. The passions generated by the womb made women lustful, deceitful, talkative, irrational, indeed—when these affects were in excess—"hysterical."

Aristotle's biology also had social and political consequences. If the male principle was superior and the female inferior, then in the household, as in the state, men should rule and women must be subordinate. That hierarchy did not rule out the companionship of husband and wife, whose cooperation was necessary for the welfare of children and the preservation of property. Such mutuality supported male preeminence.

Aristotle's teacher, Plato, suggested a different possibility: that men and women might possess the same virtues. The setting for this proposal is the imaginary and ideal Republic that Plato sketches in his dialogue of that name. Here, for a privileged elite capable of leading wisely, all distinctions of class and wealth dissolve, as do consequently those of gender. Without households or property, as Plato constructs his ideal society, there is no need for the subordination of women. Women may, therefore, be educated to the same level as men to assume leadership responsibilities. Plato's Republic remained imaginary, however. In real societies, the subordination of women remained the norm and the prescription.

The views of women inherited from the Greek philosophical tradition became the basis for medieval thought. In the thirteenth century, the supreme scholastic philosopher Thomas Aquinas, among others, still echoed

2. Aristotle, *Generation of Animals*, 2.3 737a27–28 (Barnes, 1:1144).

Aristotle's views of human reproduction, of male and female personalities, and of the preeminent male role in the social hierarchy.

ROMAN LAW AND THE FEMALE CONDITION. Roman law, like Greek philosophy, underlay medieval thought and shaped medieval society. The ancient belief that adult, property-owning men should administer households and make decisions affecting the community at large is the very fulcrum of Roman law.

Around 450 B.C.E., during Rome's Republican era, the community's customary law was recorded (legendarily) on the Twelve Tables, erected in the city's central forum. It was later elaborated by professional jurists whose activity increased in the imperial era, when much new legislation, especially on issues affecting family and inheritance, was passed. This growing, changing body of laws was eventually codified in the *Corpus of Civil Law* under the direction of the emperor Justinian, generations after the empire ceased to be ruled from Rome. That *Corpus*, read and commented upon by medieval scholars from the eleventh century on, inspired the legal systems of most of the cities and kingdoms of Europe.

Laws regarding dowries, divorce, and inheritance most pertain to women. Since those laws aimed to maintain and preserve property, the women concerned were those from the property-owning minority. Their subordination to male family members points to the even greater subordination of lower-class and slave women, about whom the laws speak little.

In the early Republic, the *paterfamilias*, "father of the family," possessed *patria potestas*, "paternal power." The term *pater*, "father," in both these cases does not necessarily mean biological father, but householder. The father was the person who owned the household's property and, indeed, its human members. The *paterfamilias* had absolute power—including the power, rarely exercised, of life or death—over his wife, his children, and his slaves, as much as over his cattle.

Male children could be "emancipated," an act that granted legal autonomy and the right to own property. Males over the age of fourteen could be emancipated by a special grant from the father, or automatically by their father's death. But females never could be emancipated; instead, they passed from the authority of their father to a husband or, if widowed or orphaned while still unmarried, to a guardian or tutor.

Marriage under its traditional form placed the woman under her husband's authority, or *manus*. He could divorce her on grounds of adultery, drinking wine, or stealing from the household, but she could not divorce him. She could possess no property in her own right, nor bequeath any to her children upon her death. When her husband died, the household property passed not to her but to his male heirs. And when her father died, she had no claim to any family inheritance, which was directed to her brothers or more remote male relatives. The effect of these laws was to exclude women from civil society, itself based on property ownership.

In the later Republican and Imperial periods, these rules were significantly modified. Women rarely married according to the traditional form, but according to the form of "free" marriage. That practice allowed a woman to remain under her father's authority, to possess property given her by her father (most frequently the "dowry," recoverable from the husband's household in the event of his death), and to inherit from her father. She could also bequeath property to her own children and divorce her husband, just as he could divorce her.

Despite this greater freedom, women still suffered enormous disability under Roman law. Heirs could belong only to the father's side, never the mother's. Moreover, although she could bequeath her property to her children, she could not establish a line of succession in doing so. A woman was "the beginning and end of her own family," growled the jurist Ulpian. Moreover, women could play no public role. They could not hold public office, represent anyone in a legal case, or even witness a will. Women had only a private existence, and no public personality.

The dowry system, the guardian, women's limited ability to transmit wealth, and their total political disability are all features of Roman law adopted, although modified according to local customary laws, by the medieval communities of western Europe.

CHRISTIAN DOCTRINE AND WOMEN'S PLACE. The Hebrew Bible and the Christian New Testament authorized later writers to limit women to the realm of the family and to burden them with the guilt of original sin. The passages most fruitful for this purpose were the creation narratives in Genesis and sentences from the Epistles defining women's role within the Christian family and community.

Each of the first two chapters of Genesis contains a creation narrative. In the first "God created humankind in his image, in the image of God he created them; male and female he created them" (NRSV, Genesis 1:27). In the second, God created Eve from Adam's rib (2:21–23). Christian theologians relied principally on Genesis 2 for their understanding of the relation between man and woman, interpreting the creation of Eve from Adam as proof of her subordination to him.

The creation story in Genesis 2 leads to that of the temptations in Genesis 3: of Eve by the wily serpent, and of Adam by Eve. As read by Christian theologians from Tertullian to Thomas Aquinas, the narrative made Eve responsible for the Fall and its consequences. She instigated the act; she deceived her husband; she suffered the greater punishment. Her disobedience made it necessary for Jesus to be incarnated and to die on the cross. From the pulpit, moralists and preachers for centuries conveyed to women the guilt that they bore for original sin.

The Epistles offered advice to early Christians on building communities of the faithful. Among the matters to be regulated was the place of women. Paul offered views favorable to women in Galatians 3:28: "There is neither Jew nor Greek, there is neither slave nor free, there is neither male nor female; for you are all one in Christ Jesus." Paul also referred to women as his coworkers and placed them on a par with himself and his male coworkers (Philippians 4:2–3; Romans 16:1–3; 1 Corinthians 16:19). Elsewhere Paul limited women's possibilities: "But I want you to understand that the head of every man is Christ, the head of a woman is her husband, and the head of Christ is God" (1 Corinthians 11:3).

Biblical passages by later writers (though attributed to Paul) enjoined women to forego jewels, expensive clothes, and elaborate coiffures; and they forbade women to "teach or have authority over men," telling them to "learn in silence with all submissiveness" as is proper for one responsible for sin, consoling them however with the thought that they would be saved through childbearing (1 Timothy 2:9–15). Other texts among the later Epistles defined women as the weaker sex, and emphasized their subordination to their husbands (1 Peter 3:7; Colossians 3:18; Ephesians 5:22–23).

These passages from the New Testament became the arsenal employed by theologians of the early church to transmit negative attitudes toward women to medieval Christian culture—above all, Tertullian ("On the Apparel of Women"), Jerome (*Against Jovinian*), and Augustine (*The Literal Meaning of Genesis*).

THE IMAGE OF WOMEN IN MEDIEVAL LITERATURE. The philosophical, legal, and religious traditions born in antiquity formed the basis of the medieval intellectual synthesis wrought by trained thinkers, mostly clerics, writing in Latin and based largely in universities. The vernacular literary tradition that developed alongside the learned tradition also spoke about female nature and women's roles. Medieval stories, poems, and epics were infused with misogyny. They portrayed most women as lustful and deceitful, while praising good housekeepers and loyal wives, or replicas of the Virgin Mary, or the female saints and martyrs.

There is an exception in the movement of "courtly love" that evolved in southern France from the twelfth century. Courtly love was the erotic love between a nobleman and noblewoman, the latter usually superior in social rank. It was always adulterous. From the conventions of courtly love derive modern Western notions of romantic love. The phenomenon has had an impact disproportionate to its size, for it affected only a tiny elite, and very few women. The exaltation of the female lover probably does not reflect a higher evaluation of women, or a step toward their sexual liberation. More likely it gives expression to the social and sexual tensions besetting the knightly class at a specific historical juncture.

The literary fashion of courtly love was on the wane by the thirteenth century, when the widely read *Romance of the Rose* was composed in French by two authors of significantly different dispositions. Guillaume de Lorris composed the initial four thousand verses around 1235, and Jean de Meun added about seventeen thousand verses—more than four times the original—around 1265.

The fragment composed by Guillaume de Lorris stands squarely in the courtly love tradition. Here the poet, in a dream, is admitted into a walled garden where he finds a magic fountain in which a rosebush is reflected. He longs to pick one rose but the thorns around it prevent his doing so, even as he is wounded by arrows from the God of Love, whose commands he agrees to obey. The remainder of this part of the poem recounts the poet's unsuccessful efforts to pluck the rose.

The longer part of the Romance by Jean de Meun also describes a dream. But here allegorical characters give long didactic speeches, providing a social satire on a variety of themes, including those pertaining to women. Love is an anxious and tormented state, the poem explains, women are greedy and manipulative, marriage is miserable, beautiful women are lustful, ugly ones cease to please, and a chaste woman is as rare as a black swan.

Shortly after Jean de Meun completed *The Romance of the Rose*, Mathéolus penned his *Lamentations*, a long Latin diatribe against marriage translated into French about a century later. The *Lamentations* sum up medieval attitudes toward women, and they provoked the important response by Christine de Pizan in her *Book of the City of Ladies*.

In 1355, Giovanni Boccaccio wrote *Il Corbaccio*, another anti-feminist manifesto, though ironically by an author whose other works pioneered new directions in Renaissance thought. The former husband of his lover appears to Boccaccio, condemning his unmoderated lust and detailing the defects of women. Boccaccio concedes at the end "how much men naturally surpass women in nobility"[3] and is cured of his desires.

---

3. Giovanni Boccaccio, *The Corbaccio or The Labyrinth of Love*, trans. and ed. Anthony K. Cassell (Binghamton, N.Y.; rev. paper ed., 1993), 71.

WOMEN'S ROLES: THE FAMILY. The negative perceptions of women expressed in the intellectual tradition are also implicit in the actual roles that women played in European society. Assigned to subordinate positions in the household and the church, they were barred from significant participation in public life.

Medieval European households, like those in antiquity and in non-Western civilizations, were headed by males. It was the male serf, or peasant, feudal lord, town merchant, or citizen who was polled or taxed or who succeeded to an inheritance or had any acknowledged public role, although his wife or widow could stand on a temporary basis as a surrogate for him. From about 1100, the position of property-holding males was enhanced further. Inheritance was confined to the male, or agnate, line—with depressing consequences for women.

A wife never fully belonged to her husband's family or a daughter to her father's family. She left her father's house young to marry whomever her parents chose. Her dowry was managed by her husband and normally passed to her children by him at her death.

A married woman's life was occupied nearly constantly with cycles of pregnancy, childbearing, and lactation. Women bore children through all the years of their fertility, and many died in childbirth before the end of that term. They also bore responsibility for raising young children up to six or seven. That responsibility was shared in the propertied classes, since it was common for a wet nurse to take over the job of breastfeeding, and servants took over other chores.

Women trained their daughters in the household responsibilities appropriate to their status, nearly always in tasks associated with textiles: spinning, weaving, sewing, embroidering. Their sons were sent out of the house as apprentices or students, or their training was assumed by fathers in later childhood and adolescence. On the death of her husband, a woman's children became the responsibility of his family. She generally did not take "his" children with her to a new marriage or back to her father's house, except sometimes in artisan classes.

Women also worked. Rural peasants performed farm chores, merchant wives often practiced their husbands' trades, the unmarried daughters of the urban poor worked as servants or prostitutes. All wives produced or embellished textiles and did the housekeeping, while wealthy ones managed servants. These labors were unpaid or poorly paid, but often contributed substantially to family wealth.

WOMEN'S ROLES: THE CHURCH. Membership in a household, whether a father's or a husband's, meant for women a lifelong subordination to others. In western Europe, the Roman Catholic church offered an alternative to the career of wife and mother. A woman could enter a convent parallel in function to the monasteries for men that evolved in the early Christian centuries.

In the convent, a woman pledged herself to a celibate life, lived according to strict community rules, and worshiped daily. Often the convent offered training in Latin, allowing some women to become considerable scholars and authors, as well as scribes, artists, and musicians. For women who chose the conventual life, the benefits could be enormous, but for numerous others placed in convents by paternal choice, the life could be restrictive and burdensome.

The conventual life declined as an alternative for women as the modern age approached. Reformed monastic institutions resisted responsibility for related female orders. The church increasingly restricted female institutional life by insisting on closer male supervision.

Women often sought other options. Some joined the communities of laywomen that sprang up spontaneously in the thirteenth century in the urban zones of western Europe, especially in Flanders and Italy. Some joined the heretical movements flourishing in late medieval Christendom, whose anticlerical and often antifamily positions particularly appealed to women. In these communities, some women were acclaimed as "holy women" or "saints," while others often were condemned as frauds or heretics.

Though the options offered to women by the church were sometimes less than satisfactory, sometimes they were richly rewarding. After 1520, the convent remained an option only in Roman Catholic territories. Protestantism engendered an ideal of marriage as a heroic endeavor, and appeared to place husband and wife on a more equal footing. Sermons and treatises, however, still called for female subordination and obedience.

THE OTHER VOICE, 1300–1700

Misogyny was so long established in European culture when the modern era opened that to dismantle it was a monumental labor. The process began as part of a larger cultural movement that entailed the critical reexamination of ideas inherited from the ancient and medieval past. The humanists launched that critical reexamination.

THE HUMANIST FOUNDATION. Originating in Italy in the fourteenth century, humanism quickly became the dominant intellectual movement in Europe. Spreading in the sixteenth century from Italy to the rest of Europe, it fueled the literary, scientific, and philosophical movements of the era, and laid the basis for the eighteenth-century Enlightenment.

Humanists regarded the scholastic philosophy of medieval universities as out of touch with the realities of urban life. They found in the rhetorical discourse of classical Rome a language adapted to civic life and public speech. They learned to read, speak, and write classical Latin, and eventually classical Greek. They founded schools to teach others to do so, establishing the pattern for elementary and secondary education for the next three hundred years.

In the service of complex government bureaucracies, humanists employed their skills to write eloquent letters, deliver public orations, and formulate public policy. They developed new scripts for copying manuscripts and used the new printing press for the dissemination of texts, for which they created methods of critical editing.

Humanism was a movement led by men who accepted the evaluation of women in ancient texts and generally shared the misogynist perceptions of their culture. (Female humanists, as will be seen, did not.) Yet humanism also opened the door to the critique of the misogynist tradition. By calling authors, texts, and ideas into question, it made possible the fundamental rereading of the whole intellectual tradition that was required in order to free women from cultural prejudice and social subordination.

A DIFFERENT CITY. The other voice first appeared when, after so many centuries, the accumulation of misogynist concepts evoked a response from a capable female defender, Christine de Pizan. Introducing her *Book of the City of Ladies* (1405), she described how she was affected by reading Mathéolus's *Lamentations:* "Just the sight of this book . . . made me wonder how it happened that so many different men . . . are so inclined to express both in speaking and in their treatises and writings so many wicked insults about women and their behavior."[4] These statements impelled her to detest herself "and the entire feminine sex, as though we were monstrosities in nature."[5]

The remainder of the *Book of the City of Ladies* presents a justification of the female sex and a vision of an ideal community of women. A pioneer, she has not only received the misogynist message, but she rejects it. From the fourteenth to seventeenth century, a huge body of literature accumulated that responded to the dominant tradition.

The result was a literary explosion consisting of works by both men and women, in Latin and in vernacular languages: works enumerating the

4. Christine de Pizan, *The Book of the City of Ladies*, trans. Earl Jeffrey Richards; foreword by Marina Warner (New York, 1982), 1.1.1., pp. 3–4.

5. Ibid., 1.1.1–2, p. 5.

achievements of notable women; works rebutting the main accusations made against women; works arguing for the equal education of men and women; works defining and redefining women's proper role in the family, at court, and in public; and works describing women's lives and experiences. Recent monographs and articles have begun to hint at the great range of this phenomenon, involving probably several thousand titles. The protofeminism of these "other voices" constitute a significant fraction of the literary product of the early modern era.

THE CATALOGUES. Around 1365, the same Boccaccio whose *Corbaccio* rehearses the usual charges against female nature wrote another work, *Concerning Famous Women*. A humanist treatise drawing on classical texts, it praised 106 notable women—100 of them from pagan Greek and Roman antiquity, and 6 from the religious and cultural tradition since antiquity—and helped make all readers aware of a sex normally condemned or forgotten. Boccaccio's outlook, nevertheless, was misogynist, for it singled out for praise those women who possessed the traditional virtues of chastity, silence, and obedience. Women who were active in the public realm, for example, rulers and warriors, were depicted as suffering terrible punishments for entering into the masculine sphere. Women were his subject, but Boccaccio's standard remained male.

Christine de Pizan's *Book of the City of Ladies* contains a second catalogue, one responding specifically to Boccaccio's. Where Boccaccio portrays female virtue as exceptional, she depicts it as universal. Many women in history were leaders, or remained chaste despite the lascivious approaches of men, or were visionaries and brave martyrs.

The work of Boccaccio inspired a series of catalogues of illustrious women of the biblical, classical, Christian, and local past: works by Alvaro de Luna, Jacopo Filippo Foresti (1497), Brantôme, Pierre Le Moyne, Pietro Paolo de Ribera (who listed 845 figures), and many others. Whatever their embedded prejudices, these catalogues of illustrious women drove home to the public the possibility of female excellence.

THE DEBATE. At the same time, many questions remained: Could a woman be virtuous? Could she perform noteworthy deeds? Was she even, strictly speaking, of the same human species as men? These questions were debated over four centuries, in French, German, Italian, Spanish, and English, by authors male and female, among Catholics, Protestants, and Jews, in ponderous volumes and breezy pamphlets. The whole literary phenomenon has been called the *querelle des femmes*, the "woman question."

The opening volley of this battle occurred in the first years of the fifteenth century, in a literary debate sparked by Christine de Pizan. She exchanged letters critical of Jean de Meun's contribution to *The Romance of the Rose* with two French humanists and royal secretaries, Jean de Montreuil and Gontier Col. When the matter became public, Jean Gerson, one of Europe's leading theologians, supported de Pizan's arguments against de Meun, for the moment silencing the opposition.

The debate resurfaced repeatedly over the next two hundred years. *The Triumph of Women* (1438) by Juan Rodríguez de la Camara (or Juan Rodríguez del Padron) struck a new note by presenting arguments for the superiority of women to men. *The Champion of Women* (1440–42) by Martin Le Franc addresses once again the misogynist claims of *The Romance of the Rose*, and offers counterevidence of female virtue and achievement.

A cameo of the debate on women is included in *The Courtier*, one of the most read books of the era, published by the Italian Baldassare Castiglione in 1528 and immediately translated into other European vernaculars. *The Courtier* depicts a series of evenings at the court of the Duke of Urbino in which many men and some women of the highest social stratum amuse themselves by discussing a range of literary and social issues. The "woman question" is a pervasive theme throughout, and the third of its four books is devoted entirely to that issue.

In a verbal duel, Gasparo Pallavicino and Giuliano de' Medici present the main claims of the two traditions—the prevailing misogynist one, and the newly emerging alternative one. Gasparo argues the innate inferiority of women and their inclination to vice. Only in bearing children do they profit the world. Giuliano counters that women share the same spiritual and mental capacities as men and may excel in wisdom and action. Men and women are of the same essence: just as no stone can be more perfectly a stone than another, so no human being can be more perfectly human than others, whether male or female. It was an astonishing assertion, boldly made to an audience as large as all Europe.

THE TREATISES. Humanism provided the materials for a positive counterconcept to the misogyny embedded in scholastic philosophy and law, and inherited from the Greek, Roman, and Christian pasts. A series of humanist treatises on marriage and family, on education and deportment, and on the nature of women helped construct these new perspectives.

The works by Francesco Barbaro and Leon Battista Alberti, respectively *On Marriage* (1415) and *On the Family* (1434–37), far from defending female equality, reasserted women's responsibilities for rearing children and managing the housekeeping while being obedient, chaste, and silent. Nevertheless, they served the cause of reexamining the issue of women's nature by placing domestic issues at the center of scholarly concern and reopening the pertinent classical texts. In addition, Barbaro emphasized the companionate nature of marriage and the importance of a wife's spiritual and mental qualities for the well-being of the family.

These themes reappear in later humanist works on marriage and the education of women by Juan Luis Vives and Erasmus. Both were moderately sympathetic to the condition of women, without reaching beyond the usual masculine prescriptions for female behavior.

An outlook more favorable to women characterizes the nearly unknown work *In Praise of Women* (ca. 1487) by the Italian humanist Bartolommeo Goggio. In addition to providing a catalogue of illustrious women, Goggio argued that male and female are the same in essence, but that women (reworking from quite a new angle the Adam and Eve narrative) are actually superior. In the same vein, the Italian humanist Mario Equicola asserted the spiritual equality of men and women in *On Women* (1501). In 1525, Galeazzo Flavio Capra (or Capella) published his work *On the Excellence and Dignity of Women*. This humanist tradition of treatises defending the worthiness of women culminates in the work of Henricus Cornelius Agrippa, *On the Nobility and Preeminence of the Female Sex*. No work by a male humanist more succinctly or explicitly presents the case for female dignity.

THE WITCH BOOKS. While humanists grappled with the issues pertaining to women and family, other learned men turned their attention to what they perceived as a very great problem: witches. Witch-hunting manuals, explorations of the witch phenomenon, and even defenses of witches are not at first glance pertinent to the tradition of the other voice. But they do relate in this way: most accused witches were women. The hostility aroused by supposed witch activity is comparable to the hostility aroused by women. The evil deeds the victims of the hunt were charged with were exaggerations of the vices to which, many believed, all women were prone.

The connection between the witch accusation and the hatred of women is explicit in the notorious witch-hunting manual, *The Hammer of Witches* (1486), by two Dominican inquisitors, Heinrich Krämer and Jacob Sprenger. Here the inconstancy, deceitfulness, and lustfulness traditionally associated with women are depicted in exaggerated form as the core features of witch behavior. These inclined women to make a bargain with the devil—sealed by sexual intercourse—by which they acquired unholy powers. Such bizarre claims, far from being rejected by rational men, were broadcast by intellectuals. The German Ulrich Molitur, the Frenchman Nicolas Rémy, the Italian Stefano Guazzo coolly informed the public of sinister orgies and midnight pacts with the devil. The celebrated French jurist, historian, and political philosopher Jean Bodin argued that, because women were especially prone to diabolism, regular legal procedures could properly be suspended in order to try those accused of this "exceptional crime."

A few experts, such as the physician Johann Weyer, a student of Agrippa's, raised their voices in protest. In 1563, Weyer explained the witch phenomenon thus, without discarding belief in diabolism: the devil deluded foolish old women afflicted by melancholia, causing them to believe that they had magical powers. His rational skepticism, which had good credibility in the community of the learned, worked to revise the conventional views of women and witchcraft.

WOMEN'S WORKS. To the many categories of works produced on the question of women's worth must be added nearly all works written by women. A woman writing was in herself a statement of women's claim to dignity.

Only a few women wrote anything prior to the dawn of the modern era, for three reasons. First, they rarely received the education that would enable them to write. Second, they were not admitted to the public roles—as administrator, bureaucrat, lawyer or notary, university professor—in which they might gain knowledge of the kinds of things the literate public thought worth writing about. Third, the culture imposed silence upon women, considering speaking out a form of unchastity. Given these conditions, it is remarkable that any women wrote. Those who did before the fourteenth century were almost always nuns or religious women whose isolation made their pronouncements more acceptable.

From the fourteenth century on, the volume of women's writings increased. Women continued to write devotional literature, although not always as cloistered nuns. They also wrote diaries, often intended as keepsakes for their children; books of advice to their sons and daughters; letters to family members and friends; and family memoirs, in a few cases elaborate enough to be considered histories.

A few women wrote works directly concerning the "woman question," and some of these, such as the humanists Isotta Nogarola, Cassandra Fedele, Laura Cereta, and Olympia Morata, were highly trained. A few were professional writers, living by the income of their pen: the very first among them Christine de Pizan, noteworthy in this context as in so many others. In addition to *Book of the City of Ladies* and her critiques of *The Romance of the Rose*, she wrote *The Treasure of the City of Ladies* (a guide to social decorum for women), an advice book for her son, much courtly verse, and a full-scale history of the reign of King Charles V of France.

WOMEN PATRONS. Women who did not themselves write but encouraged others to do so boosted the development of an alternative tradition. Highly placed women patrons supported authors, artists, musicians, poets, and learned men. Such patrons, drawn mostly from the Italian elites and the courts of northern Europe, figure disproportionately as the dedicatees of the important works of early feminism.

For a start, it might be noted that the catalogues of Boccaccio and Alvaro de Luna were dedicated to the Florentine noblewoman Andrea Acciaiuoli and to Doña María, first wife of King Juan II of Castile, while the French translation of Boccaccio's work was commissioned by Anne of Brittany, wife of King Charles VIII of France. The humanist treatises of Goggio, Equicola, Vives, and Agrippa were dedicated, respectively, to Eleanora of Aragon, wife of Ercole I d'Este, duke of Ferrara; to Margherita Cantelma of Mantua; to Catherine of Aragon, wife of King Henry VIII of England; and to Margaret, duchess of Austria and regent of the Netherlands. As late as 1696, Mary Astell's *Serious Proposal to the Ladies, for the Advancement of Their True and Greatest Interest* was dedicated to Princess Anne of Denmark.

These authors presumed that their efforts would be welcome to female patrons, or they may have written at the bidding of those patrons. Silent themselves, perhaps even unresponsive, these loftily placed women helped shape the tradition of the other voice.

THE ISSUES. The literary forms and patterns in which the tradition of the other voice presented itself have now been sketched. It remains to highlight the major issues about which this tradition crystallizes. In brief, there are four problems to which our authors return again and again, in plays and catalogues, in verse and in letters, in treatises and dialogues, in every language: the problem of chastity, the problem of power, the problem of speech, and the problem of knowledge. Of these the greatest, preconditioning the others, is the problem of chastity.

THE PROBLEM OF CHASTITY. In traditional European culture, as in those of antiquity and others around the globe, chastity was perceived as woman's quintessential virtue—in contrast to courage, or generosity, or leadership, or rationality, seen as virtues characteristic of men. Opponents of women charged them with insatiable lust. Women themselves and their defenders—without disputing the validity of the standard—responded that women were capable of chastity.

The requirement of chastity kept women at home, silenced them, isolated them, left them in ignorance. It was the source of all other impediments. Why was it so important to the society of men, of whom chastity was not required, and who, more often than not, considered it their right to violate the chastity of any woman they encountered?

Female chastity ensured the continuity of the male-headed household. If a man's wife was not chaste, he could not be sure of the legitimacy of his offspring. If they were not his, and they acquired his property, it was not his household, but some other man's, that had endured. If his daughter was not chaste, she could not be transferred to another man's household as his wife, and he was dishonored.

The whole system of the integrity of the household and the transmission of property was bound up in female chastity. Such a requirement pertained only to property-owning classes, of course. Poor women could not expect to maintain their chastity, least of all if they were in contact with high-status men to whom all women but those of their own household were prey.

In Catholic Europe, the requirement of chastity was further buttressed by moral and religious imperatives. Original sin was inextricably linked with the sexual act. Virginity was seen as heroic virtue, far more impressive than, say, the avoidance of idleness or greed. Monasticism, the cultural institution that dominated medieval Europe for centuries, was grounded in the renunciation of the flesh. The Catholic reform of the eleventh century imposed a similar standard on all the clergy, and a heightened awareness of sexual requirements on all the laity. Although men were asked to be chaste, female unchastity was much worse: it led to the devil, as Eve had led mankind to sin.

To such requirements, women and their defenders protested their innocence. Following the example of holy women who had escaped the requirements of family and sought the religious life, some women began to conceive of female communities as alternatives both to family and to the cloister. Christine de Pizan's city of ladies was such a community. Moderata Fonte and Mary Astell envisioned others. The luxurious salons of the French *précieuses* of the seventeenth century, or the comfortable English drawing rooms of the next, may have been born of the same impulse. Here women might not only escape, if briefly, the subordinate position that life in the family entailed, but they might make claims to power, exercise their capacity for speech, and display their knowledge.

THE PROBLEM OF POWER. Women were excluded from power: the whole cultural tradition insisted upon it. Only men were citizens, only men bore arms, only men could be chiefs or lords or kings. There were exceptions that did not disprove the rule, when wives or widows or mothers took the place of men, awaiting their return or the maturation of a male heir. A woman who attempted to rule in her own right was perceived as an anomaly, a monster, at once a deformed woman and an insufficient male, sexually confused and, consequently, unsafe.

The association of such images with women who held or sought power explains some otherwise odd features of early modern culture. Queen Elizabeth I of England, one of the few women to hold full regal authority in

European history, played with such male/female images— positive ones, of course—in representing herself to her subjects. She was a prince, and manly, even though she was female. She was also (she claimed) virginal, a condition absolutely essential if she was to avoid the attacks of her opponents. Catherine de' Medici, who ruled France as widow and regent for her sons, also adopted such imagery in defining her position. She chose as one symbol the figure of Artemisia, an androgynous ancient warrior-heroine, who combined a female persona with masculine powers.

Power in a woman, without such sexual imagery, seems to have been indigestible by the culture. A rare note was struck by the Englishman Sir Thomas Elyot in his *Defence of Good Women* (1540), justifying both women's participation in civic life and their prowess in arms. The old tune was sung by the Scots reformer John Knox in his *First Blast of the Trumpet against the Monstrous Regiment of Women* (1558), for whom rule by women, defects in nature, was a hideous contradiction in terms.

The confused sexuality of the imagery of female potency was not reserved for rulers. Any woman who excelled was likely to be called an Amazon, recalling the self-mutilated warrior women of antiquity who repudiated all men, gave up their sons, and raised only their daughters. She was often said to have "exceeded her sex," or to have possessed "masculine virtue"—as the very fact of conspicuous excellence conferred masculinity, even on the female subject. The catalogues of notable women often showed those female heroes dressed in armor, armed to the teeth, like men. Amazonian heroines romp through the epics of the age—Ariosto's *Orlando Furioso* (1532), Spenser's *Faerie Queene* (1590–1609). Excellence in a woman was perceived as a claim for power, and power was reserved for the masculine realm. A woman who possessed either was masculinized, and lost title to her own female identity.

THE PROBLEM OF SPEECH. Just as power had a sexual dimension when it was claimed by women, so did speech. A good woman spoke little. Excessive speech was an indication of unchastity. By speech women seduced men. Eve had lured Adam into sin by her speech. Accused witches were commonly accused of having spoken abusively, or irrationally, or simply too much. As enlightened a figure as Francesco Barbaro insisted on silence in a woman, which he linked to her perfect unanimity with her husband's will and her unblemished virtue (her chastity). Another Italian humanist, Leonardo Bruni, in advising a noblewoman on her studies, barred her not from speech, but from public speaking. That was reserved for men.

Related to the problem of speech was that of costume, another, if silent, form of self-expression. Assigned the task of pleasing men as their primary occupation, elite women often tended to elaborate costume, hairdressing, and the use of cosmetics. Clergy and secular moralists alike condemned these practices. The appropriate function of costume and adornment was to announce the status of a woman's husband or father. Any further indulgence in adornment was akin to unchastity.

THE PROBLEM OF KNOWLEDGE. When the Italian noblewoman Isotta Nogarola had begun to attain a reputation as a humanist, she was accused of incest—a telling instance of the association of learning in women with unchastity. That chilling association inclined any woman who was educated to deny that she was, or to make exaggerated claims of heroic chastity.

If educated women were pursued with suspicions of sexual misconduct, women seeking an education faced an even more daunting obstacle: the assumption that women were by nature incapable of learning, that reason was a particularly masculine ability. Just as they proclaimed their chastity, women and their defenders insisted upon their capacity for learning. The major work by a male writer on female education—*The Education of a Christian Woman: A Sixteenth-Century Manual*, by Juan Luis Vives (1523)—granted female capacity for intellection, but argued still that a woman's whole education was to be shaped around the requirement of chastity and a future within the household. Female writers of the following generations—Marie de Gournay in France, Anna Maria van Schurman in Holland, Mary Astell in England—began to envision other possibilities.

The pioneers of female education were the Italian women humanists who managed to attain a Latin literacy and knowledge of classical and Christian literature equivalent to that of prominent men. Their works implicitly and explicitly raise questions about women's social roles, defining problems that beset women attempting to break out of the cultural limits that had bound them. Like Christine de Pizan, who achieved an advanced education through her father's tutoring and her own devices, their bold questioning makes clear the importance of training. Only when women were educated to the same standard as male leaders would they be able to raise that other voice and insist on their dignity as human beings morally, intellectually, and legally equal to men.

THE OTHER VOICE. The other voice, a voice of protest, was mostly female, but also male. It spoke in the vernaculars and in Latin, in treatises and dialogues, plays and poetry, letters and diaries and pamphlets. It battered at the wall of misogynist beliefs that encircled women and raised a banner announcing its claims. The female was equal (or even superior) to the male in essential nature—moral, spiritual, intellectual. Women were capable of higher education, of holding positions of power and influence in the public realm, and of speaking and writing persuasively. The last bastion of masculine supremacy, centered on the notions of a woman's primary domestic responsibility and the requirement of female chastity, was not as yet assaulted—although visions of productive female communities as alternatives to the family indicated an awareness of the problem.

During the period 1300 to 1700, the other voice remained only a voice, and one only dimly heard. It did not result—yet—in an alteration of social patterns. Indeed, to this day, they have not entirely been altered. Yet the call for justice issued as long as six centuries ago by those writing in the tradition of the other voice must be recognized as the source and origin of the mature feminist tradition and of the realignment of social institutions accomplished in the modern age.

We would like to thank the volume editors in this series, who responded with many suggestions to an earlier draft of this introduction, making it a collaborative enterprise. Many of their suggestions and criticisms have resulted in revisions of this introduction, though we remain responsible for the final product.

PROJECTED TITLES IN THE SERIES

Giuseppa Eleonora Barbapiccola and Diamante Medaglia Faini, *The Education of Women*, edited and translated by Paula Findlen and Rebecca Messbarger

Marie Dentière, *Prefaces, Epistles, and History of the Deliverance of Geneva by the Protestants*, edited and translated by Mary B. McKinley

Isabella d'Este, *Selected Letters*, edited and translated by Deanna Shemek

Cassandra Fedele, *Letters and Orations*, edited and translated by Diana Robin

Marie de Gournay, *The Equality of Men and Women and Other Writings*, edited and translated by Richard Hillman and Colette Quesnel

Annibale Guasco, *Discussion with D. Lavinia, His Daughter, concerning the Manner of Conducting Oneself at Court*, edited and translated by Peggy Osborn

Olympia Morata, *Complete Writings*, edited and translated by Holt N. Parker

Isotta Nogarola, *Selected Letters*, edited by Margaret L. King and Albert Rabil Jr. and translated by Diana Robin, with an introduction by Margaret L. King

Christine de Pizan, *Debate Over the "Romance of the Rose,"* edited and translated by Tom Conley

François Poulain de la Barre, *The Equality of the Sexes* and *The Education of Women*, edited and translated by Albert Rabil Jr.

Sister Bartolomea Riccoboni, *Life and Death in a Venetian Convent: The Chronicle and Necrology of Corpus Domini, 1395–1463*, edited and translated by Daniel Bornstein

Olivia Sabuco, *The New Philosophy: True Medicine*, edited and translated by Gianna Pomata

Maria de San Jose, *Book of Recreations*, edited and translated by Alison Weber and Amanda Powell

Madeleine de Scudéry, *Orations and Rhetorical Dialogues*, edited and translated by Lillian Doherty and Jane Donawerth

Sara Copio Sullam, *Apologia and Other Writings*, edited and translated by Laura Stortoni

Arcangela Tarabotti, *Paternal Tyranny*, edited and translated by Letizia Panizza

Lucrezia Tornabuoni, *Sacred Narratives*, edited and translated by Jane Tylus

Juan Luis Vives, *The Education of a Christian Woman: A Sixteenth-Century Manual*, edited and translated by Charles Fantazzi

ACKNOWLEDGMENTS

I would like to express my warmest thanks to Letizia Panizza, who first introduced me to Italian Renaissance literature at Royal Holloway College, University of London and encouraged me to work on this translation. She has been a generous source of help throughout the project, on fine points of translation and on obscure references and, especially, in agreeing to write the introduction. I would also like to thank Rebecca Langlands for her enthusiastic and invaluable help over a long period of time in tracing Marinella's numerous and often obscure classical sources, and for translating many of the Latin passages into English. My thanks also to Virginia Cox for her advice and encouragement; and finally, my special gratitude to Albert Rabil Jr. for his unfailing support from across the Atlantic.

Anne Dunhill
London, 1999

INTRODUCTION TO THE TRANSLATION

Letizia Panizza

In her own lifetime (1571–1653), Lucrezia Marinella was described by Francesco Agostino della Chiesa as "a woman of wondrous eloquence and learning" who had become so famous that "it would be impossible to find anyone to equal let alone surpass her." Another contemporary, Cristofero Bronzino, pronounced her "exceptional in writing prose and poetry, most accomplished in sacred compositions, and a supreme expert in moral and natural philosophy." In addition, she was a "marvellous and truly learned woman," gifted not only with a "light, refined, elegant poetic style" but also "very well informed in philosophy, and very musical, singing and playing several instruments, particularly the lute, expertly and most harmoniously."[1] When we consider her achievements in letters and in demonstrating women's moral and intellectual equality, we realize that these words are no empty flattery. Marinella was a prolific, polished writer in many genres, and enjoyed enviable, perhaps unique, conditions for learning and writing. She was born into a professional family that encouraged her studies; she was not forced to enter the convent (like her contemporary Arcangela Tarabotti, 1604–52); neither was she pressured into early marriage nor did she die in childbirth (like her predecessor Moderata Fonte, 1555–92). She lived a

---

1. "Donna d' eloquenza e di dottrina mirabile, la quale . . . s' è inalzata tanto alto che . . . non potersi trovar chi uguagliar la possia, non che avanzarla," F. A. Della Chiesa, *Theatro delle donne letterate con un breve discorso della preminenza e perfettione del sesso donnesco* (Mondovì: G. Gislandi and G. T. Rossi, 1620), 214; "singolare nella Prosa e nel Verso, versatissima nelle sacre lettere, e peritissima nella Filosofia morale e naturale," C. Bronzino, *Della dignità e nobiltà delle donne* (Florence: Zanobi Pignoni, 1624), Week 1, Day 4, p. 82. "Donna maravigliosa e veramente dotta . . . nella poesia di leggiadro, pulito, ed elegante stile dotata, ma nella filosofia molto intendente; nella musica poi è molto versata, sonando e cantando soavemente di vari strumenti, e di liuto in particolare con molta eccellenza, e con armonia incredibile," Week 1, Day 4, pp. 112–13. Bronzino mentions her several times, always with admiration and affection; see below, notes 61–63.

long and relatively comfortable life, dying at the almost unheard-of age of eighty-two.[2]

In the praises quoted, what draws our attention is not merely the attribution of eloquence and learning to a woman, but above all expertise in ethics and natural science. Since Vittoria Colonna in the early sixteenth century, numerous women had made their mark as composers of Petrarchan lyrics; and since St. Catherine of Siena in the fourteenth century, women had laid claim to devout religious prose. But it would be hard to find a woman within living memory of Marinella called skilled in philosophy—in the sense of not just being informed about the disciplines concerned but also displaying the art of dialectic or argument, a decidedly male province. Bronzino would have had in mind Marinella's most overtly philosophical work—her dazzling *The Nobility and Excellence of Women, and the Defects and Vices of Men (La nobiltà et l'eccellenza delle donne, co' difetti et mancamenti de gli uomini)*, here presented in English for the very first time—as well as her philosophical commentaries on poetry.

Lucrezia Marinella's polemic first saw the light of day in 1600, composed at a furious rate in answer to Giuseppe Passi's diatribe about women's alleged defects, *Dei donneschi difetti*, published the year before in 1599. A second edition came out in 1601 with the addition of fifteen chapters; and a reprint with the same content but in a smaller format appeared in 1621. Marinella took the first part of her own title either from the Italian translation of a supposedly anonymous French tract, *Della nobiltà et eccellenza delle donne*, printed in Venice in 1549 (the original, written by Henricus Cornelius Agrippa in Latin as *De nobilitate et praecellentia foeminei sexus*, had appeared twenty years earlier, in 1529), or from an earlier praise of women based in part on Agrippa, *Della nobiltà delle donne* by Lodovico Domenichi.[3] The second part, on the defects and vices of *men*, is an emphatic reversal of Passi's title on the defects of *women*.

In the long polemical tradition of attacks against women, and their defense, Lucrezia Marinella's treatise occupies a unique place. It is the only formal debating treatise of its kind written by a woman; it presents a stunning range of authorities, examples, and arguments, which in sheer quantity no other woman had hitherto amassed; and it mounts a blistering attack on men for exactly the same vices Passi had dared to accuse women of. Marinella

---

2. Tarabotti's *Paternal Tyranny*, ed. and trans. Letizia Panizza, is forthcoming in this series; and Moderata Fonte's *The Worth of Women*, ed. and trans. Virginia Cox, appeared in this series in 1997.

3. For the importance of Agrippa on Renaissance disputes, see Albert Rabil's Introduction to his edition and translation of Agrippa's *The Nobility and Preeminence of the Female Sex*, in this series, 1996, 18–33.

also brings to new heights the line of argument launched by Agrippa that women are not only equal to men morally and intellectually, but in many respects excel them.

MARINELLA'S LIFE AND WORKS

Although Marinella achieved fame as an author, little biographical information about her has come to light. She was the daughter of a celebrated physician and natural philosopher, Giovanni Marinelli.[4] Nothing is known of her mother (did she die in childbirth?). Her brother Curzio was also a physician, and she married yet another physician, Girolamo Vacca. Her father was the author of several books on medicine, natural philosophy, and rhetoric. Two of his medical books were specifically concerned with women's well-being, and were composed in the vernacular, suggesting that he wanted women themselves to be enlightened about their health. One, *Women's Ornaments* (*Gli ornamenti delle donne*, Venice, 1562), is a practical manual of hygiene and beauty, from bleaching hair and whitening teeth to removing bodily odors. It is remarkable for its sane defense of women's quest for physical attractiveness, a search Marinella would also defend. The other, *Medicines Pertaining to Women's Illnesses* (*Le medicine partenenti alle infirmità delle donne*, Venice, 1563; revised and amplified, Venice, 1574), is a textbook on gynecology for the use of male physicians as well as midwives, and dedicated to women. It deals with conception, gestation, and childbirth. His last work, a commentary on the Greek physician Hippocrates, is dated 1576.[5] One of his manuals on language deserves mention here, a combination thesaurus and dictionary of Italian, aimed at improving vocabulary: *La prima [e seconda] parte della copia delle parole*, printed in Venice in 1562. It shows an author steeped in vernacular prose and poetry from Boccaccio and Petrarch to his own day, and would have been invaluable to the budding writer Lucrezia.[6]

---

4. I have respected Marinella's practice, which follows the Venetian custom of ending surnames of women in /a/, while her father and brother keep the family form ending in /i/. I have also come across /o/: see note 5 below.

5. For Giovanni Marinelli's life and works, and his significance in the history of medicine, see M. L. Altieri Biagi, C. Mazzotta, A. Chiantera, P. Altieri, *Medicina per le donne nel Cinquecento. Testi di Giovanni Marinello e di Girolamo Mercurio* (Turin: Strenna UTET, 1992), Introduction, 7–40; selections of Marinelli's *Le medicine*, 45–64.

6. The description on the title page states that in this work "is shown a new art of becoming the most copious and eloquent writer in the vernacular, which perhaps no other rhetorician in another tongue ever taught" ("si mostra una nuova arte di divenire il più copioso et eloquente dicitore nella lingua volgare che peraventura alcun Rhetore in altra [lingua] insegnasse mai").

It is not clear how much opportunity Lucrezia Marinella's father had to teach or supervise in person his precocious daughter's education. There is no record of him after 1576, and in 1600 Marinella speaks of him as already dead. Maybe she was only a young girl when he passed away, in which case her brother could have exercised a more decisive role. From his own writings and Marinella's fond references to him, Giovanni Marinelli emerges as a kind, paternal figure who promoted his daughter's studies and women's education in general. One is even tempted to read as autobiographical the sentiments expressed by a motherless, only daughter Erina regarding her beloved father Fileno, a natural philosopher, in Marinella's epic poem of 1635, *Henry or Byzantium Gained (L'Enrico overo Bisantio acquistato)*:

> And countless times while I was still a little girl, he took me with him up the mount . . . and of his knowledge imparted to me what was beautiful and good; and I, like a new Aurora, grew to virtue in the sunshine, and under the benign influences of the heavens, friend of [Apollo], the God of Delos.[7]

Marinella dedicated *The Nobility and Excellence of Women* to another doctor, Lucio Scarano (more celebrated as a man of letters), who took a particular interest in her literary formation. He may also have been the vital link between her private studies and writing and the wider world of Venetian literary circles and publishing. In the dedicatory letter found in all three editions, she writes of the exceptional friendship that Scarano had enjoyed with "the most excellent Signor Giovanni my father"—implying that her father is no more—"and that you currently have with the excellent Signor Curzio my brother."[8] Marinella also refers to Scarano as a "doctor and most noble philosopher," and expresses her deep gratitude precisely because "in a lecture of yours held in the library of Venice's most serene Signoria, you praised me to the heavens for my poetry." Through his friendship with Marinella's father and brother, Scarano would have recognized Lucrezia's talent and given her further encouragement, all the more important for a woman who would not have attended a secondary school where pupils learned Latin and often Greek.[9] In his own Latin dialogue *Scenophylax* (1601), furthermore, about

7. "Ei spessissimo volte me con seco / Condusse al monte pargoletta ancora / . . . E di quanto sapea, ne partia meco / il buono e 'l bello; e io qual nova Aurora / Crescea di virtù al sole, e ancor del Cielo / Ai cari influssi, amica al Dio di Delo." (Venice: 1635), 6.53.

8. "La singolare amicitia, ch' Ella [Scarano] hebbe con l' Eccellentissimo Signor Giovanni mio Padre, & con quella, che Hora tiene con l' Eccellentissimo Signor Curtio mio fratello." The letter is dated August 9, 1600.

9. Paul F. Grendler, *Schooling in Renaissance Italy: Literacy and Learning, 1300–1600* (Baltimore and London: Johns Hopkins University Press, 1989). On Venetian schools, geared to training boys

the classical meters used in ancient Greek tragedy and comedy, Scarano singles out Marinella as a most learned and already celebrated writer with whom he has discussed literary matters requiring acquaintance with classical philosophy. It is highly likely that Scarano introduced Marinella to the publisher G. B. Ciotti, who published both the *Scenophylax* (where Scarano presents himself as a member of an academy that includes the publisher Ciotti and a number of literary figures) and Marinella's *The Nobility and Excellence of Women* as well as an earlier work.[10]

Despite the fame bestowed on her by her publications, her own life was lived in seclusion—the norm, it must be said, for a Venetian woman of her social rank, regardless of intellectual status. She did not travel, except, perhaps, on pilgrimage to local shrines. If she participated in discussions with visitors to her father and brother in the family home, there is no evidence that she herself gathered men or women of letters around her or even that she attended meetings held in academies outside. There is no record of her corresponding with her admirer Arcangela Tarabotti, living and writing in the Convent of Sant'Anna in Castello, or of her ever paying Tarabotti a visit. On the contrary, at the very end of her life Marinella attacked Tarabotti. She does not appear to have heard of Sara Copio Sullam, a highly cultivated Jewish writer and scholar residing in Venice's Ghetto. Nor does she seem to

---

for the civil service, see 42–70; on vernacular lower schools for girls (and working- class boys), 87–108.

10. In his dedicatory letter to a young Venetian patrician, Scarano defines himself a natural philosopher, physician, and member of a literary academy: "Lucii Scarani Philosophi Medici Academici Veneti." Scarano refers both to Marinella's *Happy Arcadia* (*Arcadia felice*), for the relationship of tragedy to pastoral; and to *The Nobility and Excellence of Women* for the general principle of names signifying the nature of things: "Quare si nomina illius rei naturam sequuntur, cui fuerint imposita, quod Plato pluribus in Cratilo declaravit, & erudite satis & copiose venusta virgo Lucretia Marinella, nostri seculi decus & altera Corinna, in elegantissimo libello demonstravit, quem proxime de Mulierum nobilitate atque praestantia, multa doctrina refertum, in lucem emisit" (17). ("For if names follow the nature of the thing to which they were given— which Plato stated many times in the *Cratylus*, and the radiant maid Lucrezia Marinella, glory of our age and another Corinna, showed with much learning and abundantly in her highly polished book *On the Nobility and Excellence of Women*, full of so much learning, which she recently published.") For Scarano's reputation, see Carlo Villani, *Scrittori ed artisti pugliesi antichi, moderni e contemporanei* (Trani, 1904), who reports a seventeenth-century physician and man of letters, Giovanni Maria Moricino: "Scrisse alcune opere, nelle quali dimostra e l'elevatezza del suo ingegno, e la cognizione che aveva della lingua latina, greca e volgare e di molte scienze, onde meritevolmente, finché visse, fu da tutti amato e stimato, e dalli primi letterati di quel tempo molto onorato, e però la sua casa veniva di continuo visitata dalli migliori personaggi e letterati" (967). ("He wrote several works in which he displayed both the high level of his intelligence and his knowledge of Latin, Greek, and the vernacular as well as many disciplines, for which, deservedly, throughout his lifetime, he was loved and esteemed by everyone and much honored by the foremost men of letters of the day, while his house was continually frequented by all the best people and men of letters.")

have had any rapport with the members of the Accademia degli Incogniti, notorious writers of satire, novels, and Boccaccian *novelle*. In her eyes, they would have seemed disreputable, and both immoral and irreligious. She does not tell us, nor do we yet know from other sources (there are still archives to comb), just when she married, or when her children were born, or when her husband died. We have to turn to her will, dated 1645, to learn of the existence of her two children: Antonio, to whom as the only male heir she leaves the bulk of her possessions, and Paulina, to whom she leaves a silver goblet. As there is no mention of her husband, we may assume that he was already dead.[11] In a codicil added shortly after 1648, she leaves ten ducats to a granddaughter, Antoletta, daughter of Paulina.[12] An indication of her guarded private life comes from Bronzino, who could speak of her at fifty-three as if she were still a chaste maid, unacquainted with married life and children: [She is] "attractive, gracious, endowed with noble and religious habits, devout, humble and prudent, disdaining worldly vanities, loving spiritual matters, above all the purest of virgins."[13] Cultivating a similar image, Sansovino praised her withdrawal from the world. Indeed, he stresses, she gained "marvellous advantage from remaining enclosed in her room all day, studying literature with an eager mind."[14]

Marinella died of quartan fever in the Campiello dei Squellini in Venice, October 9, 1653, and was buried in the nearby parish church of S. Pantaleone.[15] As far as we know, there are no unpublished manuscript works, and sadly, no memoirs or letter collections.

11. Venice, State Archives (*Testamenti*, fasc. 1146), fol. 220ro. Legal custom decreed that the entire estate, apart from minor bequests like the goblet, be left to a son. Paulina would have received a dowry at marriage (which could represent a sizable portion of the estate). Another bequest of thirty ducats was left to a nephew, Gian Francesco Cantilena. A brief note on the Vacca family, stating only that Girolamo Vacca was a doctor and married to the famous literary figure Lucrezia Marinella, confirms the existence and names of the two children, but does not supply dates (Giuseppe Tassini, *Cittadini* [di Venezia], vol. 13, 2150; compiled at the end of the last century, this biographical list of Venetian families remains in manuscript).

12. *Testamenti*, fasc. 1147, fol. 221ro. A devout Catholic, Marinella also asks for masses to be said daily for her soul for the period of a month, and money to be given to the poor.

13. "Avvenente, graziosa, dotata di nobili e religiosi costume, devota, humile e prudente, delle vanità mondane spregiatrice, ma delle cose spirituali molto amatrice, ma sopra tutto vergine castissima" (*Dialogo*, Week 1, Day 4, pp. 113–14).

14. "Standosene nella sua camera tutto il giorno rinchiusa, e attendendo con vivo spirito a gli studi delle belle lettere, vi ha fatto maravigliosa profitto." ("She gained marvelous advantage from remaining confined in her room all day, studying literature with an eager mind.") Francesco Sansovino, *Venezia città nobilissima et singolare. Descritta già in XIII Libri* (Venice: Altobello Salicato, 1604), 426.

15. In the northern part of the Sestiere di Dorsoduro, the Campiello is near the Canal Grande, south of the Rio di Ca' Foscari. The parish church is adjacent to a large open space, or Campo, on the north side of the same canal.

Marinella's *oeuvre* as a whole falls within a burgeoning current of prose and both lyric and narrative poetry colored by didactic and religious hues, and taking to heart the Council of Trent's recommendations to promote Catholic doctrine and morals in literary genres of high artistic quality. The Jesuits promoted the theater in particular—"tragedia sacra" it was called—as literally the most spectacular way of reaching wide lay audiences, but the principle of using biblical stories and characters, as well as the lives of the saints and historical episodes such as the crusades, pervaded all previously secular literary genres. Frequently replacing romantic or chivalric heroines, and mythological and classical ones, for example, were virgins and virgin martyrs undergoing ever more cruel tests and trials to emerge triumphant with their crowns in the next life. (Two of the saints treated by Marinella, Columba and Justine, not to mention episodes from the life of the Virgin Mary, also supplied heroic exploits for the "tragedia sacra.")[16] Though men, too, composed in religious genres, they exhibited greater freedom in mixing such compositions with novels and short stories, satires, and erotic love lyrics.

While in some ways Marinella might seem a paragon of specifically womanly decorum in her privileging of religious subject matter, in other ways she challenges worn-out clichés of the Petrarchan love lyric and substitutes a poetics that emphasizes a woman's sensibilities and foregrounds female heroines.[17] Gender conventions represented men as the pursuers and women as the pursued, suffering male lovers and silent adored female objects, and passion felt only by men as an end in itself. Women poets could hardly find

16. For the literary historical background, see Peter Brand and Lino Pertile, eds., *The Cambridge History of Italian Literature,* (Cambridge, 1996), especially Paolo Cherchi on Seicento poetry, 303–9, and Albert Mancini on narrative and the theatre, 318–35. Pertinent for Marinella is Louise George Clubb, *Italian Drama in Shakespeare's Time* (New Haven and London: Yale University Press, 1989), especially "The Virgin Martyr and the Tragedia Sacra," 205–29.

17. Cf. what Lodovico Dolce wrote about the kind of literature appropriate for women to read in his widely diffused *Dialogue . . . on Women's Instruction (Dialogo . . . della institution delle donne)*—first published in 1545 and reprinted in Marinella's own lifetime in 1622—advice that would apply to what was appropriate for women to write. Decent women, Dolce cautions, should not be allowed to see, let alone read, Latin poets apart from selections from Virgil and Horace, historians, and moralists like Seneca and Cicero. As for vernacular genres, women "should shun all lewd books as one shuns snakes and other poisonous animals . . . all romances, the mass of knights-errant, all writers of *novelle* and similar useless books." ("Nella lingua Volgare fuggano tutti i libri lascivi come si fuggano le Serpi & gli altri animali velenosi . . . tutti i Romanci, la quantità de i Cavalieri erranti & tutti i noveglieri e simili vani libri"), *De gli ammaestramenti pregiatissimi, che appartengono alla educatione & honorevole e virtuosa vita virginale, maritale, e vedovile libri tre* (Venice: Barezzo Barezzi, 1622), 27–28. Only Dante and Petrarch are permitted, and, of course, "spiritual compositions," from which women learn how to behave morally. The new title, used only for this last edition, emphasizes that women's education is always both moral and intellectual, and is justified only if it makes them virtuous. Education for men is seldom justified in such stark terms.

such a male voice congenial, but how to find a separate one?[18] Marinella tends to assume that only by a renunciation of erotic entanglements could a woman poet find an independent voice. She favors a lyric where love means cultivating friendship based on equality and gender reciprocity, or the sublimation of erotic passion entirely. In the latter case, women direct their love to a divine person, Christ. As she oscillates between the exploration of earthly friendship on the one hand and heavenly passion typical of mystics on the other, Petrarch fades away.

The pace of Marinella's publications proceeded unevenly. In little more than a decade, between 1595 (when she was about twenty-four years old) and 1606, Marinella published ten books, including the first two editions of *The Nobility and Excellence of Women.*

Marinella made her debut in 1595 with a sacred epic poem in four cantos, each canto divided into stanzas of *ottava rima*, the established verse form for narrative and epic poetry that Marinella would prefer to all others. *The Holy Dove (La colomba sacra)* puns on the name of an early virgin-martyr, Colomba, and treats dramatically the heroic sufferings and death of a Christian heroine. Wedded to Christ, she begs only for the "costanza e fede" (p. 21) to serve her divine groom to the end. Like many of her works, it was dedicated to a woman, Madama Margherita, Duchess of Ferrara, who sent Marinella a ring by way of thanks via Ferrara's Venetian ambassador, Annibale Ariosti.[19] In the same genre and in the same meter came the *Life of the Seraphic and Glorious St. Francis (Vita del serafico et glorioso San Francesco)* two years later, reprinted in a collection of lives of St. Francis edited by Fra' Silvestro Poppi in 1606, and re-elaborated together with a life of St. Clare, foundress of the Franciscan religious order for women, in 1647.[20] *Cupid in Love and Driven Mad (Amore innamorato e impazzato)* of 1598 is a long moral allegory of ten cantos in the tradition of *psychomachia*, that is, an allegorical portrayal of interior, psychological conflicts; it was described by her publisher Barezzi as a "poem of a far more charming plot than the Cupid and Psyche story

18. For a survey of women's reworking of the love lyric in the sixteenth century, see Giovanna Rabitti, "Vittoria Colonna as Role-Model of Later Cinquecento Women Poets," in *Women in Italian Renaissance Culture and Society*, ed. Letizia Panizza (Oxford: European Humanities Research Centre, 1999).

19. *La colomba sacra, poema heroico di Lucretia Marinella* (Venice: Gio. Battista Ciotti, 1595). At an early age, Marinella mastered Petrarchan alliteration and plays on words: "L'aura con l'auro de l'aurato crine" (fol. 16ro); and her dying words, "Morend' io non morrò, ma morrà quella / Parte, che spesso fa che l'alma mora" (fol. 44vo). She dies to eternal life, and the Emperor Aurelian lives to eternal death. There are numerous references to this pure dove spreading its sacred wings before its maker in heaven.

20. *Le vittorie di Francesco il serafico. Li passi gloriosi della diva Chiara* (Padua: Crivellari, 1647).

in [*The Golden Ass* of] Apuleius."[21] Accompanied by her own commentaries in prose, it purports, as she explains to her dedicatee, Madama Caterina Medici Gonzaga, Duchess of Mantua, to depict "that glorious victory that the divine part of our being achieves against our senses."[22] In Apuleius, however, a divine Cupid subjects Psyche, the soul, to a series of trials before final heavenly nuptials; Marinella reverses the roles, and subjects an arrogant, lustful Cupid to defeat at the hands of wiser, more virtuous women. With *Cupid in Love and Driven Mad* Marinella placed herself in a distinguished vernacular literary tradition of philosophical love poetry practiced by illustrious vernacular poets like Dante, Lorenzo de'Medici, Benedetto Varchi, and Francesco de'Vieri, who treated a love poem like a sacred text to be expounded by long, densely philosophical commentaries, often Neoplatonic in perspective. While here she comments on her own poem, she would later compose commentaries on poems by Luigi Tansillo at the personal request of the publisher Barezzi (1606).

Placed in the above context, *The Nobility and Excellence of Women* was both unexpected and atypical: it was in prose, on a secular subject, and entirely polemical in spirit. Though it built on knowledge of the Italian poetic tradition shown in her three earlier works, nothing in these works could have prepared us for the fireworks display of philosophical, medical, historical, and literary texts, including misogynistic treatises, many of which she never turned to again.

Immediately after, Marinella returned to religious subject matter, composing a virtuoso double version of the life of the Blessed Virgin Mary: a sacred narrative or *historia* in prose and an epic poem in *ottava rima*, the two going under the general title, *The Life of the Virgin Mary, Empress of the Universe (La vita di Maria Vergine Imperatrice dell' universo).*[23] It may have been her most popular religious composition, to judge by the four editions of 1602, 1604, 1610, and

21. "Poema di assai più bella inventione che la Psiche di Apulegio," fol. a3vo. The centerpiece of Apuleius's novel, this fairy tale was interpreted from the early sixteenth century as an allegory of the progress of the soul from earthly attachments to divine love. Marinella's own commentary may have been inspired by Filippo Beroaldo's widely diffused Latin commentary, which first appeared in 1500. Vernacular translations of Apuleius by Matteo Maria Boiardo and Agnolo Firenzuola were also in print from 1523 and 1550 respectively.

22. "Quella gloriosa Vittoria che ottiene la divina parte nostra contra il senso" [no pagination]. 1618 Venice edition used. In line with Counter-Reformation suspicions about the use of pagan mythology, Marinella makes explicit that the names of gods and goddesses are metaphors of psychological drives, not references to true divinities. Cupid thus represents the lower appetites' desire for vain and lascivious delights; Jupiter, the intellect who puts Cupid under his control; Jupiter's Council, the union of intellect and the virtues against the senses, and so on.

23. The 1610 edition in the British Library, London, has been used for all quotations.

1617—all with the same publisher, Barezzi. Dedicated to the highest political authority in Venice, the Doge and Senate ("Prencipe e Signoria") no less, and signed by Marinella as a most loyal subject and servant ("divotissima suddita e serva"), it celebrates the historic link between the city of Venice, called "La Serenissima," and the Virgin Mary, "la serenissima Imperatrice dell'Universo." The victorious sea battle of Lepanto in 1571 against the encroaching Turks, for example, had been attributed to the intervention of the Virgin Mary on behalf of Venice.

This work also contains a further statement of Marinella's religious poetics, reiterating many of the themes found in Torquato Tasso's *Discorsi dell'arte poetica e in particolare sopra il poema eroico* of 1594, as well as the urgings of the post-Tridentine Church. Sacred, heroic, and philosophical subjects, she affirms, should be expressed with the same eloquence and poetry that classical authors used for pagan subjects. For the Empress of the Universe, it was appropriate to create monologues and dialogues that dealt with historical facts, especially when they formed part of the "marvellous" ("meraviglioso"), but which were elaborated on so as to excite readers' imaginations and arouse noble emotions.[24] An example of fictional "poetic" elaboration is Marinella's description of the young Virgin Mary at the moment of the Annunciation (pp. 54–56). In its vivid detail and use of hyperbole, it imitates portraits of secular romantic and chivalric heroines found in Boccaccio's prose novel,

---

24. For Tasso, the Christian epic should join the "verisimile," or historical credibility, with the "maraviglioso." See edition of Tasso by Ettore Mazzali (Turin: Ricciardi, 1959), 7–17. Marinella's novelty, she herself realizes, lies in applying the stylistic principles of epic poetry to prose, something which even Tasso did not attempt. Many critics, she says, "cercheranno di distruggere la grandezza di questo modo di scrivere hora da me usato, il quale, s'io non m'inganno, tiene il sommo dell'altezza dell'eloquenza; si come con l'autorità de' letteratissimi, & chiarissimi Scrittori, & con ragioni io farò manifesto ad ogn'uno" (fol. A3ro). ("Many will strive to tear down the grandeur of the style I now use, which, if I'm not mistaken, is the highest pinnacle of eloquence, as I shall make known to each and every one by the authoritative opinions of the greatest and most celebrated writers, and by arguments.") She appeals to great Greek orators like Gorgias and Alcibiades, and to Aristotle's *Rhetoric*, book 3, on prose style. Indeed, Gorgias is her ideal prose stylist, for Aristotle himself called "il di lui ragionamento 'elocutione poetica'; perciochè egli usava nella prosa tutti que' copiosi ornamenti, e tutte quelle parole magnifiche, e peregrine, che si sogliono nella poesia adoperare" (fols. A4ro and vo). " . . . his discourse 'poetic speech', since he used in prose an abundance of all those stylistic adornments, all those magnificent and rare words that one is accustomed to use in poetry.") Defining the style of all her sacred works, and herself as a sublime poet whether in prose or verse, she explains that the subject matter of Scripture and other actions "che hanno del grande, del magnifico, & del divino, e che trapassano le operationi humane, ricercano un modo di dire grande, & mirabile, molto diverso da quello che si usa nel raccontar quelle attioni, che picciole, humili, e basse sono" (fols. A6ro and vo). (" . . . which have grandeur, magnificence and the divine in them, and which surpass human operations, require a style that is grand and wondrous, very different from what is used in recounting ordinary, humble and low actions.")

Fiammetta, and in the works of Ariosto and Tasso. The "poema heroico," on the other hand, was dedicated by the publisher (not by Marinella herself) to Elena Barbariga de' Priuli. Each of the four cantos is preceded by an elegant woodcut. According to the publisher, Ciotti, the two companion pieces were such an exceptional tour de force that some said that Marinella could not have composed them—an accusation many women writers have had cast at them through the ages.[25]

In 1603 Marinella brought out her *Sacred Verses (Rime sacre)* with sonnets, madrigals, and longer poems; and in 1605, a pastoral drama in verse, *Happy Arcadia (Arcadia felice).* Both these were also published in Venice. Marinella's pastoral reforms the pre-Christian world of nymphs and shepherds who traditionally inhabit Arcadia. It is similar in structure to the earlier *Cupid in Love and Driven Mad* and the later *St. Peter's Tears (Le lagrime di San Pietro,* 1606) in that all comprise lyric poems with long prose passages of an allegorical moral-religious nature that make copious use of philosophical, theological, and poetic authorities. In the first two, the prose takes the form of commentaries; here, just as in Sannazaro's *Arcadia,* the prose supplies narrative continuity and turns the work into a pastoral novel.[26] More than any other single work, *Happy Arcadia* prefigures episodes in her later epic, *L'Enrico.* The shepherds are enlightened agriculturalists in the manner of Virgil's gentlemen farmers in the *Georgics.* The wise natural scientist Erimeno, an expert in the occult properties of plants, leads a small band to the nymph Erato (name of the Muse of scientific poetry), endowed with prophetic powers, who tends a magic garden and understands metereological secrets. Fileno and his daughter Erina of *L'Enrico* are close literary relatives.

In 1606 appeared another example of sacred poetry, *The Life of St. Justine (Vita di Santa Giustina),* printed, unusually, in Florence. A virgin-martyr of the early Church, St. Justine had one of the earliest basilicas in Padua named

---

25. See the publisher's letter to the readers in Marinella's *Arcadia felice* (Venice, 1605), where he lists her works to date, and declares that *La vita di Maria Vergine* has been "conosciuta come certamente vero parto del suo ingegno . . . a confusione de' maligni" ("recognized as undoubtedly the true creature of her mind . . . to the confusion of spiteful souls").

26. The poetry of *St. Peter's Tears,* about St. Peter's bitter tears of repentance after denying Christ in the Garden of Gethsemene, was composed by the Neapolitan Luigi Tansillo (1510–68) in 1559. Tansillo started a genre of penitential poems, *lagrime,* favored by later poets. Interestingly, Marinella never writes of women penitents, such as Mary Magdalen, preferring to portray women who remain steadfast, such as Colomba, Justine, Catherine, and the Virgin Mary. Her *Sacre rime,* which include vivid accounts of Christ's sufferings and death, may have inspired Angelo Grillo's (1550–1629) *Poesie sacre* of 1608, particularly his *Christo flagellato (Christ's Flagellation).* For *Arcadia felice,* see the new critical edition by Françoise Lavocat (Florence: Accademia toscana di scienze e lettere, "La Colombaria," vol. 162, 1998).

after her, and had also been credited with assisting Venice at the 1571 battle of Lepanto. The same year saw a reprint of Marinella's 1597 *Life of St. Francis* with a collection of other compositions honoring the saint, and edited by Fra' Silvestro da Poppi.

After this prolific burst of creativity, there followed a gap of eighteen years before a major prose life of St Catherine of Siena in 1624. In it, the publisher Barezzo Barezzi provided a list of her works to date accompanied by fulsome praise and a promise from him of more to come—almost as if the public needed to be reminded of her existence.[27] Maybe she devoted herself to marriage and bringing up her children; we do not know. At any rate, the eighteen-year silence was broken by *The Heroic Deeds and Marvellous Life of the Seraphic St. Catherine of Siena* , composed in the poetic prose Marinella had defended earlier. It was dedicated with political aplomb to Maria Maddalena de' Medici, Great Duchess of Tuscany (of which Siena is a main city) and Archduchess of Austria, and it picks up ascetic threads found in earlier lives of the saint. There were already numerous biographies and accounts of St. Catherine's visions, miracles, and torments by demons. She had been canonized in 1461 by Pope Pius II,[28] and her letters and treatises were published several times in the late fifteenth century and throughout the sixteenth. Marinella draws mainly on these sources (named in the margins), but concentrates exclusively on St. Catherine's ascetic and mystical "marvels," leaving aside her merits as a woman of letters as well as any recognition of the awesome authority she wielded in contemporary Italian religious and political history. Maybe Marinella agreed with the publisher Barezzi that the book's genre required it above all to be edifying: "full of theological wisdom, of words and actions fitting for those who wish to please God and withdraw from vain, worldly sensualities."[29]

---

27. *De' gesti heroici e della vita maravigliosa della serafica S. Caterina da Siena, di Lucretia Marinella. Libri sei. Ne' quali, non senza stupore se legge, la Nascita e pueritia di Caterina, l' Amore reciproco tra l' Eterno Signore , & Essa; le Apparitioni Divine; le Nozze Celestiali; le Astinenze incredibili; le continue Flagellationi . . .* (Venice: Barezzo Barezzi, 1624). Barezzi's letter to the reader, fols. a3ro–a4ro.

28. See entry by E. Dupré Theseider in *Dizionario biografico degli Italiani,* hereafter DBI, (22), 361–79, for the vast hagiographic literature about Catherine accumulated in the fifteenth and sixteenth centuries. A Dominican Tertiary who never joined a religious order, although she gathered a "family" around her, Catherine provided a model for laywomen wishing to lead a devout life in the world. This may explain why Marinella was drawn to her. Theseider, it must be said, presents a much more balanced, amiable, and loving "historical" Catherine than Marinella, who stresses the saint's asceticism.

29. "Pieno di Sapienza Theologica, di parole e di operationi convenevoli a coloro che desider-ano piacere a Dio, & allontanarsi dalle vane sensualità del Mondo," Barezzi's letter to the reader (note 27), fol. a3ro. In this letter, Barezzi ties the life of Catherine with the one about the Virgin Mary as Marinella's best sacred works.

Another eleven years elapsed before Marinella's masterpiece of epic poetry, *Henry or Byzantium Gained (L'Enrico overo Bisantio acquistato)*.[30] *L'Enrico* saw the light of day in 1635, when she was in her mid-sixties, and was followed by reworkings of saints' lives already published. There can be little doubt that she aimed at rivaling Torquato Tasso's *Gerusalemme liberata* and *Gerusalemme conquistata*, not only in subject matter, meter (once again, the octave) and the high style of heroic verse but also in her poetics. Marinella magnifies the minor role of twelfth-century Venice in the Crusades, turning the sacking of Byzantium (then in Greek hands) by the Venetians under the leadership of Enrico Dandolo (warrior, merchant, ambassador, and in very old age, doge) into a major triumph.[31] Dandolo's attack and conquest, Marinella patriotically intones in her introductory letter to her readers, "was without doubt the most magnificent, the most glorious, the most difficult and the most dangerous endeavor that had ever been undertaken by any great king or valiant general." The contemporary parallel with a Christian Venice engaged in wearying struggles with "infidel" Turks in a modern crusade could not be plainer. Marinella's epic offered optimistic reassurance that God would continue to be on the Venetian side (as at Lepanto). The subject matter is perfectly matched to the epic style required by decorum: "Truly [it is] the kind of enterprise that is easily capable of rendering my poem illustrious with its sublimity and splendor, and worthy of heroic grandeur, which I have wished to compose following Aristotle's testimony in his *Poetics*."[32]

30. The title page also tells us that this *Poema heroico* is dedicated *al Serenissimo Prencipe Francesco Erizzo, et Serenissima Republica de Venetia* (Venice: Ghirardo Imberti, 1635). Francesco Erizzo (1566–1646) held high offices in the republic, and was Doge when Marinella wrote her epic. See DBI (32), 450–58. On the very last page of her text, 648, Alexander Gatti makes explicit the parallel with Tasso, praising her "superbly excellent poetry": "Obstupuit, Musis astantibus, altus Apollo, / Versibus auditis, o Marinella, tuis. / Hinc subito dixit; praesertim Nomine Tassum, / Exuperat vates haec Poëtria meos. / Auratam tibi tunc citharam donavit eandem, / Donavit radios tunc tibi quoque suos." ("Sublime Apollo surrounded by his Muses was amazed, / O Marinella, after listening to your poem. / Hence he said at once: 'This poetry surpasses my inspired bards, especially one called Tasso.' / He then bestowed upon you the same golden lyre, / And he also bestowed his glory.") Marinella's epic is beginning to receive some attention. Apart from Malpezzi Price (see bibliography), 237–38, see Virginia Cox, "Women as Readers and Writers of Chivalric Poetry in Early Modern Italy," in *Sguardi sull' Italia. Miscellanea dedicata a Francesco Villari*, ed. Gino Bedani et al. (Leeds: Society for Italian Studies, 1997), 134–45, esp. 142–43.

31. On Dandolo, see entry by G. Cracco, DBI (32), 450–58. Marinella deals with an early period in his life; he became Doge only at eighty-five, when blind. She could have used medieval French accounts of Venetian conflicts with Byzantium by Godfrey of Villehardouin and Robert di Clari, as well as the many universal histories in print in her day. See note 49 below.

32. "Impresa senza dubbio la più magnifica, la più gloriosa, la più difficile, la più pericolosa che sia mai stata fatta da qual si voglia gran Rè, o valoroso Capitano. . . . Impresa veramente tale, che può di leggieri colla sua sublimità, e splendore illustrare, e rendere degno di Heroica

Compared to earlier epic and chivalric poems written by men, Marinella's *L'Enrico* alters significantly the representation of women. While tender and caring toward parents, relatives, and comrades, the three virgin-Amazons are never overcome by passion into abandoning their professional independence. Meandra, Emilia, and Claudia remain the equals, and often the superiors, of male warriors to the end. The most atypical woman character, Sibyl-like Erina (a feminist response to the Siren temptresses Alcina and Armida, and their destructive magical arts, in Ariosto and Tasso respectively), uses her gifts of prophecy and divination benignly. She is full of loving gratitude to her father, Fileno, a natural philosopher who before his untimely death instructed her in all he knew, including astronomical and astrological lore.[33] Not only is she unmarried, and not in love, she is surrounded like the goddess Diana by female virgin attendants as companions. When the shipwrecked Venetian hero Pietro Venier arrives at her idyllic realm, which is dominated by a palace with an observatory, he plays the role not of a potential conqueror, rival, or lover, but of a long-lost cousin, whom she enlightens about joint ancestors and fathers and about his future glorious destiny. Concretely illustrating women's natural dignity and equality, *L'Enrico* complements the theoretical positions of *The Nobility . . . of Women*, and reinforces earlier poems. In Marinella's epic, women do not need romantic passion, sexual liaisons, or even marriage, to make them happy; they are perfectly capable of developing morally and intellectually as men's equals and therefore of cultivating abiding friendship with men without erotic attachments if they so wish. Marinella's advancement of friendship between

---

maestà il mio Poema; il quale ho voluto formare secondo li documenti di Aristotile nella sua Poetica" (*L'Enrico*, 3). Marinella declares that she also adheres strictly to the Aristotelian unities of time, place, and action (4). Since the Venetian episode involved just as much relentless warfare and unstinting bravery as better-known ones, Venetians have every right to rejoice proudly. Marinella concludes: "Con l'acquisto della maggior Città dell' Europa, apparve il vittorioso Dandolo suprema meraviglia a gli occhi di Dio, e del mondo" (6). ("By gaining the major city of Europe, our victorious Dandono showed himself the highest marvel in God's eyes and the world's.") She also draws a further parallel between Dandolo and modern Venice by pointing out that Doge Erizzo has rescued Italy from a similar peril in combating the Turks (canto I, 5).

33. As stated above (p. 4), the figure of Fileno could well be a tribute to Marinella's own father. Fileno is in the tradition of the natural philosopher as delineated in Virgil's celebrated account in *Georgics*, book 3, line 490: "Felix qui potuit rerum cognoscere causas" ("Happy is he who can understand the causes of the universe")—and who finds his highest happiness in probing the secrets of nature. Erina remarks of her father, "Non da gli effetti a le cagioni occulte; / Ma da le cause a manifesti segni / Passò l'acuto spirto . . ." (canto VI, 58). ("Not from effects to hidden causes / But from causes to their visible manifestations / Did his fine mind proceed . . .") Erina's father seems to belong to the Neoplatonic school, able to grasp the Ideas directly, and not needing to learn first from the senses, empirically.

men and women, whether married or not, was a radical goal, denied by law, custom, and assumptions of misogynistic treatises.

Out of character with her bold polemics of *The Nobility and Excellence of Women* and all her female figures was Marinella's final *addio* to the world in 1645 advancing submission and domesticity for women. *Essortazioni alle donne e agli altri* praises a life of seclusion, *retiratezza*, for women, as part of God's and nature's design. Contradicting what she had said earlier, Marinella here accepts a gender-based moral code. Women would do well to stick to traditional domestic tasks of spinning and weaving. Subservience for the sake of preserving the social order is honorable. She is even disillusioned with literary pursuits, "a useless vanity and of little comfort" ("una vanità inutile e di poca consolatione").[34] If we recall the tension in Marinella's writings between secular values and spiritual, otherworldly ones, these exhortations could be seen as taking the latter values to their extreme and thus seem appropriate for an old woman who had only death to hope for. Afterward, there are only spiritual writings promoting renunciation, such as a further celebration of St. Francis together with a new praise of St. Clare published in 1647,[35] followed by more mystical poetry in honor of St. Justine, whom Marinella had written about forty years before.[36]

ORIGIN OF MARINELLA'S
THE NOBILITY AND EXCELLENCE OF WOMEN

Marinella's *The Nobility and Excellence of Women* had a precise occasion and purpose: the overturning of Giuseppe Passi's *The Defects of Women (Dei donneschi difetti)*, printed in 1599. Passi's was a repugnant diatribe, even by Renaissance standards.[37] Known in the Ravenna Accademia de' Signori Informi as "The

---

34. (Venice: Valvasense, 1645); quotations from Emilia Biga, *Una polemica antifemminista del '600: La maschera scoperta di Angelico Aprosio*, Quaderno dell' Aprosiana, 4, Pinerolo, Civica Biblioteca Aprosiana, 1989, 38–40. A vehement misogynist, the Augustinian friar Aprosio (1607–81) frequented Loredan's Accademia degli Incogniti in Venice, where he came to know and correspond with Marinella and Tarabotti. He joined sides with Marinella in criticizing Tarabotti for her denunciation of the custom of constraining young girls to enter the religious life against their will. For Aprosio, see entry by A. Asor Rosa, DBI (3), 650–53.

35. See note 20 above.

36. *Holocausto d'amore della vergine Santa Giustina* (Venice: M. Leni, 1648).

37. *Dei donneschi difetti* went through at least three editions: 1599 (the one used here), 1601, and 1618. Occasionally, a 1595 edition is mentioned. Passi later attempted a feeble defense of marriage, which concluded that there are more disadvantages than advantages to the state: *On the Married State (Dello stato maritale)* (Venice: J. A. Somasco, 1602, 1617). Addressing the reader, Passi explicitly rejects the view that he wished to dissuade men from marriage in the earlier work. But

Bold" ("L'Ardito"), Passi attacked women's alleged evil nature, perverse emotions, and especially their incapacity—"proved" by countless authorities, arguments, and examples—to behave in civilized, social, and benevolent relationships with men. Passi deserves our thanks for one reason only: his virulence provoked Marinella (urged on by others, including the publisher Ciotti) into swift and intense combat, driving her to bring all her wealth of learning and all her consummate debating skills against Passi to crush him resoundingly. As Marinella states in her introduction, "It is the custom for those who write on any subject or topic to be driven or motivated by a specific goal." Hers, she says, "is to make this truth shine forth to everybody, that the female sex is nobler and more excellent than the male" (p. 39).

Passi had written thirty-five chapters about various kinds of women's wickedness, some only a few pages long, others up to forty. After one chapter on women's nature, there follows a doleful litany: women are proud, avaricious, lustful and depraved, wrathful, gluttons and drunkards, envious, vain and boastful, ambitious, ungrateful, cruel, adulterous and roaming "vagabonde" (chapters 2 to 13). Then come invectives against whores and courtesans, procuresses, witches and fortune-tellers, the use of cosmetics (the longest chapter), the use of jewelry and other lavish adornments, women's very beauty, and women's general untrustworthiness (men should never confide in their wives nor take advice from them, chapters 14 to 20). Women are also jealous, inconstant and fickle, inquisitive, quarrelsome, hypocritical, vain, cowardly, good-for-nothing, stubborn, idle, thieving, tyrannical, fraudulent, liars and chatterboxes. Finally, they are unable to resist the blows of fortune—part of their feebleness (chapters 21 to 35). Passi drew on classical and modern authorities, Latin and vernacular ones, the Bible, Fathers of

---

the dialogue form of the debate arguing the pros and cons of matrimony allows Passi plenty of scope to recycle the same material from *Dei donneschi difetti* while granting that there may be some value in taking a wife. The conclusion lists examples of women whose love for their husbands far surpassed their husbands' love for them (176), an indication that he had read Marinella's criticisms and was making some amends. A Latin translation of 1612 enabled it to reach a wider, more professional and clerical audience than the Italian original. In 1603, after the first and second editions of Marinella's response, Passi was forced to compose a proper recantation, *The Monstrous Smithy of Men's Foul Deeds (La mostruosa fucina delle sordidezze de gl' huomini)* (Venice: Somascho, 1603), in which the vices he condemned in women are now condemned in men—with some significant differences. Whereas thirty-five vices were attributed to women, only eighteen are allowed to men. (Men are not accused of inconstancy, loquacity, quarrelsomeness, curiosity, hypocrisy, deceitfulness, or laziness.) Nowhere is Marinella mentioned by name. Nor does he provide a praise of women's virtues (which would have made his recantation complete), merely announcing that in the future he will compose *The Haven of Women's Perfections (Il porto delle perfettioni donnesche)* (59). Finally, whereas in his first chapter he attacked women's nature—and therefore soul—as base, there is no equivalent first chapter in *The Monstruous Smithy* attacking men's nature. They remain superior.

the Church, theologians and jurists. He also used historians and poets. St. Augustine was his favorite Latin Church Father, and St. Chrysostom, who has harsh things to say about women's fashions and cosmetics, a favorite Greek one. His Greek sources are rendered in Latin, though Latin sources are sometimes quoted or paraphrased in the vernacular, and sometimes not. Characteristic of Passi's method is the piling up of legal sources, a practice meant to dazzle the nonprofessional but which often leads to obfuscation.

Passi is concerned about the dangers that young men expose themselves to daily in their encounters with women and also in taking a wife. They need to be warned "to shun women's wiles," he explains to his patron, Colonel Mario Rasponi, even if it means bringing to light a deformed and grotesque literary creation. To his (male) "benevolent readers," he assumes the role of the elder man revealing the "truth" about women that only he and a few other men know, and which women themselves studiously conceal. Just as it would be impossible to count the stars or the grains of sand on a shore, so it is equally impossible "to relate the infinite evils of wicked women." By desiring women, men "cause the downfall of their own houses, make their own children and their desolated household suffer, and by following down this path so frequently they open death's door before the time to their doleful fathers and woeful mothers, nor do they give a thought to honor (worth much more than gold). And what's worse, they take their own lives, like the lowest brute beasts. . . . Women . . . are the cause in all things of men's ruin." There are moments when Passi seems to be condemning only bad women, that is, a small percent, but more often than not he slides into blanket condemnations, as with the Latin saying, "Nulla mulier bona" ("There is not a single good woman").[38] Fleetingly, Passi allows that there are illustrious men who have praised famous and honorable women. He is not deflected; compelled by righteous indignation he has turned against women for showing little concern for their honor and less for their family.

It is hard to believe with Passi that the evil nature of women posed such a threat to the moral stability of Venetian society. Yet a five-page catalogue of authorities, double columns to a page, most of the nine sonnets from fellow

---

38. "I giovani fra tanto leggano il libro, e da quello imparino a schifare gl'inganni delle Femine" (fol. a3vo). Rasponi was an illustrious military officer in the service of the Papal States. In his letter to readers, "Sarà impossibile gl' infiniti mali delle malvaggie donne raccontare"; by loving them, men "le proprie case mandono in ruina, e fanno patire i proprii figliuoli, e la sconsolata sua fameglia, e così spessissime volte innanzi al tempo per questa strada aprono le sepulture ai dolenti padri & alle mestissime madri, né manco mirano all' honore, ch' assai val più che l' oro; e quel ch' è peggio si danno la morte come vilissime bestie. . . . Le Donne . . . sono causa in tutte le cose della ruina loro" (fol. a4vo).

academicians (a couple, it must be said, call for restraint), another eight-page index in double columns (in finer print than any other introductory matter) of all the women and topics treated, plus 296 pages of the diatribe itself move us toward that conclusion. What would Passi have men do? (Women themselves are beyond reform in his moral universe.) A layperson, Passi does not recommend the monastery; his invective, however, aims at putting women in their place within marriage and a wider social context, and gives support to the subordination and segregation of wives as animals without reason and morality, whose only purpose is the propagation of the species. True friendship and noble feelings are found with other men, in public affairs, professional activities, and institutions like academies. Although rarely spelled out, such invectives provided ammunition for an abhorrence of the married state that encouraged turning to homosexuality.[39] (Conversely, some encomia of women aimed at drawing men to women and married life.[40]) No wonder Marinella responded with such indignation.

Marinella's treatise was one of the last distinguished chapters in the history of Renaissance praises and defenses of women (see the Editors' Introduction to the Series). Although she names authors who attack women beginning with Aristotle, she is not explicit about authors who praise them. Even when referring to her contemporary, Moderata Fonte, Marinella quotes Fonte's chivalric poem, *Floridoro*, rather than the longer prose dialogue, *The Worth of Women*.[41] Marinella's arguments about the superiority of women had

---

39. One explicit treatise is the anonymous *Manganello*, written in the vernacular between 1430 and 1450, and refuted by Antonio Cornazzano (c. 1430–c. 1480) after 1457. The two were then printed together in the sixteenth century. See the critical edition by Diego Zancani, *Il Manganello. La reprensione del Cornazano contra Manganello* (Exeter: University of Exeter, 1982). On Cornazzano, see entry by P. Farenga, DBI (29), 123–32. In *Manganello*, 6–9, an old man wanting to take a wife is shown that young men are much better companions than bothersome women. In his reply, Cornazzano clearly links the vituperation of women with sodomy, which he roundly condemns, 56–60. See also above, the Editors' Introduction to the Series, especially pp. viii–xv, "The Misogynist Tradition."

40. For a survey of how attitudes toward marriage changed in a more positive direction after the Council of Trent, so making Passi's outburst anachronistic in his own day, see Brian Richardson, "Advice on Love and Marriage in the Second Half of the Sixteenth Century," in Panizza, ed., *Women in Italian Renaissance Culture and Society*; and Daniela Frigo, "Dal caos all' ordine: sulla questione del 'prender moglie' nella trattatistica del sedicesimo secolo," in *Nel cerchio della luna. Figure di donna in alcuni testi del XVI secolo*, ed. Marina Zancan (Venice: Marsilio Editori, 1983), 57–93.

41. See pp. 55, 78–79, and 80–81 of this translation. The passages quoted refer to women easily becoming the equals if not betters of men if only they received an education. Marinella may have known of Moderata Fonte's *The Worth of Women* through mutual acquaintances such as Lucio Scarano. See Cox's introduction to her translation of Fonte, 21–22 and notes 32 and 33.

their origin in Agrippa, whom Marinella could have read in an anonymous Italian translation of 1549. It is even more likely that she used Lodovico Domenichi's *The Nobility of Women (La nobiltà delle donne)* of 1549, the longest Renaissance dialogue in praise of women, and one which makes copious use of Agrippa. She may have read as well Tommaso Garzoni's *Lives of Illustrious Women from Holy Scripture with a Discourse . . . on the Nobility of Women (Le vite delle donne illustri della scrittura sacra con un discorso . . . della nobiltà delle donne)* of 1588.[42] Surprisingly, she does not make use of Castiglione's ample vindication of women's equality in book 3 of *Il cortegiano*, maybe because it had been censured or had simply fallen out of favor by Marinella's day, or because Domenichi has a speaker declare that his own treatise makes Castiglione's redundant.[43] On the other hand, Ariosto's narrative poem, *Orlando furioso*, is a rich mine for Marinella of opinions, episodes, and characters that bring into the foreground women's moral and intellectual eminence.[44] She also makes use of her literary, historical, and philosophical education in the debate, particularly her knowledge of the flourishing Italian lyric tradition that she herself was part of.[45]

CONTENT AND ANALYSIS OF
THE NOBILITY AND EXCELLENCE OF WOMEN

Marinella's answer to Passi is divided into two symmetrical parts, which together constitute a double refutation. Where Passi attacked women for their vices, Marinella in part I praises women for their virtues—termed the *pars construens*, the positive or constructive side of the argument; in part II she condemns men for their vices—the *pars destruens*, the negative or destructive side. Passi had not composed a praise of men's virtue, but as male and female

42. (G. Giolito, first edition, 1549, reprint, 1552). Domenichi ties the praise of women to attracting men toward them and the married state. Garzoni's work was published in Venice by Imberti. Note that Agrippa, Domenichi, and Garzoni all call attention to woman's *nobility*. On Domenichi (1515–64), see entry by A. Piscini, DBI (40), 595–600.

43. Castiglione's dialogue was placed on the Index in 1590 because of remarks considered critical of the Church and the clergy. Only an edition expurgated by the theologian Antonio Ciccarelli was permitted. It was published four times between 1584 and 1606. See Peter Burke, *The Fortunes of the Courtier* (Cambridge: The Polity Press, 1995), 100–104.

44. See Pamela Joseph Benson on Ariosto in *The Invention of the Renaissance Woman* (University Park: Pennsylvania State University Press, 1992), 91–155.

45. The richness of Marinella's poetic culture has been investigated by Adriana Chemello in "La donna, il modello, l'immaginario: Moderata Fonte e Lucrezia Marinella," in *Nel cerchio della luna*, 150–70. See also Chemello's "The Rhetoric of Eulogy in Marinella's *La nobiltà et l'eccellenza delle donne*," in *Women in Italian Renaissance Culture and Society*, ed. L. Panizza.

were assumed to be opposites poles, any vituperation of women by men took for granted male excellence. Marinella, a woman, makes this implicit binary opposition explicit by performing both a praise of women and a vituperation of men.

An appreciation of Marinella's refutation, furthermore, requires a minimal understanding of how she matches Passi. His list of women's vices was preceded by a general chapter, "What Is Woman?" investigating woman's nature—for Passi, the sum of all evil. Passi relies on etymologies of the various names for woman, *donna, femina, mulier,* a practice bolstered up by the widely accepted belief that names are signifiers revealing the innermost nature of the signified. His second arm is the use of supposedly authoritative quotations, in his case the haphazard throwing together of Aristotelian commonplaces about woman as a mutilated, imperfect male (*mas laesus*) and an error of nature (*animal occasionatus*), as well as others of a philosophical, theological, and occasionally literary attribution. The level of the debate can be judged by a few examples. According to the Greek philosopher Alexander of Aphrodisias, women are "saints in church, angels when they greet you, demons in the home, chatterboxes at the gate, goats in the field and stench in bed." Similar lists from an early Greek theologian, St. John Chrysostom, prove that woman is a "necessary evil"; and, juxtaposed to the ancients is the misogynistic wish of a fictitious character Rodomont: life would be so much better if only men could reproduce without women, like pears from grafted tree branches! (Ariosto, *Orlando furioso* 27:120). The quotation is out of context—Rodomont is shown up to be a fool and his opinions are declared absurd.

Marinella's lucid, point-by-point reply is divided into three chapters. (In her edition of 1600, she briefly engaged in religious polemics, dropped in 1601 and 1620.) In chapter 1, "On the Nobility of the Names Given to the Female Sex," she gives a soberer account than Passi of the divine power of names and finds positive interpretations of names of women, not only *donna, femina, mulier,* but also *Eva* and *Isciab.* She has an empirical sense of etymology, drawing on how words are used in literary texts. Thus she correctly derives *donna* from the Latin *dominus/domina* (master/mistress), and quotes from medieval poets to show that it means a superior. Directly or indirectly, she is indebted to Agrippa, who also used etymology, and/or, closer to home, possibly Garzoni's *Discourse . . . on the Nobility of Women* (1588). Garzoni derived *femina* from the Greek *phos* (fire), pointing out that fire was a symbol of a divine and intellectual nature, an interpretation Marinella follows (p. 49). (Passi had argued that *phos,* and therefore *femina,* signified a destructive force consuming all around it.)

Against Passi's ranting about woman's innate evil tendencies, Marinella is concerned in the next two chapters with demonstrating the nobility and excellence of woman's soul by considering its causes (chapter 2), and nature (chapter 3), and then by providing examples and quotations from authorities that illustrate woman's rational and ethical faculties. Marinella accepts the traditional Aristotelian doctrine of four causes—material, formal, efficient, and final—with the Christian gloss that God is the efficient cause of everything, and therefore of woman. To argue that excellent causes give rise to excellent effects, she also incorporates the Neoplatonic theory of forms or Ideas as causes, another fundamental doctrine passed down from antiquity and Church Fathers like Augustine. Woman is thus the manifestation of a perfect Idea or form existing in the mind of God. Marinella deals with Passi's three central chapters on the vileness of women's beauty and bodily adornment in the more important context of this second chapter on the excellence of woman's soul. Poets like Dante, Petrarch, and Boccaccio acknowledge that women are more beautiful than men, Marinella points out by numerous quotations; and since beauty according to the Neoplatonists manifests virtue, women must proceed from nobler Ideas than men. Marinella refers to distinguished Renaissance Neoplatonists like Marsilio Ficino and Leone Ebreo, whose vernacular expositions on love leading to spiritual nobility and union with God were staple ingredients on the subject for poets and philosophers.[46]

Chapter 3, "Of the Nature and Essence of the Female Sex," reiterates a basic argument that as the souls of men and women belong to the same human nature, they are therefore equal. (This doctrine, of impeccable Aristotelian derivation, had been diffused in the vernacular since the early sixteenth century by Castiglione's *Book of the Courtier.*) If we consider the nature of woman's soul, affirms Marinella, "and if we speak as philosophers, we will say that man's soul is equally noble to woman's, because both are of the same species, and therefore of the same nature and substance" (p. 55). Gender, in other words, does not constitute a difference of species. Whatever differences

---

46. Ficino's Latin dialogue-treatise *De amore*, a version of Plato's *Symposium* with contemporary Florentines delivering speeches on the various aspects of Love, was composed in Latin in 1475 and followed almost immediately by an Italian translation, *Sopra lo amore*, which was not in print, however, until 1544. For the Latin text, English translation, and introduction, see Sears. R. Jayne, *Marsilio Ficino's Commentary on Plato's Symposium* (Columbia: University of Missouri Press, 1944); followed by Jayne's completely revised English translation, with new introduction, notes, and bibliography (Dallas, Texas: Spring Publications, 1985). Marinella quotes from the Latin. Leone Ebreo's *Dialoghi d' amore* were first published in 1535; see critical edition by S. Caramella (Bari: Laterza, 1929).

there are between men and women—following the standard terminology—
are not about substance or nature but accidents or qualities. Marinella now
returns to the notion of woman's greater beauty to argue for her greater
nobility, and applies Ficino's metaphor of beauty as a divine ray to woman's
body and soul: "the more beautiful the woman, the more . . . it is her soul that
renders grace and loveliness to her body" (p. 57).[47] An abundant selection of
poetry quotations are adduced to affirm that woman's beauty is not a devil's
snare trapping innocent men into sin, but rather a divine gift drawing men
into a noble love for women.

Added to the 1601 edition, chapter 4 is specifically directed at Passi's
assertions that men do well to shun women as shameless creatures. On the
contrary, Marinella shows, in all known societies men have honored women.
Aristotelian opinions, not women, are to blame for promoting the view that
women are depraved. Marinella enjoys showing up inconsistencies, boldly
accusing Aristotle of adulating his own sex with too much fervor (p. 74).

Once Marinella has affirmed the dignity of woman's soul in theoretical
terms, she turns her attention in chapter 5 to woman's reason and will, the two
faculties of the rational soul denied by Passi to women. These are equal, if not
superior, to men's, Marinella hammers home in the following eleven subdivi-
sions of this chapter (the sections on women of learning and achievement and
on the cardinal virtues of prudence, temperance, and fortitude are included
in this translation). Like a vast tapestry cutting across centuries, countries,
and social classes, Marinella's work holds up illustrious women: queens,
saints, goddesses, philosophers, poets, scholars, courtesans, wives, mothers,
grandmothers, and peasant girls, all of whom embody specific virtues or skills.
Marinella had access to numerous historical and biographical reference works
to assist her in her display. Many of her examples in these chapters have been
derived from Boccaccio's famous collection of biographies, *De claris mulieribus*
(*Concerning Famous Women*), composed from 1361 to 1375, and its numerous
additions. Boccaccio's collection of 104 lives of exceptionally brave, chaste
women concentrated on pagan antiquity with the exception of Eve and five
medieval examples. Translated into Italian, and printed, it continued to grow.
Marinella would have had at her disposal a late sixteenth-century edition with
fifty more lives of contemporary women added by Giuseppe Betussi and still
further additions by Francesco Serdonati.[48]

---

47. For beauty as a divine ray, see Jayne's 1985 edition of *Marsilio Ficino's Commentary*, speech 5,
chapters 1–4, 83–91; and discussion in Introduction, 13–16.

48. Such a bumper edition came out in 1596 (Florence: F. Giunti). Betussi deserves credit for
choosing secular women who were powerful or learned rather than ascetic ones. He does not

Modern readers are often dismayed at the medieval and Renaissance practice of indiscriminately lumping together historical and fictional, pagan-mythological and Christian, ancient and contemporary figures. How can such a flawed mixture constitute valid "proof"? Three considerations may be pertinent. First of all, historical rigor was not seen to be as necessary as it is nowadays. Except for a handful of scholars, it was perfectly acceptable to juxtapose disparate categories of documents, accounts, and witnesses. Since the purpose of recounting a life was largely edification, poetry with its fictional characters was thought to offer truthful insights about human nature. Even Marinella's favorite historian, the sixteenth-century Giovanni Tarcagnota, wrote ambitious *Histories of the World* that started with Adam and Eve and reported soberly Greek and Roman myths. Giovanni Niccolò Doglioni likewise wrote *A Universal Compendium of History*, beginning with creation and arriving up to 1600.[49]

Second, Marinella's *The Nobility and Excellence of Women* fell within a genre governed by a system of rhetorical assumptions and strategies that was accepted by her peers and by herself as entirely valid. When dealing with probable rather than certain truths, the important skill was in making a better case for the side you were defending than your opponent made for his. In the context of refuting generalizations about women's nature, of shifting the argument from "all" to "some," or from universals to particulars as logical terminology put it, it would be satisfactory to find examples from any acceptable source, especially an "authority." Hence the sometimes tedious batting to and fro of classical and Christian authorities, as if a famous name would clinch an argument rather than the argument itself. It was also considered acceptable for opposing sides to use quotations from the same authority. Both Passi and Marinella use Aristotle and Ariosto for different ends.

Finally, rhetoric required the author to present a case in a persuasive manner that appealed to imagination and feeling. Style was therefore important. Marinella's letter to Bronzino about a draft of his treatise *The Dignity and Nobility of Women* affords an insight into what was valued in a polemical prose work very much like her own. She has read and re-read it "with admiration for the height and charm of your style, its method full of amazing rhetorical display in its composition. . . . I say that it is a most complete work in every

---

add moralistic comments about woman's flawed nature as does Boccaccio. Betussi (1512–73) also wrote on Platonic love and on beauty, and may have been read by Marinella. See entry by C. Mutini, DBI (9), 779–81.

49. Tarcagnota's *Delle istorie del mondo* came out in 1562, and was brought up-to-date roughly every ten years (1573, 1585, 1598). Doglioni's *Compendio historico universale* appeared at least in 1594 and 1601. Both histories were printed in Venice.

aspect, enjoyable, full of information and learning, and of many authorities."
(It is the only letter of hers, apart from dedicatory ones, we have in print.)⁵⁰

Marinella concludes her proof of the nobility and excellence of women,
and of women's exercise of all the intellectual and moral virtues, by then,
and only then, answering the objections of Passi and the Aristotelians, "our
slanderers," in chapter 6. What has motivated them? Marinella warns us
that we should not be under the delusion that reason has guided men like
Aristotle to vituperate women; rather, it has been "anger, self-love, envy,
and insufficient intelligence" (p. 119). By accusing women of being more
deceitful and garrulous than men, more envious and evil-tongued, Aristotle
"did not see that in calling them slanderous, he too was joining the ranks of
the slanderers" (p. 120). Marinella locates the fundamental reasoning error
committed by Passi and other misogynists (alluded to above, p. 23): that of
generalizing from the example of *one* woman or *some* women to *all* women, or
jumping from a handful of anecdotes to a condemnation of woman's nature
as such. If there are some bad women, there are not only many more good
ones, rebuts Marinella, but also many more bad men! She sums up about
Passi: "It is reprehensible of him to jump from the particular to the universal,"
and therefore the inscription of the book would have been more appropriate
if it had read 'the defects of wicked women'"(p. 127).

Marinella may have drawn confidence in insisting on male envy and
men's false generalizations about women from her favorite narrative poet,
Ariosto. In this same chapter, she notes satirical parallels between the fictional
pagan warrior Rodomont—quoted, remember, by Passi with approval for
his misogyny—and Passi himself. Jilted by *one* woman, Doralice, Rodomont
launches into vituperative complaints to a like-minded innkeeper about *all*
women. The ensuing *novella*, and interventions by a wise and fair listener as
well as by Ariosto himself, underline the blind irrationality of condemning
all for the guilt of one or two; and of condemning women for sexual misde-
meanors committed far more frequently and universally by men. Marinella's
extensive quotations from this episode indicate how much better than Passi
she knew her Ariosto.⁵¹

50. "[L' ho letto e riletto] . . . per ammirare la grandezza e dolcezza dello stile, e l' ordine
piena di mirabil maniera nel comporre. . . . dirò ch' è opera perfettissima in ogni dottrina, e di
scienza e di molte autorità" (Week 1, Day 4, p. 89). For the development of historical method in
the Renaissance, see E. Cochrane, *Historians and Historiography in the Italian Renaissance* (Chicago:
University of Chicago Press, 1981). In his chapter on biography, he distinguishes this activity
from writing "lives," where edification was paramount.

51. *Dei donneschi difetti,* 17. Ariosto accuses male envy of concealing women's achievements in
Orlando furioso 20:1–3, but especially 37:1–23, where he opines that if women had been able
to receive an education, their reputation would perhaps be more exalted than men's. Ariosto

This rebuttal chapter was meant to complete her task of praising women; but in 1601 she extended the scope of her replies to misogynists by adding four other chapters, each one taking on a renowned author and treatise slandering women: Boccaccio's *Corbaccio*, composed in 1355, and known in the Renaissance as *Love's Labyrinth* (*Labirinto d'amore*); Sperone Speroni's *Dialogue on the Dignity of Women* (*Dialogo della dignità delle donne*) of 1542; Torquato Tasso's treatise *On Female and Womanly Virtue* (*Della virtù feminile e donnesca*) of 1585; and Ercole Tasso's *On Taking a Wife* (*Dello ammogliarsi*) of 1595 (in which Torquato Tasso is also implicated). Arrigo di Namur's *Woman's Wickedness* (*La malvagità delle donne*)—a work whose identity poses several puzzles—is briefly mentioned in the chapter on Ercole Tasso as being composed in 1428 and saying much the same thing.

Underlying Marinella's choice was her awareness of how much Passi owed to both Aristotle and Boccaccio (indeed, he says so), and an equally strong awareness that offensive attitudes of Aristotelian origin about women were being revived and strengthened in her own time by Sperone and Tasso. Representing very diverse genres, her selection shows how widespread misogyny was and how variegated were its species. The texts she attacked, furthermore, were written in Italian, not Latin, and thus formed part of a nonspecialist culture that laymen and -women of letters would have access to. Her choice poses yet again the issue of why Marinella studiously avoids engaging with ecclesiastical writers like St. Jerome or St. Chrysostom, or writings of professional jurists like the Italian Giovanni Nevizzano, whose vast compendium on marriage and the "problems" of taking a wife, *Silva nuptiarum*, was printed several times in the sixteenth century. Her lack of formal professional university training needed to enter combat as an equal on that territory may have deterred her. As a woman and devout layperson, moreover, she might not have wanted to challenge directly by name authoritative religious writers and saints revered by the Church and so risk censure if not condemnation. Nevertheless, her dismantling of Aristotle, the cornerstone of theologians and jurists alike, should not be underrated. It meant dismantling the disciples and followers of Aristotle as well.

The treatise of Ercole Tasso, subtitled *An Amusing Debate between the Two Contemporary Tassos, Ercole and Torquato* (*Piacevole Contesa fra i due moderni Tassi, Hercole e Torquato*), was published only once (Bergamo, 1595). It may have been called "amusing" because composed around a paradox: Ercole, a younger cousin of the poet, composed this rhetorical declamation against marriage

---

accuses men, furthermore, of not just ignoring the good that women do, but actually putting women down when they can. Every age produces outstanding women who have not been more known simply "per invidia di scrittori" ("because of male writers' envy"), stanza 23.

and taking a wife on the occasion of his own marriage; while Torquato, himself unmarried, responded by defending marriage and the taking of a wife.[52]

The debate was always conducted from the point of view of the husband-to-be and his future "quality of life." No one ever asked whether a woman should take a husband or whether she had any point of view at all on the issue. The conclusion was inevitably that the disadvantages outweighed the advantages, regardless of the wife's conditions—rich or poor, beautiful or ugly, learned or ignorant, virtuous or vicious. Friendship was not possible in marriage, for women were unfit for any other role or task than sex (and in this respect they were bound by nature to cuckold their husbands), and childbearing. An incensed Marinella refutes the false reasonings point by point, especially the specious accusations that women, innately drawn to deceit and wickedness, do not love their husbands and strive to harm them (Passi dwelled on this point). The commonplaces of this genre are not only untrue, she maintains, but wildly anachronistic. Look at our own experience of seventeenth-century Venice, Marinella tells her readers: in the vast majority of cases, Venetian wives find themselves maltreated by their husbands, who dissipate their wives' dowries in gambling and drink! And why shouldn't the many young, rich, attractive, and educated women alive in Venice have even more right to complain about being led into matches with physically and morally repulsive husbands? (pp. 135–36). At this point, Marinella tags on Arrigo di Namur's *Malvagità delle donne*, assuming he is a known figure.[53]

---

52. The genre, whether a wise man, meaning a philosopher, should marry (called in Latin *An uxor ducenda*), goes back to classical antiquity, and was diffused in the Latin Middle Ages and Renaissance by Juvenal's Satire VI, and sections in St. Jerome's *Adversus Jovinianum* attributed to the Greek philosopher Theophrastus. Passi makes use of many of the authorities and quotations used by Ercole, perhaps directly or from common sources. A sixteenth-century version had been penned in Latin in 1537 by Giovanni Della Casa (1503–56), author of the famous Italian manual of good manners, *Il galateo*. For the autograph, see Florence, Biblioteca Nazionale Centrale, MS XXX, 111, "Dialogus de uxore non ducenda" (note the negative—"Dialogue about *not* taking a wife"). The modern Italian translation by Ugo Enrico Paoli tames the original title: *Se s'abbia da prender moglie* (*Whether One Should Take a Wife*) (Florence: Le Monnier, 1946). Paoli's introduction charts the genre's history in antiquity and the Renaissance up to Della Casa, and lists Petrarch, Boccaccio, Leon Battista Alberti, Francesco Barbaro, Guiniforte Barzizza, and in the sixteenth century, Nevizzano, Bembo, and Filippo Beroaldo. On Della Casa, see DBI (36), 690–719.

53. We have not been able to find any work matching the author, title, and date given by Marinella. Countless vernacular poems bear the same title or similar ones like *La malizia delle femmine* (Women's Malice), but they tend to be bawdy, short, and with no pretense to learning. An example of a very diffused, anonymous popular poem of twenty-eight "ottave" warns of the disadvantages of marriage, but the conclusion urges the husband to satisfy his wife sexually and not seek other women: *Le malitie delle donne, con la superbia e pompa che usano. Et insegna alla gioventù a trovar buona moglie con un' essempio a maritati di attender a casa sua. Opera nuova, e piacevole, honesta, e da*

The next two "opinions" Marinella refutes are those of Sperone Speroni and Torquato Tasso. Both works differ from Ercole Tasso's and Boccaccio's in that they are written without vituperation. These two neo-Aristotelians, outstanding men of letters, learned, urbane, articulate prose writers of Italian, offer a superficially reasonable assessment of woman's ethical possibilities in the light of the latest philosophical trends. They are careful to make clear that woman's nature is good, not evil, but at the same time they rationalize inequality.

In Sperone's dialogue, two distinguished Aristotelians from Padua, Michele Barozzi and Daniele Barbaro,[54] find that their doubts are resolved, implausibly, by a woman interlocutor of impeccable character speaking against her own sex. "A pretty fiction," comments Marinella, unimpressed by Signora Beatrice Obiza's acceptance of woman's subservient relation to man, in which he was born to command and she to obey, he to stand for reason and she emotion. Speroni has his lady speaker sugar the bitter pill of servitude: the rule of a husband is like Christ's yoke, sweet and light, Beatrice explains, so much so that she does not even wish liberty. "And so the wife should serve, for she is born for that purpose, but such servitude should not be a burden since she does not serve as one deprived of liberty like a slave,

---

ridere (Women's Malice, with the Pride and Pomp They Employ; and [the Poem] Teaches Young Men to Look for a Good Wife by an Exemplum to Husbands to Look after Their Own House. A New, Pleasant and Decent Work to Make One Laugh) (Bologna, Venice, Padua, Bassano: G. Antonio Remondin, no date or place). The exemplary tale recounts how a young bride became jealous when her husband returned at midnight and fell asleep without making love to her. She got a razor and cut off his nose ("nose" standing for the male member?), after which he died. The refrain reads: "De le donne non ti fidare / Che son troppo vitiose / Di natura son gelose / E ben pronte al vendicare." ("Don't trust women / They're far too depraved / They're jealous by nature / And quick to take revenge.") The Italianized French name (Henri of the city of Nemours) leads us to consider that Marinella may have had in mind a French work, related to the infamous Latin diatribe of the fourteenth century by Matheolus, translated into French by Jean le Fèvre, printed in 1492, then several times after, and translated further. See *Les lamentations de Matheolus et le livre de Leesce de Jehan le Fèvre, de Resson*, ed. A. G. van Hamel (Paris: Emile Bouillon, 1892). The aim is close to Boccaccio's and Passi's: to dissuade young men from hasty marriage by illustrating the ways women are inclined to evil, never love their husbands, will always be unfaithful, and so on. Marriage, however, is declared better than becoming a cleric. Christine de Pisan (1365–1431), author of *La cité des dames (The City of Ladies)*, confesses to having been shocked and depressed on reading Matheolus and similar diatribes. Another candidate remains the *Manganello*, also known as *La malvagità delle femine*, mentioned above (note 39) as a possible inspiration, among others, for Passi.

54. See "Della dignità delle donne," in *Trattatisti del Cinquecento*, ed. Mario Pozzi (Milan- Naples: Ricciardi, 1978), I, 565–84. Michele Barozzi was a noted philosopher, commentator on Aristotle's Ethics. Daniele Barbaro, close friend of Speroni, founder of an Academy, published his ancestor Ermolao Barbaro's commentary on Aristotle's *Art of Rhetoric* and wrote prolifically on literary and philosophical topics. See entry by G. Alberigo in DBI (6), 89–95. Beatrice degli Obizzi was a noble Ferrarese lady of the Pio family, whose country house was a meeting place for scholars and writers. Bembo and Speroni wrote works in her honor.

but as a creature for whom being free in any amount or to any degree is not fitting, as of her very nature she is deficient in that part of the soul concerned. Whence it has been decreed that you men should be the lords and masters."[55]

Marinella has no patience with paradoxical utterances by women characters set up by men to turn the rhetorical sword of argument against themselves. She refutes Beatrice's case by an alternative set of quotations from Aristotle, and asserts that wives are equal partners, "compagne" and friends, not servants—a relationship she upholds in all her writings. She also delivers the sharp retort to Speroni that perhaps he was influenced not so much by Aristotle and Christ as by "the tyrannical insolence of those many men who make not only their wives serve them but also their mothers and sisters, showing greater obedience and fear than that [with which] humble servants and slaves serve their lords and masters" (p. 138). Having constrained women into service, men then imagine themselves to be "naturally" superior.

Torquato Tasso's treatise/oration to a noble lady continues along these alarming lines to develop a separate moral code for men and women, based like Sperone on the supposition that the female soul is naturally more deficient than the male. For Tasso, her soul is not suited for the exercise of intellectual virtues like philosophical speculation (and she doesn't need to use intellect anyway), nor for the practice of the three main cardinal virtues of fortitude, justice, and prudence. Only the fourth cardinal virtue, temperance, is properly within her grasp. Marinella pounces on Tasso's invention of two souls for human beings based on gender, exacerbated by the further novelty of ordinary female virtue for most women and "womanly" ("donnesca") heroic virtue for exceptional women like queens and rulers, who are apportioned "virile" souls.[56] Marinella refers to her earlier chapters proving that women have given abundant evidence of their achievements in the intellectual sphere and in the cardinal virtues of fortitude, prudence, justice, and temperance, and reiterates the basic tenet that men and women are of the same species, humankind, and therefore have the same soul (p. 140).

Marinella dismisses *Il corbaccio* on the sane grounds that one cannot reason with irrational abuse: "Boccaccio reviled the female sex with indecent words full of poison and envy rather than true or apparent reasoning, and thus presumed many things that required actual proof" (p. 141). In

---

55. "Serva adunque la donna, poi che a servire è creata, ma non l' aggravi tal servitù, conciosiacosa ch' ella non serve sì come priva di libertà e a guisa di schiava, ma come cosa cui l'esser libera tanto o quanto non si convenga, mancando per sua natura di quella parte dell' anima, onde è dato a voi uomini che voi debbiate signoreggiarne," "Della dignità della donne," 583.

56. *Discorso della virtù feminile e donnesca* (Venice: B. Giunti, 1582). Critical edition with introduction and notes by Maria Luisa Doglio (Palermo: Sellerio Editore, 1997).

Boccaccio's dream-fiction, a dead husband appears to warn the new lover (the unfortunate narrator) of his ex-wife about her deceptions and generally depraved character.[57] The earliest of the texts singled out by Marinella, its influence was incalculable because of Boccaccio's literary stature. She lists the insults—Passi had made them his own—and makes her case by appealing to the unreliability of male narrators and the evidence of everyday experience. Women are not perverse in themselves; they have been made to seem so by men. "I do not see that discreet, benign women usurp their husbands' patrimonies," since they bring with them dowries for their own expenses; "Furthermore, you will never find a woman who dissipates her husband's assets the way husbands do their wives'" (pp. 142–43). Boccaccio contradicted himself in the *Decameron*—and so invalidates his argument—for there men confess that they cannot help desiring women.[58] In her final rejoinder to the dreamer/narrator, she exposes further absurdity in medieval and Renaissance love codes: men are wont to insult women who do not respond to their lustful pleadings. But these same men should realize that, on the contrary, women are under no obligation to do so!

MARINELLA'S REPUTATION IN THE QUERELLE DES FEMMES

Marinella was celebrated by contemporaries and posterity, both within the Italian peninsula and outside, though hardly anyone engaged with and followed up the issues addressed in *The Nobility and Excellence of Women*. It is only now, in the last quarter of the twentieth century, that she is receiving the serious attention she merits. This present volume is the very first translated work of hers. There has only just appeared the very first modern Italian edition of one of her writings, *Arcadia felice*.

Marinella's contemporaries understood her best. Lucio Scarano, we have seen, appreciated her exceptional talents, calling her "the adornment of our century" and comparing her to the Greek poetess Corinna.[59] For Sansovino, the three great Venetian women of letters were Cassandra Fedele, a Latin humanist writer of the late fifteenth century; Moderata Fonte, who died in 1590 and is mentioned affectionately by Marinella; and Marinella herself. He drew

---

57. See *The Corbaccio*, trans. and ed. by Anthony K. Cassell, 2nd rev. ed. (Binghamton, N.Y.: Medieval and Renaissance Texts and Studies, 1993).

58. Boccaccio dedicated the *Decameron* to women for the benefits they had bestowed on him; in addition, the introduction to Day IV praises love for women as a natural irresistible force, universally felt by all mankind.

59. See *Scenophylax*, p. 12, and note 10 above.

attention to her solitary life, leading us to believe that it was this condition above all that enabled her to write so much so soon (his history was published in 1604, at the end of Marinella's most prolific decade).[60] Della Chiesa paid Marinella his glowing tribute in his 1620 *Theatre of Literary Ladies*, a list in alphabetical order beginning with Anna, the mother of Samuel, and ending with Queen Zenobia. The entries for Marinella and Moderata Fonte are among the longest, but strangely, after listing most of her writings, he is not sure whether Marinella is dead or alive: "She lives—if she did not die a short while ago—the immortal glory of the female sex, the only phoenix of our age." He does describe the main features of *The Nobility and Excellence of Women*.[61]

Her greatest admirer was Bronzino; not only did he speak of her several times in *The Dignity and Nobility of Women*, he sent her a partial draft of his book for her comments and then included her answer with gratitude in the printed text. Bronzino's testimony confirms the success of both Moderata Fonte and Marinella in overturning traditional Renaissance misogyny; he plainly enjoys reporting their victory in shutting up Passi, whom he describes as a madman struggling to shore up a pack of cards.[62] Their works, in the words of Bronzino's spokesman Onofrio, "serve, and according to reason ought to serve, to gag the unfortunate Passi and shatter whatever pile he amassed to damage and prejudice these happiest of ladies. Once aware that the engine he constructed on falsehood would easily and quickly fall, he thought he could revive it by mounting lies upon lies, as if adding weight to an already collapsing (and now collapsed) edifice would not hasten its downfall."[63] Another interlocutor, Vittorio, singles out for special praise Marinella's didactic poem, *Cupid in Love and Driven Mad*.[64]

---

60. See note 14 above. Sansovino lists *The Nobility and Excellence of Women*, and her religious poems about Saints Columba and Francis, and the Virgin Mary—all of which were completed by 1602.

61. "Vive (se non è morta da poco tempo in qua) con immortal gloria del feminile sesso, e unica fenice dell' età nostra," 215. See note 1 above. The work is dedicated to Margherita of Savoy, Duchess of Mantua, described as a conspicuous example of a "donna letterata." For Marinella, see pp. 214–15; for Fonte, 242–43.

62. This remark about Fonte has led to some confusion. Fonte died in 1590, before Passi wrote his diatribe. Strictly speaking, she could not have intended to answer him. But as *The Worth of Women* was printed in 1599, and Marinella's discourse in 1600, it would seem to the public that both works were in effect refuting Passi, whose *Defects of Women* first appeared in 1599.

63. "Servono e ragionevolmente devono servire per otturar la bocca e atterrare qualsivoglia mole fatta dall' infelice Passi a danno e disfavore delle felicissime Donne; il quale, accorgendosi che agevolmente e presto caderia la macchina da lui fabricata sul falso, si diede a credere d' ingagliardire il suo artificioso edificio con aggiugner menzogne a menzogne, come che l' accrescer peso ad una già cadente (ed ora caduta) mole non affrettasse la ruina che soprastava alla sua mal fondata fabrica," Week 1, Day 1, p. 30.

64. Week 1, Day 4, p. 44.

Fonte, Marinella, and Tarabotti represent a high tide of feminist consciousness and articulateness in Venice. Italian women do write in later centuries, but not until the nineteenth century is there a similar momentum and abundance of discussions on women's liberty and equality.[65] Yet after her own century, Marinella's name and *The Nobility and Excellence of Women* become items in catalogues. When the Neapolitan scholar and editor Antonio Bulifon turned his attention to rediscovering and editing sixteenth- and seventeenth-century texts by women that were already proving difficult to find, it was their lyric poetry that interested him. In 1693, for example, he published *Rime di Lucrezia Marinella, Veronica Gambera, Isabella della Morra, Maria Selvaggia Borghini.*[66]

Outside Italy, two outstanding women scholars contemporary with Marinella, Marie de Gournay, adopted daughter of Montaigne, and Anna Maria van Schurman in Holland (regarded as the most learned woman of her age), show scant familiarity with the Italian scene. The former does not seem to have heard of any Italian women writers, while the latter names *The Nobility and Excellence of Women* and Gournay's *The Equality of Men and Women* (*L'Egalité des hommes et des femmes*), published in Paris in 1622, to disapprove of both of them. Schurman's essay-letter to Andrea Rivetus dated 1638 discusses whether a Christian woman should be educated. While answering in the affirmative, and impressed enough with Marinella's polemic to call it "outstanding," she is at the same time apparently shocked by the Venetian woman's impudence: "Lucrezia Marinella's otherwise outstanding treatise, in my judgment, is so far removed from being compatible with virginal modesty, or at least an innate reticence, that it bothers me even to read it." Gournay's shorter and milder work is also damned with faint praise: "As for her little treatise, just as I cannot disapprove in any way of its elegance and wit, so I neither wish nor dare to approve of all its contents."[67] The

---

65. See Marina Zancan's survey of the highs and lows of women's writing in Italy, "La donna," in *Le questioni*, vol. 5 of *Letteratura italiana*, ed. A. Asor Rosa (Turin: G. Einaudi, 1986), 765–827.

66. Bulifon's burst of publishing women's verse started in 1692 with the poems of Vittoria Colonna and Laura Terracina in one volume; in 1693 he published Tullia d' Aragona; in 1694, Laura Battiferri; in 1695, an important anthology of women poets, *Rime di cinquanta illustri poetesse*, duplicating Lodovico Domenichi's *Rime diverse d' alcune nobilissime e virtuosissime donne* (Lucca, 1559). All were published in Naples, with the sign of 'La Sirena.' For Bulifon, see entry by G. De Caro in DBI (15), 57–61.

67. "Tantum vero abest ut hoc cum virginali modestia aut saltem innato mihi pudore congruere arbitrer, ut vel perlegere pigeat tractatum caetera insignem Lucretiae Marinellae (cui titulum fecit *La nobiltà & l' eccellenza delle donne con i difetti e mancamenti de gli huomini*). [Nobilissimae Gornacensis] dissertatiunculam, *De L'egalité des hommes & des femmes*, uti ab elegantia ac lepore improbare minime possum, ita eam per omnia comprobare nec ausim quidem, nec velim," *Dissertatio de ingenii muliebris*

French Protestant scholar and philosopher Pierre Bayle, author of the major encyclopedia of the late seventeenth century, *Dictionnaire historique et critique,* supplies a brief entry for Marinella, concentrating on *The Nobility and Excellence of Women.* He admires her high intelligence while remaining doubtful about her subject matter. Indeed, what he says about Marie de Gournay's *The Equality of Men and Women* could be applied with equal relevance to Marinella: "A person of her sex must scrupulously avoid these kinds of disputes."[68] The victories that Italian women gained in challenging men intellectually were thus disregarded.

In the eighteenth century, Marinella's works all but disappeared from sight. Indicative is Rosa Califronia's *Brief Defense of Women's Rights* of 1794, composed in the heat of the French Revolution. Defending women's rights against misogynists, including Giuseppe Passi, she takes the trouble to compile a bibliography of all writings favorable to women that she and her sister have found. Neither Marinella nor Moderata Fonte nor Arcangela Tarabotti is mentioned.[69] A few years earlier, however, in 1773, Abbate Conti had provided a few footnotes on Marinella, Fonte, and Bronzino in his Italian translation of a noted French essay on women by Thomas, who now found reasons for women's inferiority in physiology.[70] In Ginevra Canonici Fachini's biographical compilation of women writers of 1824, there is a short paragraph on Marinella.

---

ad doctrinam & meliores litteras aptitudine, in *Epistolae* (Louvain: Elzevir, 1641), 71–72. For Gournay, see Mario Schiff, *La fille d'alliance de Montaigne Marie de Gournay, essai suivi de L'Egalité des hommes et des femmes (1622) et au Grief des dames (1626)* (Paris: Librairie Honoré Champion, 1910). Gournay's arguments, including the one that women have been held back by men, resemble Marinella's and Tarabotti's, but her modern sources, she states, are Erasmus, Agrippa, Poliziano, and Castiglione—roughly a century old. No Italian women authors are mentioned; indeed, she claims that English and French women have the advantage over Italian women "en esprit et galanteris," though Italians in general are "le plus subtil peuple de l' Europe" (65).

68. For Gournay, see the *Dictionnaire,* vol. 7 (Paris, 1820), 184–91; for Marinella, vol. 10 (1820), 307. Bayle defines Marinella "dame vénitienne qui avait beaucoup d' esprit," who "portait les prétentions de son sexe non-seulement à l' égalité, mais aussi à la superiorité," and was disapproved of by Schurman. His discussion of Gournay is ambivalent. On the one hand, he admits that she was without doubt an extraordinary literary figure; on the other hand, he does not approve of her. The issue is one of decorum and taboo: women transgress a social code when they challenge men intellectually.

69. *Breve difesa dei diritti delle donne* (Assisi, 1794). Little is known about Califronia, called a "Roman Countess" on the title page. The arguments for women's education are similar to those of Marinella, Fonte, and especially Tarabotti, two centuries before.

70. *Saggio sopra il carattere, i costumi, e lo spirito delle donne ne' varii secoli del sig. Thomas* (Venice: G. Vitto, 1773), 92–93. Thomas/Conti find the rhetorical mode of using examples and authorities in debating unconvincing: maybe a reason for the whole genre falling into disrepute in the eighteenth century.

It was only in the 1970s with the advent of the feminist movement that serious critical interest in Marinella began to flourish; first in Italy with Marina Zancan, Ginevra Conti Oderisio, and Adriana Chemello, and then in the United States, with Patricia Labalme and Margaret King, both Venetian historians, who set Marinella in a sociohistorical context. There are other more recent studies by Chemello, Cox, Jordan, Malpezzi Price, and others (see bibliography), opening up new vistas on Marinella's achievements. Work is in progress, but in a sense it has only begun.

A NOTE ON THE TEXT

Of the three editions of 1600, 1601, and 1621 mentioned earlier in this Introduction, the enlarged 1601 edition has been used as the basis for this translation. The third edition is identical to that of 1601.

The additions of 1601 are substantial: fifty-six chapters as opposed to forty-one; in particular chapter 4 on the reasons for men's poor treatment of women (partly devoted to refuting Aristotle and partly to examining the position of women in other countries), the four sections in chapter 5 refuting the misogynistic opinions of Boccaccio, Speroni, Ercole and Torquato Tasso, and extra chapters on the vices of men. Other, already existing chapters have been augmented by Marinella with further illustrative material, for example, the chapter on learned women.

Given the daunting length of Marinella's work, a selection has had to be made for this translation. The chapters where she is arguing about the nobility and excellence of women and refuting the opinions of learned male writers and philosophers were felt to be of most interest to modern readers. Many of the chapters on the individual virtues of women and vices of men have been omitted, as these tend to become catalogues of examples with quotation following quotation, a formula that can become repetitive.

Marinella quotes from Latin and Italian sources, all of which have been translated. On occasion, she gives both Latin and contemporary Italian translations, a practice which indicates that she did not assume her readers could follow Latin easily. As far as possible, the sources of quotations and names have been identified in the Notes and their spellings standardized.

Much deliberation has gone into the choice of an appropriate English "register" to correspond to Marinella's written Italian. Marinella, born and bred in Venice (a city proud of its own language and literature) always wrote in the accepted literary Italian of primarily northern Italy—a tuscanized Italian canonized in the sixteenth century by the Accademia della Crusca and its dictionary. She writes so fluently in it that often we have the impression of a text dictated at high speed with frequent exclamations and asides. The English striven for is, allowing for the exigencies of a close translation, that of a contemporary educated person, not archaic but not employing slang either. The printed work is marked furthermore by a conspicuous lack of punctuation, even by Renaissance standards, which would be intolerable if carried over into English. Likewise, there are often no paragraphs within the individual chapters. Here, editorial policy has also decided in favor of the kind of sentence and paragraph length used by an educated person today. Marinella is a delight to read in the original; without sacrificing accuracy, the English is meant to be so as well.

THE NOBILITY AND EXCELLENCE OF WOMEN, AND THE DEFECTS AND VICES OF MEN

A DISCOURSE IN TWO PARTS

by
Lucrezia Marinella

TO THAT EXCELLENT GENTLEMAN,

Signor Lucio Scarano,
Doctor,
and most noble philosopher

If a person, having received an honor from someone, is to be considered ungrateful and discourteous for not returning the favor—or at least for not excusing themselves with innumerable and infinite thanks for their inability to do so—I shall thus far undoubtedly have merited rebuke. For your worthy Lordship has already praised me to the heavens for my poetry, in a lecture of yours held in the library of Venice's most serene Signoria, and I have neither thanked you nor given you any other courteous acknowledgment. Now, wishing to make amends for my fault, I dedicate my work on the Nobility of Women to you in order to release myself in part from my obligation.

If the gift seems small in comparison with your great praises, I hope you have been compensated in part by the exceptional friendship that you had with the most excellent Signor Giovanni, my father, and that you currently have with the most excellent Signor Curzio, my brother, and beg you to accept as well the eager spirit of she who is in debt to you. May God send you happiness.

Written at home, August 9, 1600.
To Your Most Worthy Lordship
As from a daughter,
Lucrezia Marinella

In the first part women's nobility is demonstrated with the aid of powerful reasoning and countless examples. Not only is Boccaccio's opinion confuted —as well as Tasso's, Speroni's, and those of the Monsignors Namur and Passi—but also the great Aristotle's.

In the second part it is proved, through true reasoning and using varied examples from innumerable ancient and modern texts, that men's defects far surpass those of women.

Venice, 1601

OF THE NOBILITY AND EXCELLENCE OF WOMEN AND OF THE MOST SERIOUS FAULTS OF MEN

Discourse by Lucrezia Marinella
Divided into two parts

DIVISION OF THE ENTIRE COMPOSITION

It is the custom for those who write on any subject or topic to be driven or motivated by a specific goal. Many authors desire that the truths they write about should be known by everybody, and so labor "days and serene nights,"[1] employing every effort not only in composing their material but also in rendering it in an elegant fashion so that it is clear and accessible to diligent readers. Others, scorning philosophical truths and driven only by vivacity and readiness of wit, attempt to convince the world in all seriousness that the true is false, that good is bad, and that the ugly is beautiful and lovable. Using specious reasoning, they often obtain the end they so desire. Several others can be found who, moved by envy, seek with biting pen to obscure and annihilate another's noble actions, which, to their shame, often far surpass their own and soar nearer to heaven. Finally, there is no lack of writers who, stimulated by hate or proud disdain, proceed to detract from others' fame and honor with copious lies. The first are worthy of praise on their own account. The second should not be wholly condemned, since they are gifted with such noble wits. But all those who are motivated by envy or some particular hatred are indeed deserving of blame by everyone.

As for myself, I wish to follow the first group in my discourse. My desire is to make this truth shine forth to everybody, that the female sex is nobler and more excellent than the male. I hope to demonstrate this with arguments

---

1. This is a reference to Lucretius, *De rerum Natura* (*On the Nature of Things*) 1.14: Marinella writes "dies noctesque serenas" where Lucretius's line reads "nocte vigilare serenas." He relates how he stayed awake night after night while striving to compose in the clearest and most accessible way possible this poetic work designed to teach his friend Memmius about Epicurean philosophy.

and examples, so that every man, no matter how stubborn, will be compelled to confirm it with his own mouth.

Those who come near to recognizing this truth include Plutarch and the great Plato in book VII of his *Republic* and in many other works, where he shows that women are equal to men in valor and wit.[2] I say that they "come near" because they did not arrive at the full realization that women are nobler and more excellent than men.

I am not moved by hate or scorn, still less by envy. On the contrary, these are far from my mind, because I have never wanted nor do I want nor will I ever want to be a man, even if I should live longer than Nestor.[3] But I truly believe that Aristotle was led by scorn, hate, or envy in many of his books, to vituperate and slander the female sex, just as on many occasions he reproved his master Plato.[4] So too, I believe, was Giuseppe Passi of Ravenna, when he wrote his book entitled *Dei donneschi difetti*, though whether he was moved by envy or scorn or something else, I cannot tell.[5] May God forgive him.

2. Plato, *Republic* 7. The argument in Plato is not quite this, but that women as well as men may possess the qualities necessary to be trained as "philosopher-kings" for his utopian republic. Marinella refers to Plato, *Republic*, 540c, where Socrates tells his audience: "You must not forget that some of [the philosopher-kings] will be women. All I have been saying applies just as much to any women who are found to have the necessary qualities." The full argument for this case takes place at 4.445b–5.457b. Plutarch (a second century C.E. Greek writer who spent some time in Rome) wrote a work entitled *The Bravery of Women* (*Moralia* 242e–263c), a collection of historical tales about great deeds of women, illustrating his opening thesis that women are equal to men in every virtue.

3. Nestor, a Greek elder at Troy who was a son of Neleus and Chloris, and grandson to Neptune. The ancients are all agreed that he lived three generations of men, which some suppose to be three hundred years.

4. Unlike Plato (note 2 above), Aristotle holds that the virtues of men are separate and different from those of women (see *Economics* 1.3 [1343b7–1344a8] [not by Aristotle but still regarded so in the seventeenth century], or *History of Animals* 9.1 [608a20–b18]) and often states that women are naturally weaker than, inferior to, and less capable than men. Aristotle was Plato's pupil, and most contemporary accounts treated him as a devoted supporter of his master (see, for example, the account of their relationship in Marsilio Ficino's *Letters*). However, Diogenes Laertius, a Greek biographer from the third to fourth century C.E., claims that Aristotle left Plato's Academy while Plato was still alive, and attributes this remark to Plato: "Aristotle spurns me as colts kick out at the mother who bore them" (Diogenes Laertius, *Life of Aristotle*, in book 5, chapters 1–37, of his *Lives of Eminent Philosophers*). As we have no way of knowing which Latin translation of Aristotle Marinella used, all references to Aristotle have been checked against *The Complete Works of Aristotle*, tr. and ed. Jonathan Barnes, 2 vols. (Princeton: Princeton University Press, 1984). The line numbers key the translation to Immanuel Bekker's standard edition of the Greek text of Aristotle of 1831 and are used by all scholars who write about Aristotle.

5. Giuseppe Passi, *Dei donneschi difetti* (Venice: I. A. Somascho, 1599). Marinella's discourse was written in response to Passi's book (see Introduction to the Translation). An opening sonnet dedicated to Passi by Giulio Morigi (see book I, chapter 6, note 29 of this translation) implies that Passi has been unhappy in love.

I will divide my discourse into two main parts. In the first I shall speak of the nobility and excellence of women. This will be divided into six principal chapters, of which the fifth alone will contain enough for eleven separate sections. In the second part I shall explain the defects and faults of men, which I shall divide into thirty-five chapters. Beginning with the excellence of women, I shall show that they surpass men in the nobility of their names, causes, nature, operations, and the things men say about them. Finally, I shall reply to the superficial reasoning that is employed every day by imprudent and unwise men.

PART I

THE NOBILITY AND
EXCELLENCE OF WOMEN

I

ON THE NOBILITY OF
THE NAMES GIVEN TO
THE FEMALE SEX

There is no doubt that the names by which things are called reveal their true natures. This is affirmed by many learned philosophers, such as Averroës, using as his authority book VIII of Aristotle's *Metaphysics*.[1] Thus it is right, even necessary, to believe that names are not chosen by chance, as the less scientifically minded may believe, but with the greatest foresight.

The ancient Egyptians and wise Chaldeans believed that proper names, by which we designate creatures possessed with reason, were not chosen by man but imposed by a divine power that possessed the soul of the person choosing the name and forced him to bestow one particular name on a man or woman. Through long experience and observation of names and their workings, they developed a new art or science named Onomancy. This science of the power of names was learned by the great Hebrew theologians, as Iamblichus demonstrates in the *De mysteriis Aegyptiorum*. This work states that names reveal and prove not only the essence and power of the objects named but also God's.[2]

We may affirm therefore, without any doubt, that the more dignified and honored the name, the nobler and more remarkable the object. Who will ever deny that the feminine sex is adorned with worthier and more illustrious names than the masculine sex? Nobody, in my opinion. Let us consider the strength of the names that render the former sex worthy of honor. They are

1. Aristotle, *Metaphysics* 2 (1043a–1044b). Averroës was a twelfth-century Arabic writer from Cordoba who played a major part in the transmission to the West of the ancient Greek philosophy preserved in Arabic tradition. He wrote commentaries on many Aristotelian and Platonic works, Latin translations of which were available in Europe from the thirteenth century.

2. Iamblichus (a Neoplatonic philosopher who came from Chalcis in Syria and lived in the fourth century C.E.), *The Mysteries* 7.4–6, on the divinity of names.

five in number, taken from different languages, and all noble: *Donna, Femina, Eva, Isciah,* and *Mulier.*

To begin with the first, *donna* derives from the Latin *domina,* which means lady and mistress. Not only in the present day does it have imperial connotations and regal power; it also had them in ancient times. In the *Life of Lycurgus,* Plutarch writes that the Spartan name for women signified "lady."[3] In Epictetus's *Enchiridion,* chapter 55, he writes these words: "From the age of fourteen women are called this [*dominae*] by men."[4] Claudius Caesar, recognizing women's excellence, called his wife "my lady." Emperor Hadrian did the same.[5] Even in Homer's time women were honored with illustrious names. In book III of the *Odyssey,* we read of Nestor's wife in Latin translated from the Greek: "by him his lady wife who had laid out the bed."[6] and in book VIII, speaking of Alcinous, that: "his lady had made it with her own hands."[7]

The name *donna* is so noble that great kings and dukes usurp it. Don Cesare d'Este, Duke of Modena; Don Vicenzo Gonzaga; and Philip of Spain join with poets in recognizing the excellence of the name and bestowing it on gods and other symbols of dominion or lordship. Thus Petrarch, speaking of love:

Through deception and force he has made himself lord,[8]

and Dante:

who held his lord's enemies in his hands,[9]

and Torquato Tasso, talking of sleep in *Gerusalemme liberata:*

3. Plutarch, *Life of Lycurgus* 14.1: "[The Spartan husbands] paid [their wives] greater deference than they deserved, and addressed them as 'mistress' [*despoina*]." (Although Marinella cites what Plutarch writes as evidence for the excellence of women, it actually occurs in an unflattering context, as do several other of her citations.)

4. Epictetus, *Enchiridion* or *Handbook* 40 (not 55 as Marinella writes): "Mulieres a tertiodecimo anno vocantur." The mistake of chapter may have occurred in whichever Latin translation Marinella used, while the sense of the Greek is: "From the age of fourteen women are called 'mistress' by men," rather than from the age of thirteen as in the Latin phrase that Marinella uses.

5. Claudius was emperor of Rome from 41–54 C.E., and Hadrian from 117–38 C.E., but Marinella's reference to them in this context is obscure: Claudius divorced his first two wives and his third was executed, while Hadrian was said to have been more interested in young men.

6. Homer, *Odyssey* 3.403. Marinella's Latin translation reads: "Cui domina uxor lectum suum stravit."

7. Homer, *Odyssey* 7.347 (not book 8): "Quem suis ipsa manibus domina construerat."

8. Petrarch, *Canzoniere* 360:65: "Per inganni e per forza è fatto donno."

9. Dante, *Inferno* 22:83: "Ch'ebbe i nemici di suo donno in mano."

Little by little it steals upon him and makes itself lord of his senses, mighty and strong.[10]

Not content with having masculinized the noun, they have also made verbs and adverbs from it, all denoting lordship and dominion. Thus Boccaccio, wishing to convey grandeur, says that the Queen turns to Elissa almost "*donnescamente.*"[11] Petrarch substitutes the word "*indonnare*" for "*signoreggiare,*" writing:

flame of love, making itself lord on high over my heart.[12]

And Dante:

for that reverence which makes itself lord.[13]

It is clear, according to these illustrious writers, that the name *donna* (truly, as Guarini, secretary of the great Duke of Tuscany, says, a gift from heaven),[14] denotes lordship and imperiousness. But this is a peaceful dominion, corresponding to the nature of she who dominates. If she were to rule by tyranny, as does the less courteous male, perhaps the detractors of this noble sex would remain silent.

There are those who believe that the name *donna* does not suit the whole of the feminine sex and who exclude virgins from sharing it. Among them is Giuseppe Passi.[15] It seems to him that such a name is too noble to include the whole sex. I, however, using the authority of poets and prose writers, will show clearly that the name *donna* can also be used by virgins. Ariosto refers to Angelica as "*donna*" in *Orlando furioso*, canto I, 13, having already said she was a virgin.

The lady turned her palfrey back.[16]

Referring to Bradamante in canto II, 32, he writes:

---

10. Tasso, *Gerusalemme liberata* 14:65: "Quel serpe a poco a poco, e si fa donno / Sopra i sensi di lui, possente e forte." All quotations from Tasso have been checked against the modern critical edition by Claudio Varese and Guido Arbizzoni (Milan, 1972).

11. Boccaccio, *Il decameron* Day 3, Story 5: "Quasi donnescamente la Reina impose ad Elissa."

12. Petrarch, *Canzoniere* 127:25: "Fiamma d'Amor, che'n cor alto s'indonna."

13. Dante, *Paradiso* 7:13: "Per quella riverentia, che s'indonna."

14. Battista Guarini, *Pastor fido*, act 3, chorus (line 30): "O donna, o don del Cielo."

15. Giuseppe Passi, *Dei donneschi difetti*, chapter 1, p. 1.

16. Ariosto, *Orlando furioso* 1:13: "La donna il palafreno a dietro volta." All quotations have been checked against the modern critical edition of *Orlando furioso*, ed. Marcello Turchi (Milan: Garzanti, 1974).

The lady was loved by a knight who had come from Africa with King Agramante,[17]

and elsewhere, still writing of Bradamante:

Thus removing her helmet the lady showed a glimpse of paradise.[18]

He writes of Marfisa:

I wish to follow the warlike lady[19]

whom he called the virgin Marfisa.

Trissino, speaking of the virgin Sophia, refers to her many times as *"donna"* in canto III of *Italia liberata*.[20] Tasso, writing of the virgin Sophronia, refers to her as "proud lady."[21] In canto XIII, 53, he says of Clorinda, who is fighting with Tancredi:

The intrepid lady does not surrender,[22]

and in canto XII, 69:

So passes the lovely lady, and seems as if she sleeps.[23]

Erminia is also referred to thus.[24] Mirtillo, lamenting about Amarilli in Guarini's *Pastor fido*, says:

my lady more cruel than hell.[25]

Speaking of Dorinda, Guarini writes:

since you have transformed yourself from a lady to a wolf.[26]

These are just a few of the countless examples available in verse, while among prose writers Boccaccio provides many more in the *Decameron*, the *Corbaccio*, and the *Amorosa Fiametta*, as well as in all his other books. There

17. Ibid., 2:32: "La donna amata fu da un Cavaliero / Che d'Africa passò col Rè Agramante."
18. Ibid., 32:80: "Così l'elmo levandosi dal viso / Mostrò la donna aprirsi il paradiso."
19. Ibid., 20:106: "Voglio seguir la bellicosa donna."
20. Giangiorgio Trissino, *Italia liberata dai Goti*, 3.
21. Tasso, *Gerusalemme liberata* 2:19: "altera donna."
22. Ibid., 13:53: "La fortissima donna non diè crollo." I cannot trace this quote.
23. Ibid., 12:69: "Passa la bella donna, e par che dorma."
24. Ibid., 3:12: "Erminia bella." 6:100: "così disse la donna."
25. Guarini, *Pastor fido* 3.6.6: "La mia donna crudel più dell'inferno." See above, chapter 1, note 14.
26. Ibid., 4.2.38: "Già che [. . .] di donna in lupo ti trasformi."

seems little point in continuing to offer proof of a fact that is well known to everybody, nor is it contradicted by Petrarch in the line:

the beautiful young girl who is now a lady,[27]

because he was looking at the girl's age rather than the fact of her being a virgin. At thirty or forty, she would not be referred to as a girl, but as a lady, as can be seen from the previous lines of the verse:

Thus if I see in youthful guise the world starting to clothe itself in green I seem to see at that same immature age the beautiful young girl who is now a lady.[28]

Enough now of the name *donna*. The second name derived from Latin is *femina*, the significance of which is so noble and elevated that few names can equal it. It is derived both from the latin *fetu*, or foetus, as stated by Isidore of Seville,[29] and from the Greek *phos*, meaning fire.

In the first case, therefore, *femina* denotes reproduction or generation, as Plato writes in the *Cratylus*.[30] This, of all human acts, is one of the most worthy, and it can only be performed by perfect beings such as women. This being so, who will dare to deny that the name *femina* is both noble and excellent?

In the second case it denotes fire, one of the most beautiful and useful things in this unworthy world. Anyone showing agility, promptness of action, or greatness of spirit resembles fire, which is the most active and perfect of the elements. Many, indeed, believe that the soul is composed of fire. Two marvels occur as a result of fire, heat and brightness. Both are excellent things and most useful to all living creatures. What could be more productive and fertile than heat, what more beautiful and useful than light? The name *femina* is, therefore, far nobler than *donna*. The latter may signify lordship and dominion, but the former signifies reproduction and fire, without whose heat we could not live and without whose light nature and the world would languish.

27. Petrarch, *Canzoniere* 127:22: "La bella giovanetta, c'hora è donna."

28. Ibid., 127:19–22: "Onde s'io veggio in giovinil figura / Incominciarsi il mondo a vestir d'herba / Parmi vedere in quella etade acerba / La bella giovinetta, c'hora è donna."

29. Isidore of Seville, *Etymologies* (also called *Origines*) 11.2.24. He puts forward both these etymologies for the word *femina*, but the linking of it with the Greek word for fire, *phōs*, is not interpreted as flatteringly here as it is in Marinella's text: "Other people think that in Greek etymology *femina* comes from the force of fire, because females lust so fiercely."

30. Plato, *Cratylus*, 414A. In the Greek the link is between the words *gune* (woman) and *gone* (birth). Perhaps in the translation that Marinella read the terms *femina* (woman) and *fetus* (offspring) were used to create a similar effect.

It saddens me that such a richly endowed name as *femina* should not be in greater use. This neglect has come about because of certain pejorative connotations that it has unfortunately acquired, even though Boccaccio, unlike Passi, often wrote favorably of noble and honorable females and Ariosto, speaking of two women who brought about the death of Marganore's rascally sons, wrote:

Two females had brought him to this pass.[31]

Guarini too uses the name female without pejorative additions, introducing the Satyr:

Accursed Corisca, and I would almost say every female in the world, . . . [32]

while Torquato Tasso speaks of *"femine Norvegie"* in *Torrismondo*.[33] Thus the name *femina* can be used both positively and negatively, like *donna*.

The third and most ancient name, *Eva*, means life. Everything on earth, and especially all animate beings, depend on it for their existence. In fact many people contend that only animate creatures should be described as living. It is hardly necessary for me to say what a noble and excellent name this is, seeing that every action depends on life, and it is only right that this name should be given to the feminine sex, considering that it gives life to the masculine one. This name surpasses the two previous ones because the first means lordship, the second production and fire, but the third means life and soul, the supreme perfection of all these inferior things.

The fourth name, *Isciah*, also means fire, but a very different fire from the first one. This fire is holy, divine, and incorruptible. Its purpose is to purify our souls, to excite and illuminate them, and to render them worthy of participating in divine perfection, far from the ugliness of earth. This holy fire can be seen in the beauty that shines forth from women's bodies, as I will prove. What more can be said of this name? As heavenly things are nobler than earthly ones, so this name far surpasses all the others, because it enables men to participate in divine excellence. Unfortunate indeed is the man whose house lacks such a fire, stimulating and forcing him to look upward and contemplate the heavens

---

31. Ariosto, *Orlando furioso* 37:76: "Due femine a quel termine l'han spinto."

32. Guarini, *Pastor fido* 3.9.46–47): "Maladetta Corisca, e quasi dissi / Quante femine ha il mondo."

33. Tasso, *Il re Torrismondo* 5:4.52.

The fifth and last name is *mulier*,[34] from the Latin, which, when applied to the body, means soft and delicate, but when applied to the soul, means gentle and benign. Thus, in both senses, it praises women, because a soft delicate skin denotes a mind that is readier to understand than one that is enclosed in a harsh, rough skin. This is taught by Aristotle, who said: "Soft skin, able mind."[35] As regards the soul, what could be more praiseworthy than gentleness and mercy?

Thus these two excellent qualities are united in the name *mulier*. In fact, it would not really be possible for one to exist without the other. Who can imagine a grim, steely soul in a soft, delicate body or a benign and gentle one in a rough, hideous exterior? We conclude that the name *mulier* has considerable merit and is hardly less important than those names that have preceded it.

These are the names with which this honorable sex is adorned. In my opinion, as I have clearly shown, they are among the most illustrious and remarkable that can be expressed by man. Such rare, wondrous, worthy names, which denote every excellent quality that is found, or can be found, in the world! All other names must yield to them, signifying, as they do, production and regeneration, earthly fire and light, soul, life, divine radiance, delicacy and mercy, and, finally, lordly dominion.

In the combination of all these names it can be seen that woman brings forth the ungrateful male, gives him life and soul, illuminates him with the splendor of divine light, confers earthly heat and light on him, renders him (contrary to the inclinations of his soul) affable and courteous, and finally rules over him with a sweet, nontyrannical dominion. Oh immortal God, what more illustrious names than these can be found in the world? What can be nobler than Life, Fertility, Fire, Mercy, and Dominion?

I will now pass from the declaration of names attributed to the female sex to the consideration of their causes.

---

34. This etymology again comes from Isidore of Seville, *Etymologies* 11.2.18, and states that the other Latin word for woman, *mulier*, derives from the term *mollitia*, which means softness (and also cowardice).

35. Aristotle. The Latin phrase quoted, "Molles carne apti mente," seems to be a paraphrase of Aristotle's *History of Animals* 9.1 (608a23–25), where he states "the character of females is softer and . . . quicker to learn."

II

THE CAUSES THAT PRODUCE WOMEN

There are two causes that produce women—not just women but every creature inhabiting the world. One of them is known as the efficient or productive cause, and the other the material one.[1] If I speak of procreation, there can be no doubt that the sole cause and productive origin is God. Thus it would almost seem at first as if all things were of equal perfection, considering that they depend on the same cause. But if we reflect more deeply it becomes obvious to us that though they have been created or generated by the same cause, our Eternal Maker had different ideas for them when He produced them. That same courteous hand created angels, heavens, men, and the rude, dull earth, all in varying degrees of perfection. Angels are extremely noble, man less noble, the heavens noble, the earth extremely ignoble, and yet all are created by the same maker.[2] It is the creator who decides which things are of less value and which are worthier, and more particularly, which have a less noble purpose and which a more remarkable one. Thus Dante, wishing to demonstrate the different effects of the supreme good, writes in *Paradiso:*

> His glory, which moves everything, pervades the universe, and shines
> more brightly in one part and less in another.[3]

1. Here Marinella refers to Aristotle's theory of causation, which was still very influential on Renaissance thought, although it had been adapted to suit Christianity. See also Introduction to the Translation.

2. Renaissance beliefs about the creation of the universe also saw it as having been created with a hierarchical structure in which man is superior to animals but inferior to heavenly beings such as stars and angels.

3. Dante, *Paradiso* 1:1–3: "La gloria di colui, che'l tutto move / Per l'universo penetra, e risplende / In una parte più, e meno altrove."

Different degrees of perfection can be found, therefore, not just in the things already named, but in everything in the world. Among the many kinds of living animals, for example, some are more and some less perfect. All, however, depend on the same cause. If this is the case, as in truth it is, why should not woman be nobler than man and have a rarer and more excellent purpose than he, as indeed can be manifestly understood from her nature? I will discuss this at length in the chapter that follows.

According to Platonists, Ideas are the eternal exemplars and images of things, whose proper place lies in the mind of the supreme power before their creation.[4] Leone Ebreo, however, refers to Ideas as divine precognition of things produced, because before God creates things He has an image in His mind of what He wants to create.[5] To give you a clearer example of this sort of Idea, let us pretend that an artist wishes to paint a beautiful Venus or that an architect wishes to design a beautiful palace. There is no doubt that before the artist begins to draw or paint he will have fixed in his mind the sort of figure he wishes to paint and only then will proceed to bring this image to life, as will the wise architect. This thing or image that they have in their minds is designated the Idea or pattern of the goddess Venus or of the palace and is found in the mind of the maker before he makes or paints it. I believe that this example of an Idea is familiar to everybody, and I also believe, and will explain, that the Idea of a superb, well-proportioned palace is nobler than that of a poor, disproportionate hovel and that the Idea of a lovely nymph is nobler than that of a rustic and deformed satyr.

Now, applying the example to my subject, I say that the Idea of women is nobler than that of men. This can be seen by their beauty and goodness, which is known to everybody. There is not a philosopher or poet who fails to attribute these qualities to them, rather than to men. I can confirm, furthermore, that the Idea of a charming woman adorned with beauty is nobler than that of a less beautiful and pleasing one, because Ideas exist of particular people, as Marsilio Ficino and many holy doctors confirm, and as Luigi Tansillo, a most learned Platonist, demonstrates clearly in one of his songs:

Among the most sacred Ideas, among the most beautiful that are reserved in the bosom of the divine and foremost mind of their eternal

4. This refers to the Platonic theory of forms as set out by Plato in his *Republic*. According to this theory, each object or person that exists in the physical world is a manifestation or example of a perfect Idea or Form of such an object or person. In Renaissance thought such an Idea exists before creation in the mind of the creator, God.

5. Leone Ebreo (Juda Leon or Leo Hebraeus, ca. 1460–ca. 1521), *Dialoghi d'amore* 3:4e: Teorie delle Idee.

maker, ours shines no less in heaven than the moon in beautiful serenity among the stars.[6]

It can be understood from these words that particular women exist as Ideas in the supreme mind. Petrarch writes this too, praising Laura in these words:

In what part of the world, in what Idea was the pattern from which nature copied that lovely face, in which she has shown down here all that she is capable of doing up there?[7]

Thus he explains in a most scholarly way the nature of the Idea and the fact that it comes before the created object, which he refers to as the pattern, and the mind as the Idea, which was the customary way of speaking. Boccaccio also shows this in *L'amorosa visione*, with these words:

And from what Idea it could take the form and so beautiful a design, and brilliant light I, defeated by doubt, could not say.[8]

Enough of the efficient or productive cause. I will now pass to the remote material cause from which woman is composed. I do not need to make an effort over this since, as woman was made from man's rib, and man was made from mud or mire, she will certainly prove more excellent than man, as a rib is undoubtedly nobler than mud.

6. Luigi Tansillo, *Poesie, canzone* 3 (lines 65–69): "Tra le più sante Idee, tra le più belle / Che in grembo alla divina, e prima mente / Riserbasse l'eterno lor fattore / Splendea la nostra in Ciel non altramente, / Che in bel seren la Luna tra le stelle."

7. Petrarch, *Canzoniere* 159: "In qual parte del mondo, in qual' Idea / Era l'esempio, onde natura tolse / Quel bel viso leggiadro, in ch'ella volse / Mostrar qua giù quanto lassù potea?"

8. Boccaccio, *L'amorosa visione*, canto XXIX (lines 61–63): "Et da cui Idea pigliasse la misura / Et così bel disegno, e chiara luce / Sapria'l mal dir vinto da dubbia cura."

III

OF THE NATURE AND
ESSENCE OF THE FEMALE SEX

Women, like men, consist of two parts. One, the origin and cause of all noble deeds, is referred to by everyone as the soul. The other is the transitory and mortal body, which is obedient to the commands of the soul, just as the soul is dependent on the body.

If we consider the first, that is woman's soul, and if we speak as philosophers, we will say that man's soul is equally noble to woman's because both are of the same species and therefore of the same nature and substance. Knowing this, Moderata Fonte, to demonstrate that women are as noble as men, wrote in *Floridoro*:

And why if their nature is shared, if their substances do not differ? . . . [1]

and subsequently goes on to show that they are part of the same species.

For my part, I do not agree with this opinion. I say that it is not impossible that within the same species there should be souls that are from birth nobler and more excellent than others, as is written by the Master of Sentences, Peter Lombard.[2] Given this fact, I would say that women's souls were created nobler than men's, as can be seen from the effect they have and from the beauty of their bodies. That souls differ among themselves is known by many, among them poets, who are inspired by their own ardor, which reveals to them the highest and most mysterious secrets of nature and the supreme good. This is shown by these words from Remigio Fiorentino's sonnet:

1. Moderata Fonte, *Tredici canti di Floridoro* (Venice, 1581), 4.1: "E perché se commune è la natura / Se non son le sostanze variate?" Marinella substitutes the word "natura" for Fonte's "figura."

2. Peter Lombard, *Sentences* 2.32

Among the beautiful souls intended by nature to give things life are the beautiful and rare forms that have come down to animate the beautiful and dear limbs of my lady.[3]

That the souls of women possess an excellence which men's do not is shown in several of Guarini's stanzas:

In your pure souls a ray shines of that sun which in heaven illuminates the blessed, so that the warmth is born which descends from you to those who are born to burn in such a beautiful fire. This is what adorns you and lights the sparks of love in beloved eyes, and this is the reason for those sighs in which lovers breathe their great desire.[4]

Not only Guarini and Remigio Fiorentino but many other poets are aware of this truth. In one of his sonnets Bernardino Tomitano shows how the Eternal Mover sometimes sends creatures who are worthier both in mind and body:

He who with infinite great government and with immense providence and art shows us his admirable virtue, holy, wise, divine Eternal Mover, you gave Lucrezia to our age so that your inner valor would resound in a thousand verses and gradually bring to life everything of yours that is light and heavenly.[5]

Padre Angelo Grillo also shows us this in these verses:

Ah who has forced the most beautiful soul to part from the most beautiful limbs and in a single flash extinguish all my light? Ah heaven and nature's greatest creation, are you too merely shadow and bone?[6]

---

3. Remigio Fiorentino, Sonnet in *Rime di M. Remigio Fiorentino* (Venice, 1547): "Tra le belle alme, ch'a far vive intese / Son di natura le belle opre, e rare / A dar vita a le membra e belle, e care / De la mia donna la più bella scese."

4. Battista Guarini: "Nelle vostre pure alme un raggio splende / Di quel sol, che nel Cielo arde i beati, / Onde nasce l'ardor, che da voi scende / Ne così in si bel fuoco ad arder nati. / Questo è quel, che v'adorna, e quel ch'accende / Le faville d'amor ne' lumi amati, / E questa è la cagion di quei sospiri / Ch'esalan gl'amorosi alti desiri."

5. Bernardino Tomitano, Sonnet 4 in *I fiori delle rime de poeti illustri*, vol. 8 (Venice, 1558): "Quel che con infinito alto governo, / E con immensa providenza, ed arte / Sua mirabil virtute a noi comparte / Santo, saggio, divin Motore eterno, / Vi diede a questa età, perche l'interno / Vostro valor Lucretia in mille carte / Per voi rimbombi, e viva a parte, a parte / Tutto quel, ch'è di voi chiaro, e superno."

6. Angelo Grillo, *Pompe di Morte, canzone* 2, "In morte della Signora D. Leonora Cibo." Stanza 6 (lines 16–20): "Ahi chi la più bella alma / De le più belle membre a partir sforza / E in un sol lume ogni mio lume ammorza? / Ahi del Ciel, di natura ultima possa / Sarete adunque voi nud'ombra, e ossa?"

Women's souls can, therefore, be nobler and more prized in their creation than men's. Now, if we wished to apply the common reasoning, we would say that women's souls are equal to men's. But the complete falseness of this opinion will become apparent to everyone whose mind is not totally committed to the opposite point of view if we consider the body, because the nobility of the soul can be judged from the excellence of the body—which is ornamented with the same character and beauty as the soul, "which such a body manifests in itself."[7] The greater nobility and worthiness of a woman's body is shown by its delicacy, its complexion, and its temperate nature, as well as by its beauty, which is a grace or splendor proceeding from the soul as well as from the body. Beauty is without doubt a ray of light from the soul that pervades the body in which it finds itself, as the wise Plotinus writes, following Plato in this case, in these words:

> There is a natural exemplar of beauty, a more beautiful rational principle in the soul, from which beauty flows.[8]

Marsilio Ficino writes in his *Letters*:

> Bodily beauty lies not in the shadow of matter, but in the light and grace of form.[9]

And what is the form of the body if not the soul?

The greatest poets teach us clearly that the soul shines out of the body as the rays of sun shine through transparent glass. The more beautiful the woman, the more they affirm that it is her soul that renders grace and loveliness to her body. Petrarch demonstrates this a thousand times, especially when talking of Madonna Laura's eyes, or rather, her two bright suns. He writes:

> My noble lady, I see in the movement of your eyes a sweet light that shows me the way that leads to heaven.[10]

Francesco Rainieri writes in one of his sonnets:

---

7. The phrase in quotation marks here is in Latin: "que parat sibi tale corpus."

8. Plotinus, *Enneads* 5.8 ("On the Intellectual Beauty"), following Plato's *Symposium*: "Exemplar pulchritudinis naturalis est ratio quaedam in anima pulchrior, a qua profluit pulchritudo."

9. Marsilio Ficino (1433–99), *Letters* 47: "Pulchritudo corporis non in umbra materiae, sed in luce, et gratia formae." Ficino was head of the Platonic Academy in Florence. He made translations of the works of Plato, Plotinus, and other ancient thinkers. His *Letters* were printed in 1495 but some date from as early as 1470, and his translation of Plato's *Dialogues* was completed in 1469.

10. Petrarch, *Canzoniere* 72: "Gentil mia donna, i'veggio / nel volger de'vostri occhi un dolce lume / che mi mostra la via ch'al ciel conduce."

> If from your beautiful eyes in which can be seen all the beauty which nature and art can make . . . ,[11]

and in another sonnet:

> Fair soul wrapped in a flimsy veil that shines gold as if enclosed in glass.[12]

Tasso, too, demonstrates this in his sonnets:

> Fair soul, whose splendor is transparent, a sun through the clouds of its hazy veil,[13]

in which he shows that the soul shines forth through a lovely, well-composed body, rather like the sun when veiled by flimsy clouds. The soul, therefore, is the cause and origin of physical beauty, as I have demonstrated. And not only the soul.

If we take our reasoning further, we will see that God, the stars, the sky, nature, love, and the elements are the origin and source of beauty. Beauty, the home of the graces and of love, is dependent on the supernal light. Platonists affirm that it is an image of divine beauty with the words:

> External beauty is the image of divine beauty.[14]

Dionysius writes:

> Through participation in the first cause, all things are beautiful in themselves and in their own way.[15]

Leone Ebreo reveals this to us abundantly in *De amore*, affirming that that the corporeal beauty which shines in bodies is a shadow and image of incorporeal

---

11. Francesco Rainieri, Sonnet in *Rime di M. Anton Francesco Rainerio Gentilhuomo Milanese*, p. 9 (Venice, 1554): "Se da' begli occhi vostri in cui si mira / Tutto il bel, che può far natura e arte."

12. Ibid. (p. 10): "Alma gentil in sottil velo involta, / Che come in terso cristal chiuso auro splendevi." (The lines Marinella quotes are slightly different: "Alma leggiadra in sottil velo involta, / Che come in vetro chiuso auro splendevi," and may have come from a different edition.)

13. Tasso, Sonnet dedicated to La Signora Vittoria Scandiana Tassona in *Scielta delle rime del Sig. T. Tasso*, part 1, p. 69 (Ferrara, 1582): "Alma leggiadra, il cui splendor traluce / Qual sol per nubi dal suo vago velo."

14. "Pulchritudo externa est divinae pulchritudinis imago." This is a reference to the Platonic theory of Forms (see chap. 2, note 4 above). Physical beauty is a manifestation of the divine, abstract Idea or Form of beauty.

15. Dionysius the Areopagite, *The Divine Names*, 704a: "Per participationem causae primae omnia pulchra sunt pro suo cuique modo." Dionysius was a Greek writer from the fifth or sixth century C.E. who wrote on theological themes with Christian and Neoplatonic influences.

beauty.[16] If it came solely from the body, each body would be beautiful, which it is not. Beauty and majesty of body are, therefore, born of superior reason as Giovanni Guidiccioni states, like a good Platonist wondering if beauty is the image of God:

> The beautiful and pure light that shines in you almost awakes in my bosom an image of God.[17]

But Claudio Tolomei demonstrates clearly that earthly beauty is an important part of God's beauty with these words:

> Of the beauty that great God possesses such a bright ray shines in you, lady, that he who is worthy to look on you sees the true source of eternal light.[18]

This shows, as Dionysius the Areopagite states, that the greatest beauty is given to creatures who are worthy of it, as women are.[19] This is also confirmed by Francesco Maria Molza, who writes:

> Lady in whose bright and divine splendor God proposed to give himself pleasure, at the time when he created both the hemispheres and whatever within them was exotic or ornate.[20]

Celio Magno, secretary of the Signoria of Venice, also expresses this opinion in one of his sonnets:

> Did not God create beauty to arouse love in us once the lustful fire has been extinguished?[21]

In a *canzone* praising the beauty of the woman he loves, and in particular her eyes, he writes:

---

16. Leone Ebreo, *Dialoghi d'amore* 3.E.d: "Teoria della bellezza."

17. Giovanni Guidiccioni, Sonnet in *Rime diverse di molti eccellentiss autori*, p. 154 (Venice, 1565): "La bella e pura luce che in voi splende / Quasi imagin di Dio nel sen mi desta."

18. Claudio Tolomei, *Ottava* 1 in *Rime di diversi nobili buomini et eccellenti*, vol. 2 (Venice, 1547): "De la beltà, che Dio larga possiede / Si vivo raggio in voi donna riluce / Che chi degno di quel vi guarda, vede / Il vero fonte dell' eterna luce."

19. Dionysius the Areopagite. See note 15 above.

20. Francesco Maria Molza, Sonnet 2 in *Rime di diversi nobili buomini et eccellenti*, vol. 2 (Venice, 1547): "Donna nel cui splendor chiaro, e divino / Di piacere a se stesso Dio propose, / Allor che gli Emisferi ambi dispose / E quanto hanno d'ornato, e pellegrino."

21. Celio Magno, Sonnet, "In reply to Sig. Valerio Marcellini," in *Rime di Celio Magno e Orsato Giustiniano* (Venice, 1600): "Non creò Dio bellezza, accioché spento / Sia'l fuoco in noi, che per lei desta amore."

Your other honors are miracles of nature. This one seems to have descended from God himself.[22]

This is also stated by Remigio Fiorentino in his sonnets:

Lady, they [your eyes] are the image of that serenity, of that beauty, of that charm, and that divinity which His goodness alone pours into us.[23]

Bernardo Rota demonstrates it also, with these words:

If from the eye of heaven the wondrous great light shines upon and nourishes both good and evil, noble lady, in you alone shines all the beauty that God sees and possesses within himself.[24]

Guarini writes in *Pastor fido*:

Oh lady, oh gift from heaven, or rather of Him who created you both and made you more beautiful . . . [25]

In short each writer, Platonist, and poet affirms that beauty comes from God. This is shown by Petrarch in his *Canzoniere*, 73, which begins "Since through my destiny," in these words:

since God and nature and love wished to place completely every virtue in those lovely lights on account of which I live in joy.[26]

Divine beauty is, therefore, the first and principal cause of women's beauty, after which come the stars, heavens, nature, love, and the elements. As Petrarch writes of Madonna Laura:

The stars and the heavens and the elements vied with all their arts and put every ultimate care into that living light where Nature is mirrored—and the sun, which finds its equal nowhere else.[27]

22. Celio Magno, *canzone* beginning "Quanto in voi Donna io miro," in *Rime di Celio Magno e Orsato Giustiniano*, lines 14–16 (Venice, 1600): "Son gli altri vostri honori / Miracol di natura / Questo par che da Dio proprio discenda."

23. Remigio Fiorentino, Sonnet beginning "Se quel seren, ch'a bei vostri occhi intorno," in *I fiori delle rime de poeti illustri*, vol. 8 (Venice, 1558): "Donna l'imagin son di quel sereno, / Di quel bel, di quel vago, e quel divino, / Che sol s'infonde in noi per sua bontade."

24. Bernardo Rota, Sonnet in *I fiori delle rime de poeti illustri*, vol. 8: "Se dell'occhio del Ciel l'alma gran luce / Quale al rio, tale al buon giova, e risplende, / Donna gentil, s'in voi sola riluce / Tutto il bel, che in se Dio vede e possiede."

25. Guarini, *Pastor fido*, act 3, chorus (lines 30–33): "O donna, o don del Cielo, / Anzi pur di colui / Che'l tuo leggiadro velo / Fe' d'ambo creator più bel di lui."

26. Petrarch, *Canzoniere* 73: "Poi che Dio, e natura, e amor volse / Locar compitamente ogni virtute / In quei bei lumi, ond'io gioioso vivo."

27. Petrarch, *Canzoniere* 154: "Le stelle, il Cielo, e gli Elementi a prova / tutte lor arti et ogni estrema cura / poser nel vivo lume in cui Natura / si specchia e'l sol, ch'altrove par non trova."

Petrarch also demonstrates in many other places that this beauty comes from heaven. Similarly, Bembo writes:

> All the love that heaven can gather was shown to me within the space of a beautiful face and courteous, humble conversation, so that all other dear beings would become vile to me.[28]

Petrarch writes in his *Canzoniere*, 325, that beauty is created in the stars:

> The day she was born the stars that produce happy effects in us were in high and elect places. They turned toward each other with love.[29]

Tansillo, in a *canzone* that begins "Love which lives and lodges within my breast," discovers the same thing:

> But when my mind leads me to penetrate the high virtue which encloses the beautiful soul, it seems to me then that the mouth, eyes and laughter and the limbs made in Paradise by the hands of the angels and God are the least cause of my ardor. Who could ever describe the high infinite graces of heaven, dealt you with a generous hand by all the best planets, Venus beauty, Mercury judgment, and the words that if heard in hell would comfort those who suffer most?[30]

Nature's role is shown by Petrarch in this sonnet:

> In what part of Heaven, in what Idea was the pattern from which Nature copied that lovely face in which she wished to show down here all that she is capable of doing up there?[31]

And finally the same author demonstrates that love is the origin and cause of beauty in this sonnet:

> Where and from what mine did Love take the gold to make two blond tresses? Among what thorns did he pluck the rose and on what slope the fresh and tender frost, to give them pulse and breath? Where the pearls

28. Pietro Bembo, Sonnet 69: "Mostrommi entro a lo spazio d'un bel volto, / E sotto un ragionar cortese umile / Per farmi ogn'altro caro essere a vile / Amor quanto può darne il Ciel raccolto."

29. Petrarch, *Canzoniere* 325:60: "Il dì che costei nacque eran le stelle, / Che producon fra noi felici effetti, / In luoghi alti, e eletti. / L'una ver l'altra con amor converse."

30. Luigi Tansillo, *Poesie, canzone* 3.32–44: "Ma quando mi conduce / La mente a penetrar l'alta virtude, / che la bella alma chiude. / Parmi allor, che la bocca, e gl'occhi, e'l riso / E i membri in Paradiso / Fatti per man de gl'angeli, e di Dio / Sien la minor cagion dell'ardor mio. / Chi potria mai narrar l'alte infinite / Gratie del ciel, ch'a larga man vi denno / Alma real tutti i miglior pianeti? / Venere la beltà, Mercurio il senno, / E le parole, ch'a l'inferno udite / Quei c'han pena maggior farien più lieti."

31. Petrarch, *Canzoniere* 159: "In qual parte del Ciel, in qual' Idea / era l'esempio onde Natura tolse / quel bel viso leggiadro in ch'ella volse / mostrar qua giù quanto lassù potea?"

with which he breaks and reins in sweet words, chaste and strange? Where the beauties, so many and so divine, of that forehead brighter than the heavens? From what angels and what sphere did he send that heavenly song which so melts me that by now little remains to melt? From what sun was born the high kindly light of those lovely eyes from which I receive war and peace, that burn my heart in ice and fire?[32]

To create this rich and esteemed treasure house of beauty, therefore, it is necessary to look for it in all the most excellent and noble places, such as God, the stars, nature, the elements, and love—the minister who takes it from the different bodies and from every other source of perfection and excellence. Tasso concludes in his sonnets that every good thing in the world is contained in beauty. He uses these words:

Beautiful lady, in your fair face is seen the splendor of paradise, so that when my thoughts dwell on you it seems to me that I see every good gathered there.[33]

So if women are more beautiful than men, who, as can be seen, are generally coarse and ill-formed, who can deny that they are more remarkable? Nobody, in my opinion. Thus it can be said that beauty in a woman is a marvellous spectacle and a miracle worthy of respect, though it is never fully honored and respected by men.

But I wish to go further and show that men are obliged and forced to love women, and that women are not obliged to love them back, except merely from courtesy. I also wish to demonstrate that the beauty of women is the way by which men, who are moderate creatures, are able to raise themselves to the knowledge and contemplation of the divine essence. Everybody will be convinced of these matters one day, and the obstinate oppressors of women who trample on their dignity with greater insolence each day will be overcome.

That women's pleasing qualities and lovely, delicate faces force and oblige men to fall in love with them against their wills is very clear. To affirm this appears to me an easy undertaking, because beauty is by nature

---

32. Petrarch, *Canzoniere* 220: "Onde tolse Amor l'oro e di qual vena / per far due treccie bionde? e'n quali spine / colse le rose, e'n qual piaggia le brine / tenere e fresche, e diè lor polso e lena? / Onde le perle in ch'ei frange et affrena / dolci parole oneste et pellegrine? / Onde tante bellezze et sì divine / di quella fronte più che 'l ciel serena? / Da quali angeli mosse e da qual spera / quel celeste cantar che mi disface / sì che n'avanza omai da disfar poco? / Di qual sol nacque l'alma luce altera / di que'belli occhi ond'io ho guerra e pace, / che mi cuocono il cor in ghiaccio e 'n foco?' "

33. Torquato Tasso, Sonnet dedicated to La Serenissima Duchessa di Ferrara, in *Scielta delle rime del Sig. T. Tasso*, part 2, p. 24: "Bella Signora nel tuo vago volto / Sì vede lo splendor del Paradiso, / Sì che qual' ora il mio pensier v'affiso / Parmi vedere il ben tutto raccolto."

lovable, or truly worthy of love, as Marsilio Ficino states in these words in his translation of Plato's *Symposium*:

> Beauty is a kind of human splendor that ravishes the soul, and whose nature is lovable.[34]

Man needs to love beautiful things, and what more beautiful thing adorns the world than woman? Nothing in truth, as is admitted by all those opposed to us, who affirm that women's lovely faces shine with the grace and splendor of paradise and that they are forced to love them for this beauty, while women are not forced to love men, because that which is less beautiful, or ugly, is not by nature worthy of being loved.

I say that compared to women all men are ugly. They would not be loved by women were it not for our courteous and benign natures, to which it seems discourteous not to love our male admirers a little. Let the complaints, laments, sighs, and exclamations of men cease, therefore. They mistakenly seek to make women love them by saying that women are cruel, ungrateful, and wicked. This cast of thought can be plainly seen in men's poetry and is merely laughable. That women's beauty leads to the knowledge of God and the supernal intelligence, and shows the way to heaven, is demonstrated by Petrarch, who, in the movement of Madonna Laura's eyes, saw a light that showed him the way to heaven and caused him to add:

> And through long custom within myself, where I sojourn alone with love, your heart shines almost visibly. This is the sight that leads me to do good and that shows me a glorious goal: this only distances me from the common herd.[35]

Further down he adds:

> I think: if up there—from where the eternal mover of the stars deigned to show his work on earth—the other works are as beautiful, let the prison open in which I am closed.[36]

From these words it can be understood that Petrarch was saying to himself: "If this unique beauty that I have discovered in the graceful, sparkling eyes

---

34. Marsilio Ficino, translation of Plato's *Symposium* (see note 8 above): "Pulchritudo est quidam splendor humanus ad se rapiens animam, et amabilis sua natura."

35. Petrarch, *Canzoniere* 72:1.4: "E per lungo costume / dentro là dove sol con amor seggio / quasi visibilmente il cor traluce, / questa è la vista, ch' al ben far m'induce / e che mi scorge a glorioso fine: / questa sola dal vulgo m'allontana."

36. Ibid. 2:1: "Io penso se là suso / onde il motore eterno delle stelle / degnò mostrar del suo lavoro in terra / son l'altre opre sì belle, / aprasi la prigione, ov'io son chiuso."

of Madonna Laura is so worthy and deserving of respect, what must that which is in heaven be like?" and that thinking of this made him want to die. In sonnet 13 he thanks fortune, or God, who has made him worthy of seeing Laura, through whose means he has been guided toward the supreme good:

> From her comes the amorous thought that, while I follow it, sends me toward the supreme good, little valuing what other men desire. From her comes fair courage, which guides me to heaven by the straight path.[37]

In sonnet 289 he writes:

> I thank her and her lofty counsel, which with her beautiful face and with gentle anger forced me while burning to think of my salvation.[38]

Shortly afterward he writes:

> That sun which showed me the straight path to go to heaven with glorious steps.[39]

Dante, in a ballad, writes that in contemplating the face of his lady he becomes beatified, like an angel.

> Since my eyes can never have enough of looking at my lady's beautiful face I will look at it so fixedly that I will become blessed while looking at her. As an angel, who, by nature living on high, becomes blessed just by looking at God, thus being a human creature looking at the face of this lady who holds my heart, I could become blessed here.[40]

Caro, speaking to Love in a *canzone*, says:

> Who guides us down here, who raises us to heaven? For from pole to pole dark fog envelops us. With these guides Love leads us from ardor to ardor. From one splendor to another he leads us to gaze at

---

37. Ibid. 13:9: "Da lei ci vien l'amoroso pensiero, / Che mentre il segui al sommo ben t'invia, / Poco prezzando quel, ch'ogn' uom desia. / Da lei vien l'animosa leggiadria, / Che'al Ciel ti scorge per destro sentiero."

38. Ibid. 289:9: "Lei ne ringrazio, e 'l suo alto consiglio, / Che col bel viso, e co'soavi sdegni / Fecemi ardendo pensar mia salute."

39. Ibid. 306: "Quel sol, che mi mostrava il camin destro / Di gire al Ciel con gloriosi passi."

40. Dante, *Ballate* 9: "Poi che saziar non posso gli occhi miei / Di guardare a Madonna il suo bel viso / Mirerò 'l tanto fiso, / Ch'io diverrò beato lei guardando. / A guisa d'angel, che di sua natura / Stando su in altura / Divien beato sol vedendo Dio; / Così essendo humana creatura / Guardando la figura / Di questa donna, che tene il cor mio / Potria beato divenir qui io." This ballad is now regarded as spurious. See *Le Opere de Dante, Testo Critico della Società Dantesca Italiana* (Florence: R. Bemporad, 1921).

the eternal sun; thus mortal beauty, which comes from him, seems to awaken us to him: thus celestial light derived from above, is honored here below. Now who is to raise us up, and who from on high look down on us if our beloved sun offers us no light?[41]

In one of his sonnets we read:

I see well how she inspires and how she shines, because with remembrance and desire of her beautiful eyes and her sweet smile she leads my thought so high that it draws near to her, and perceives in that beautiful face the brightness of angels, and of God.[42]

Bernardo Tasso writes a whole *canzone* demonstrating that beauty is a stairway which leads to heaven, and then adds:

Oh noble lady, oh my shining sun, safe and solid stairway to heaven, sun of my life, sweet support: Nature gave life to you for no other reason, rare virtue, unique beauty, and sun, if not to enrich this unworthy world and show it a pattern of angelic and divine beauty.[43]

Molza makes similar points in his sonnets, and Guidiccioni says the same thing in a very beautiful sonnet of which I will quote only three lines:

He does it so that the mind, passing from one likeness to another, unites itself with God, not for purposeless desire as others believe.[44]

What poet is there, however coarse, who does not state openly that beauty is the path that guides us directly to the contemplation of divine wisdom (even though Passi, writing in ignorance, dares to affirm that beauty

41. Annibale Caro, *canzone* beginning "Amor, che fia di noi se non si sface," in *Rime* (Venice, 1572): "Chi ne guida qua giù, chi n'erge al Cielo? / Poi ch'ambi i nostri poli / Atra nebbia c'involi / Con queste scorte Amor di zelo, in zelo. / D'una in altra chiarezza / Ne conduce a mirar l'eterno sole; / Così mortal bellezza / Che da lui viene, a lui par che ci deste: / Così lume celesto / Che di la sù deriva, qui si cole / Or chi s'inalza, e chi d'alto ci scorge / Se'l nostro amato sol lume non porge."

42. Annibale Caro, Sonnet beginning "O d'umana beltà caduchi fiori," in *Rime:* "Ben veggio come spira, e come luce / Che con la rimembranza, e col desio / De' suoi begli occhi, e del suo dolce riso / Il mio pensier tanto alto si conduce, / Che le s'appressa, e scorge nel bel viso / La chiarezza de gli angeli, e di Dio."

43. Bernardo Tasso, *canzone* dedicated to la Signora Ginevra Malatesta (lines 79–86) in *Rime,* book 2: "O nobil Donna, o mio lucente sole, / Scala da gir al Ciel salda, e sicura, / Sol de la vita mia dolce sostegno: / Per altro no vi diè l'alma natura / Rare virtù, bellezze uniche, e sole / Se non per arricchire il mondo indegno / E mostrarne un disegno / De la bellezza angelica, e divina."

44. Giovanni Guidiccioni, Sonnet beginning "Sì come il sol, ch'è viva statua chiara," in *Rime diverse di molti eccellenti autori* (Venice, 1545): "E'l fa perché la mente oltre passando / D'una in altra sembianza a Dio s'unisca / Non già per van desio com'altri crede."

is the cause of infinite evils)? Beauty should be looked at dispassionately and without lascivious, vain thoughts, as Petrarch writes:

> I gave him wings to fly above the heavens through mortal things that,
> if judged rightly, are the staircase to the Creator.[45]

I would not merely call beauty a staircase. I believe it to be the golden chain referred to by Homer that can always raise minds toward God and can never, for any reason, be dragged down toward earth. This is because beauty, not being earthly but divine and celestial, always raises us toward God, from whom it is derived. This is shown in the following lines by Petrarch:

> From one beauty to another I raise myself gazing on the first cause.[46]

This means, "I ascend from beauty to beauty," that is, from link to link, "and I base myself on the first cause." The first link of our golden chain that, descending from heaven, gently carries away our souls, is corporeal beauty. This is gazed at and considered by the mind, through means of the outer eye, which enjoys and finds moderate pleasure in it, but then, conquered by supreme sweetness, ascends to the second link and contemplates and gazes with the internal eye at the soul that, adorned with celestial excellence, gives form to the beautiful body. Not stopping at this second beauty or link, but avid and desirous of a more vivid beauty and almost inflamed by love, the mind ascends to the third link, in order to compare earthly and celestial beauties and raise itself to heaven. From there it contemplates the angelic spirits, and finally this contemplative mind seats itself within the great light of the angels, and thus of the one who supports the chain. So the soul, taking delight in Him, is made happy and blessed.

I will say no more for now of this chain, but may speak of it at greater length further on. I believe that through my reasoning I have clearly demonstrated that the beauty of a lovely face, accompanied by a graceful appearance, guides every man to the knowledge of his maker. What a gift and what a dowry these women have, and in what abundance, that with their beauty they can raise men's minds to God! Who could ever praise you enough, rich treasure of the world? I confess that if I spoke as many languages as there are leaves on the trees in the laughing springtime, or grains of sand in sterile and infertile Libya, I could never begin to sing your

45. Petrarch, *Canzoniere* 360:137: "Da volar sopra il Ciel gli havea dat'ali / Per le cose mortali / Che son scala al Fattor, chi ben l'estima."

46. The lines Marinella quotes are: "D'una in l'altra bellezza / M'alzo mirando la cagion primiera." The nearest quote I can find to this is in Petrarch, *Canzoniere* 360:142: "D'una in l'altra sembianza / Potea levarsi a l'alta cagion primiera." (From one likeness to the next he could have risen to the high First Cause).

praises sufficiently. Not only does your beauty raise cold minds to God, but it renders even the most crude and obstinate heart humble and meek. What more? Oh marvel! It adorns the primitive with pleasing habits, renders the foolish prudent and wise, and in short has moved every poet to write verses to women's beauty. Petrarch, for example, in his *Canzoniere*, 360, which begins "My old sweet cruel Lord," demonstrates that it is the cause of all his virtues in the words:

Risen to some fame only through me, who have raised up his intellect to where it could never have raised itself.[47]

In order to praise the divine beauty of Madonna Laura he composed a poem that was greatly esteemed by the world. If she had not pushed him to this honor with her beauty he might have been, as Love says in the same poem:

who now perhaps would be a hoarse murmurer of the courts, one of the mob![48]

Sperone Speroni confesses that women give poets their voices and intellects:

so I may see you assemble the beautiful array of all your beloved goddesses who give to poetry its voice and intellect.[49]

Other poets have done the same, recognizing their obligation to praise and bow to women's beauty, which lives even when they are dead. A beautiful face can conquer the proudest, most haughty kingdom of the world, as well as the one most scientific and literate. Tasso demonstrates the greatness and majesty of this gift in *Torrismondo*:

This beauty is the particular benefit, dowry and gift of women, oh daughter, and the particular object of praise. And this makes us equal, even superior, to the rich, wise, fertile, industrious, and strong. And victories, triumphs, spoils and palms are ours and are more dear and more beautiful and greater than those boasted of by men, who are stained with blood and overflowing with anger.[50]

47. Petrarch, *Canzoniere* 360:88: "Salito in qualche fama / Solo per me, che 'l suo intelletto alzai / Ov'alzato per se non fora mai."

48. Petrarch, *Canzoniere* 360:116: "Ch' or saria forse un roco / Mormorador di corti, un uom del vulgo!"

49. Sperone Speroni: "Ch'io vi veda adunar la bella schiera / Di tutte queste vostre amate Dive / Che danno a poetar voce e' intelletto."

50. Tasso, *Il re Torrismondo* 2:4.28–36: "Questa bellezza / Proprio ben, propria dote, e proprio dono / È de le donne, o figlia, e propria laude / Et agguagliam, anzi vinciam con questa / Ricchi, saggi, facondi, industri, e forti. / E vittorie, e trionfe, e spoglie, e Palme / Le nostre sono e son più care, e belle / E maggiori di quelle, onde si vanta / L'uom che di sangue è tinto, e d'ira colmo."

In these few words he has shown the marvellous ways in which beauty works, how it has tamed the pride not only of men, but also of the ancient gods.

I would wish now to exalt and praise you, but I lack the words, and the more I spread the wings of my too audacious thoughts, the more there remain, so I would merely say with Petrarch:

> Silent I cannot be, and I fear that my tongue may produce an effect contrary to my heart, which would wish to honor its lady, who listens to us from Heaven. How can I if love does not teach me with mortal words to equal divine works.[51]

I can even say that I diminish beauty's praises by speaking them, and that it is better therefore to be silent and bow before it and gaze at it and worship it while it stupefies me. I worship and bow before it as before something holy.

Let us conclude, therefore, that women, being more beautiful than men, are also nobler than they are. The reasons for this are first because God's power can be discerned in a blooming and delicate face, which also raises men's minds toward divine goodness; second, because beauty is lovable by nature and attracts every heart, however rigid or bitter; and finally, because beauty is adorned with and full of goodness, being a ray and splendor of excellence. As Marsilio Ficino states: "For all beauty is good."[52] Speusippus and Plotinus say the same, and everyone clearly appreciates how rare it is for an evil soul to dwell in a pleasing, graceful body.

It is for this reason that nature, knowing the perfection of the female sex, produces a greater abundance of women than of men, as it always, or nearly always, does on occasions when objects are better or closer to perfection. Thus it appears to me that Aristotle goes against all reason, and even against his own theory that nature always, or almost always, designs more nearly perfect objects, when he states that women are imperfect in comparison to men.[53] Moreover, I would say that as nature produces smaller numbers of men than of women, that men are the less noble sex, since nature chooses not to produce large or copious quantities of them. And now enough of the singular nature of the female sex.

---

51. Petrarch, *Canzoniere* 325: "Tacer non posso, e temo non adopra / Contrario effetto la mia lingua al core, / Che vorria far onore / A la sua donna, che dal Ciel n'ascolta. / Come poss'io se non m'insegna amore / Con parole mortali aguagliar l'opre / Divine."

52. "Omne enim pulcrum est bonum." See, for example, Ficino's *Letters* 19: "Beauty follows the light of the good as its splendor." Also Plotinus, *Enneads* 1.6.7: "Anyone who has seen [the good] knows what I mean when I say that it is beautiful."

53. See, for example, Aristotle, *Generation of Animals* 4.6 (775a5–15): female nature is "a sort of natural deficiency." (Cf. Marinella's Introduction, note 4, where Aristotle's misogynist philosophy is referred to by Marinella and especially the following chapter.)

IV

THE REASONS FOR MEN'S NOBLE TREATMENT OF WOMEN AND THE THINGS THEY SAY ABOUT WOMEN

Even though men upbraid and defame the female sex each day in garrulous and biting language, and search in every possible way to obscure the noble actions of women, they are forced in spite of themselves, by consciences that are governed by truth, to honor worthy women and praise them to the skies. They do this in words and in writings that demonstrate women's superiority beyond any doubt.

We see constantly and in every place and occasion that women are honored by men. That is why men bow to them and make way for them when walking, why they raise their hats to them and wait on them at table like servants, accompany them bareheaded in the streets, and give up their seats to them. These obvious signs of honor are performed toward women not merely by low, plebeian men but also by dukes and kings, who raise their hats whether greeting princesses or ladies of mediocre condition. It may be superfluous, but I will give two examples of these princes. The first is the King of France, who honors every lady with bows and salutations; the second the King of Spain, who, though extremely powerful, raises his cap or hat on meeting a noblewoman, which is something he would not do to any male subject, even if he were a prince. Uncovering the head, standing up, and giving way are undoubtedly signs and proofs of honor, and since they are signs of honor, women must be nobler than the men who honor them, because the object of such honor is always more nobler than the person who honors them. Nobody honors another person unless they know that the person has some gift or quality that is superior to his own, as Aristotle writes in book IV of the *Ethics:* "Everything that excels in some way

is more honorable."[1] Honor is nothing other than the reward or benefit of
the virtue that shines forth from somebody as he states in the *Ethics,* book
VIII, chapter 16: honor "is the prize appointed for the noblest deeds."[2] It is
necessary therefore to conclude that women are nobler than men because
they are honored by men.

Further indications of honor are the ornaments bestowed on women,
who are permitted to dress themselves in purple and cloth of gold with
diverse embroideries decorated with pearls and diamonds, and to adorn their
heads with pretty gold ornaments and finest enamel and precious stones.
These things are forbidden to men, apart from rulers. If any other man dared
to dress himself in cloth of gold or such like, he would be mocked and
pointed out as light-minded or a downright buffoon. It was the ancients
who bestowed these ornaments on women. The Romans in particular made
decrees and laws about it. Ornaments were forbidden to women under the
Oppian law because of a most urgent need for money during the war against
Carthage, but when the war ended women were allowed ornaments once
more. This reversal was forced, in fact, by women, who were jealous of their
dignity, though they did so with great danger of incurring some sinister
event. For the truth of this, read the words of Livy in the fourth decade,
book IV:

> The matrons could not be kept at home until they again had leave to
> wear their ornaments, neither by the authorities, nor out of respect for
> or by commandment of their husbands. They crowded into every street
> of the city and neck of the squares, demanding that men should give
> back the ornaments that they had taken from them. This constant
> attendance of women increased each day, because not only Roman
> women but also women from the country and neighboring villas joined
> together and dared to exhort the consuls, so that Cato, in his oration
> against women, said that he would suspect them of civil sedition and
> turmoil if they did not check their pride. Lucius Valerius, the tribune
> of the Plebs, spoke against him, praising the women lavishly. The
> following day a much greater number of women showed themselves in
> public and, all in formation, surrounded the tribunes' houses, protesting
> against the law and not ceasing to clamor until it was quashed and

---

1. Aristotle, *Nicomachean Ethics* 4.3 (1124a23): "Omne quod aliquo excellit, est honorabilius."

2. Aristotle, *Nicomachean Ethics* 4.3 (1123b35) (not book 8 as stated): "est virtutis premium et
benefitii."

annulled by the patricians, who were able to do this by reason of the well-known nobility and merits of women.[3]

This law was subsequently upheld and is observed in every city. In Germany, where men are not permitted any sort of festive attire unless they are noble, every little woman adorns herself with festive drapes and different types of necklace, as is the habit all over the world. Women are honored everywhere with the use of ornaments that greatly surpass men's, as can be observed. It is a marvellous sight in our city to see the wife of a shoemaker or butcher or even a porter all dressed up with gold chains round her neck, with pearls and valuable rings on her fingers, accompanied by a pair of women on either side to assist her and give her a hand, and then, by contrast, to see her husband cutting up meat all soiled with ox's blood and down at heel, or loaded up like a beast of burden dressed in rough cloth, as porters are. At first it may seem an astonishing anomaly to see the wife dressed like a lady and the husband so basely that he often appears to be her servant or butler, but if we consider the matter properly, we find it reasonable because it is necessary for a woman, even if she is humble and low, to be ornamented in this way because of her natural dignity and excellence, and for the man to be less so, like a servant or beast born to serve her.

As well as in the ways already narrated, women have been honored by men with great and eminent titles that are used by them continually, being commonly referred to as *donne*, for, as was demonstrated in the first chapter, the name *donna* means lady and mistress. When men refer to women thus, they honor them, though they may not intend to, by calling them ladies, even if they are humble and of a lowly disposition. In truth, to express the nobility of this sex men could not find a more appropriate and fitting name than *donna*, which immediately shows women's superiority and precedence over men, because by calling women mistress they show themselves of necessity to be subjects and servants.

Besides this, they have often been called other names, and even if only by certain men, this matters little because these men have been among the

---

3. In 215 B.C.E., because of the financial demands on the state made by the war with Hannibal, a sumptuary law—the so-called Oppian Law—was passed in Rome, stating that no women should possess more than half an ounce of gold, wear a multicolored dress, or ride a carriage in the city or within a mile of its limits except during public religious ceremonies. Twenty years later, with the wars over, the Roman women petitioned successfully to have the law repealed. The story is told in Livy, *History of Rome, From the Founding of the City,* book 34, and Marinella here quotes a severely shortened paraphrase of chapters 1.5–8.3, leaving out the long speeches from Cato the Elder and Lucius Valerius on both sides of the question. The conclusion that it was because of the "well-known nobility and merits of women" that the law was repealed is not, however, found in Livy's version, but appears to be supplied by Marinella herself.

most wise and powerful in the world and their addresses determine to whom is due dignity and precedence. It should not be the task of the stupid, ignorant commoner to give new titles to emperors and kings in order to recognize them. Plebeians are better at filling their sacks with food than at discussing such matters. These names, which denote sublime excellence and that woman is the glory of man, were given to women even by Aristotle, their enemy, who allowed them precedence in some things even while upbraiding them, by granting them the virtue of diligence. This is something that men are far from possessing, as can be read in *Economics*, book I, chapter 3: "Woman is more assiduous, but man less so."[4] From these words it can be understood how much he errs in other directions when he states that women are fickle and changeable, and should make diligence, firmness, and stability their goals. He also says in several chapters of the same book that women conserve the benefits of fortune. This virtue of conservation is at least equal to, if not nobler than, that of acquisition, as he relates in *Economics* I.6, the book on caring for the family, in this way:

> For one should be fit no less to conserve than to provide, otherwise all the labor of providing would be in vain.[5]

And who conserves things with her rare virtue? The woman. "The male sex supplies the necessities . . . and the female conserves them."[6]

Having said that women are good companions, he confirms in the *History of Animals*, book IX, chapter 1, that they are wiser and more perspicacious than men.[7] I need not exert myself by recounting what a useful quality of the

---

4. Aristotle, *Economics* 1.3 (1344a4): "Mulier ad sedulitatem optima, at vir deterior." This translation may well be a confusion between the Latin word *sedulitas*—assiduity or zeal—which Marinella takes to be the meaning, and the word derived from *sedes*—chair—used to translate the original Greek sentiment that women are excellent in sedentary occupations. The *Economics* is nowadays not considered to be a genuine Aristotelian work.

5. Aristotle, *Economics* 1.6 (1344b23): "Nam non minus ad servandum quam ad comparandum idoneum esse oportet, alioquin vanus fuerit omnis labor comparandi." The more colorful quotation in the original goes: "[The head of the household] must have the faculty of preserving what he has acquired; otherwise, there is no more benefit in acquiring than in baling with a colander."

6. Aristotle, *Economics* 1.3 (1344a2), "Suppeditat enim masculus necessaria . . . et femina conservat ea." The *Economics* sets out in this passage the differentiated roles for the two sexes within the household: the man is to bring in from outside the necessities of life and the woman to remain within looking after them.

7. Aristotle, *History of Animals* 9.1 (608a15–b18). Marinella moves from the use of the word *socia* (companion) in *Economics* 3 to describe a wife to Aristotle's description of sex differences throughout the animal kingdom, which are seen as following a pattern. In *History of Animals* 9.1 he sets out the general characteristics of the female sex, and states: "Among the Laconian

brain perspicacity is, for in it consists the subtlety of the intellect and good judgment, as Aristotle says himself in the *Ethics*, book VI, chapter 10. Not only does he judge women to be wiser than men, but also much more astute, saying: "Females are more astute than males,"[8] which attribute of the soul, for its activity and excellence, has come to be called *calliditas* (cleverness) by the Latins. This gift is always joined with prudence, as he demonstrates in *Ethics*, book VI, chapter 11. Women are also more vigilant. Aristotle states: "for they are more vigilant"—and more docile and kindhearted in their customs than men. In the same chapter we read: "Females are gentler in their behaviour, easier to tame and more compassionate,"[9] qualities that are not found in men, belonging more to wild beasts than to men, who are ferocious, bloody, and pertinacious. What is the importance of mercy? Hear what Aristotle says in his *Physiognomy*, reasoning on the compassionate: "The compassionate are naturally ingenious and clever," and a little later he adds: "Compassion goes with wisdom and propriety while hardness of heart goes with stupidity and effrontery,"[10] that is to say that those who pity the sorrows of others are clever, wise, and modest. It can be said, therefore, that woman, being more compassionate than man, is consequently wiser, cleverer, and more modest than he.

In *History of Animals*, book IX, chapter 1, Aristotle recounts something so whimsical as to make him seem mad and unworthy of himself. What am I saying? Unworthy? On the contrary. He says similar things in other places. He states that women are less modest than men. What a ridiculous judgment! His words are "more shameless than the males."[11] No matter that this is contrary to every opinion and contrary to experience and that it was difficult

---

breed of dogs, the females are cleverer than the males." Marinella takes this to apply to females in general and compares it to a line in the *Ethics*, where Aristotle praises the quality of cleverness.

8. Aristotle, *History of Animals* 9.1 (608b4): "Sunt feminae maribus astutiores." This precise phrase cannot be found in Aristotle, but in the *History of Animals* 9.1 he includes among the characteristics of females that they are less simple than males, more cunning, and quicker to learn.

9. Aristotle, *History of Animals* 9.1 (608b13): "Ad haec vigilantiores," and *History of Animals* 9.1 (608a21–b18): "Sunt enim feminae moribus mollioribus, mitescunt enim celerius, et magis misericordes."

10. "Sunt misericordes ingeniosae et callidae" and "misericors est sapiens, et modestus, immisericors, insipiens, et inverecundus." The idea that the compassionate are more ingenious and clever is not to be found in Aristotle, but in *Physiognomy* 3 (808b1–2) we find the statement: "Compassion goes with wisdom, with cowardice and with propriety, while hardness of heart goes with stupidity and effrontery." Of course Marinella does not mention the association with cowardice, but only that with the more positive qualities!

11. Aristotle, *History of Animals* 9.1 (608b11): "impudentior maribus."

even for Aristotle to illustrate his opinion with a thousand illustrations—more so as in other places he affirms the opposite. It is hardly surprising that he said this, since he loved his own sex with too much fervor. In the same chapter he lets slip that women allow themselves to be deceived more often than men, saying "who are also more easily deceived,"[12] not remembering that he had said earlier that they were more astute, wiser, and more insidious than men, very gifted at opposing deception and deceit and anticipating the wise and astute swindler and the frauds of others. So this astute person tries to deceive others who are more astute by concluding that men are wiser than women. What can I say? I cannot believe that even Demosthenes could defend him over this error.[13]

But now let us leave the slanderer aside. Has not Plato praised women in a thousand ways? Has not Lycurgus exalted them?[14] All the great poets and honored writers have praised them to the skies, putting the malicious to shame.

Women's nobility and excellence is recognized by the French and Spanish more than by the Italians. In these countries they are allowed to inherit estates, succeeding not only to dukedoms but to principalities exactly as men do. Not only to principalities, but to the monarchy itself, like the sister of the King of Spain, who was able to ascend to the monarchy, as well as have dominion over numerous other principalities. Women who inherit estates can be seen every day in France and England. The Germans too recognize women's superiority.[15] The women there conduct all the business dealings and mercantile transactions in the cities while the men remain at the stoves. This also occurs in Flanders and in France. In France men may not spend even a *centime* unless at the request of their wives, and women not only administrate business dealings and sales but private income as well. What do you think? Are not women, as I have proved, known by men to be nobler

12. Ibid. (608b12): "quinetiam facilior decipi." In the text that we possess Aristotle merely says that women themselves are more deceptive.

13. Demosthenes was a famous Athenian orator who lived 384–322 B.C.E., many of whose legal and political speeches are still extant. He was considered by posterity the greatest orator and legal speaker of all time.

14. For Plato's praise of women in the *Republic*, see Marinella's Introduction, note 2. Lycurgus was a mythical founder or "law-giver" of Sparta whose policy of training women along with the men in the traditionally male sports of riding and gymnastics is praised by Plato in *Laws* 7 (804d–5c). See notes 7, 8, and 9 in chapter 5 below. Agrippa referred to Plato and Lycurgus together in this context.

15. There are several sources, classical and contemporary, which refer to the greater liberty of German women. A recent one for Marinella would be Giovan Maria Cecchi, *Compendio di più ritratti nelle cose della Magna, Fiandra* . . . , composed about 1575 (Archivio storico italiano, 1993).

than them, seeing that they confess it with their own mouths? What more is there for me to say?

Some obstinate people might say that in order to remove all doubt on this matter they would like to see an actual judgment, authenticated by a king or other great man, conferred on women in the presence of many wise and great men. I intend to appease them fully, even if I am not obliged to do so, because I wish to satisfy them and remove every occasion for doubt. Listen to what Tarcagnota writes. After Darius inherited the kingdom of Persia, he held a magnificent banquet, worthy of such a king, for the governors of the hundred and twenty-seven provinces that were subject to him. After the sumptuous banquet he proposed to his noble vassals, all of whom were of royal lineage, a riddle, promising great rewards to whoever was able to solve it. The riddle was this. Which of the following four things did they believe to be the most powerful, wine, the King, woman, or truth? The first person to speak was full of praise for wine, which could turn the head of every man were he king or servant, make the unhappy happy, the timid audacious, and, most miraculous of all, remove the fear of death. The next, reasoning in favor of the King, said royal power was the greatest. Nothing was superior to it, since mortal men obeyed it implicitly and foreign nations were subject to it, as were mountains from foothill to peak. It altered the course of rivers, and held the life and death of others in its hands. The third, speaking in favor of woman, said that undoubtedly wine was very powerful and the King more so, but that woman was far, far more powerful than either because she gave birth to and brought up powerful kings as she gave birth to the person who discovered wine. Man serves other men against his will, but obeys and serves woman with all his heart, desiring only to please her and gather riches for her, and consigning not only his friends but the whole of the rest of the world to oblivion for her sake. Finally, he depends on her and always attempts to do whatever she wants, and his father leaves his mother everything he possesses in the world. He added that not only did he remember having read that many kings and heroes had served women and, for the sake of their love, dressed themselves as women and allowed themselves to be commanded by them, but that with his own eyes he had seen the daughter of Robezaci slap the face of a great king, tear the crown from his head, and put it on her own, while the king remained humble and calm, and anxious to placate her and melt her anger, recognizing her as his 'lady.

When the third speaker had finished talking about the power of women, he added that all the things which had been said were true, but that compared with the power of truth all these things were as nothing. This reasoning was much applauded by the hundred and twenty-seven provincial governors, by many scholars and powerful men, and above all by the King himself, who rose from his golden seat to embrace and kiss him, and who made him sit next to him and not only gave him great quantities of gold and silver but cities and great honors similar to his own.[16]

16. M. G. Tarcagnota, *Delle istorie del mondo* 1.1, p. 269 (Venice, 1585). This vast work was begun by Tarcagnota, who wrote the history of the world from the creation to 1515. The first edition is unknown, but a later edition was published in Venice in 1562. Mambrin Roseo continued the History from 1518–58, publishing it in Venice in 1559, and then continuing it to 1571, published 1573. It was then continued from 1571–82 by Bartolomeo Dionigi da Fano.

V

OF WOMEN'S NOBLE ACTIONS AND VIRTUES, WHICH GREATLY SURPASS MEN'S, AS WILL BE PROVED BY REASONING AND EXAMPLE

Small honor is mine in proving through reasoning and example that the female sex is, in its actions and transactions, more singular and excellent than the male sex. I say that I will acquire small honor because the proving of it will be even easier than to prove that the sun is the brightest body in the world or that the delectable spring is the mother of flowers and leafy branches. However, to proceed on my established route—and also to enlighten certain, I will not say men but rather pale shadows of men, so that they may abandon their appalling obstinacy and lament their error—I will in this section, provide irrefutable reasons and in other sections I will offer examples of women worthy of being sung in the best poetry and in history.

I claim that every operation performed by the human race depends either on the soul or on the body, or on both of these principles united together. I also affirm that the closer to perfection these principles are, the nobler and more excellent will be the actions depending on them. I believe these suppositions to be absolutely true. Is it not so, oh men? Who can deny them? It follows that I am the victor, since both women's souls and their bodies are nobler than men's and therefore the whole compound must be nobler, as can be seen from the splendor of their beauty.

I have proved clearly in the preceding chapter that women possess all these gifts within themselves and that as a result their actions are more esteemed than men's. But it is necessary that I should clarify to some extent the nature of the body, because nearly all of its virtues and defects depend on its temperature, so that reason, even though it is master, is frequently dazzled and blinded by the senses. Why should some people be unstable, others great gluttons and guzzlers, others lively and audacious, and others unbridled and given wholly to concupiscence and pleasure? I believe, as all writers who describe people's customs confirm and as can be seen by experience, that in general the origin and cause of these matters are one's country of birth and one's bodily temperature.[1] For this reason a temperate body like a woman's is most adapted to moderate workings of the soul, which do not accord with men's hot temperature, as we will show when the time comes.

That women possess this nature can be seen from their soft and delicate flesh, their pale color mixed with vermilion, and finally from the whole composition of their body, a fitting shelter for kindness and virtue. If with these gifts and marvels given to them by nature they should practice the sciences and military arts, what could men do all day but raise their eyebrows and remain stupefied and full of admiration, as Ariosto knew when he said in *Orlando furioso*:

> Their name would soar to heights perhaps beyond the reach of any of the male sex.[2]

He did not, however, need to add the word perhaps, because women would certainly be victorious in any honored and esteemed action. The same author shows in canto XXXVII, 1, that women have succeeded triumphantly in those works they have undertaken, stating:

> Since in acquiring some other gift that nature cannot bestow except on the industrious the valiant women have labored night and day with greatest diligence and long attention, if they have met with good success, no humble work has been accomplished.[3]

In canto XX we read:

> Women have become excellent at every art that they have attempted and to those who study history their fame is clearly apparent.[4]

Moderata Fonte, who was aware to some extent of the excellence of our sex, leaves us these words:

---

1. The notion that personal characteristics are largely the result of the country of birth and its climate and of body temperature derives from ancient medical and ethnographical works. See for example the Hippocratic Corpus (*Airs, Waters, and Places* 12–24): "the temperate climate of Asia means that its inhabitants are milder natured and more prone to luxury because there are no violent extremes of temperature."

2. Ariosto, *Orlando furioso* 37:2: "Tanto il lor nome sorgeria, che forse / Viril fama a tal grado unqua non sorse."

3. Ibid., 37.1: "Se come in acquistar qualch'altro dono / Che senza industria non può dar natura / Affaticate notte, e dì si sono / Con somma diligenza, e lunga cura / Le valorose donne, e se con buono / Successo, n'è uscit'opra non oscura."

4. Ibid., 20.2: "Le donne son venute in eccellenza / Di ciascun'arte, ove hanno posto cura, / E qualunque all'istorie habbia avvertenza / Ne sente ancor la fama non oscura."

It has always been seen, and can still be seen provided that a woman has determined to set her mind to it, that more than one has enjoyed military success and stolen the praise and applause from many men: and they have done the same at letters, and in every undertaking that men practice and talk about. Women's efforts have been and are so good that they have no need at all to envy men.[5]

But in our times there are few women who apply themselves to study or the military arts, since men, fearing to lose their authority and become women's servants, often forbid them even to learn to read or write. Our good friend Aristotle states that women must obey men everywhere and in everything and not search for anything that takes them outside their houses.[6] A foolish opinion and cruel, pedantic sentence from a fearful, tyrannical man. But we must excuse him, because, being a man, it is only natural he should desire the greatness and superiority of men and not of women. Plato, however, who was truly great and just, was far from imposing a forced and violent authority. He both desired and ordered women to practice the military arts, ride, wrestle, and, in short, to instruct themselves in the needs of the Republic. The truth of this can be read in *Laws*:

The female must share with the male, both in education and in all other things.[7]

In the *Republic*, book VII, he writes:

In the Republic, the women no less than the men, if they are distinguished by valor and are of a ready nature, will hold an equal position with men.[8]

Oh, how many women there are, who with their greater prudence, justice, and experience of life, would govern empires better than men! It was

---

5. Moderata Fonte, *Tredici canti di Floridoro* (Venice, 1995), 4.2: "Sempre s'è visto, e vede (pur ch'alcuna / Donna v'habbia voluto il pensier porre) / Ne la militia riuscir più d'una / E 'l pregio, e 'l grido a molti huomini torre: / E così ne le lettere, e in ciascuna / Impresa, che l'huom pratica, e discorre / Le donne sì buon frutto han fatto, e fanno / Che gli huomini a invidiar punto non hanno."

6. Aristotle, *Economics* 3.1: "In all other things [the wife] should obey her husband, and not listen to outside influences. . . . It is unseemly for women to go looking for things out of doors." This book survives only in Latin translation. It is not included in Bekker's edition, so the customary Bekker references are absent.

7. Plato, *Laws* 7 (805c): "Foemineum genus eruditionis, et aliorum studiorum societatem cum virili genere habere debet."

8. Plato, *Republic* 7 (540c): "Foeminae non minus, ut viri in Republica virtutu in ornande, ut que prestantes natura sunt, principatum gerant equaliter cum viris."

not only the wise Plato who was of this opinion, but many, many others before him, such as Lycurgus. In *Laws*, dialogue 7, Plato states:

> I am persuaded by the ancient stories that horsemanship and gymnastics are as suitable for women as for men.[9]

From these words it can be seen that before the advent of Plato women in many places were practicing the military arts. A little later he speaks of the foolish opinion of his own times that did not allow women to do the things imposed on them by the ancients. He says:

> I declare that this practice which at the moment prevails in our country is extremely irrational—that men and women do not follow the same pursuits together to the best of their abilities.[10]

Would to God that in our times it were permitted for women to be skilled at arms and letters! What marvellous feats we should see, the like of which were never heard, in maintaining and expanding kingdoms. And who but women, with their intrepid spirits, would be the first to take arms in defense of their country? And with what readiness and ardor they would shed their blood and their lives in defense of males. I have proved that women are nobler than men in their dealings. If they do not show their skills, it is because men do not allow them to practice them, since they are driven by obstinate ignorance, which persuades them that women are not capable of learning the things they do. I would like these men to try the experiment of training a good- natured boy and girl of about the same age and intelligence in letters and arms. They would see how much sooner the girl would become expert than the boy and how she would surpass him completely. Moderata Fonte, though content with proving them equal, writes this in *Floridoro*:

> If when a daughter were born to a father he imposed the same tasks on her as on his son, she would not perform greater or lesser duties in an inferior manner or unequally to her brother, or if he placed her among armed troops with him, or to learn the liberal arts. But since she is brought up to perform different tasks, she receives scant respect for her education.[11]

9. Plato, *Laws* 7 (804e): "Foeminis non minus, quam viris decoram esse equestrem disciplinam, et gymnasticam ex veteribus narrationibus persuasus sum." The actual quotation from Plato translates as: "I will unhesitatingly affirm that neither riding nor gymnastics, which are suitable occupations for men, are unsuitable for women."

10. Ibid. (805a): "Stolidissime omnium nunc in regionibus nostris censeo fieri, quod non omni robore uno consensu mulieres, ac viri eadem studia tractent."

11. Moderata Fonte, *Tredici canti di Floridoro* 4.4: "Se quando nasce una figliuola al padre, / La ponesse col figlio a un opra eguale / Non faria ne le imprese alte, e leggiadre / Al frate inferior,

The reason we do not daily see memorable feats and acts of heroism from women is, therefore, because they do not put these skills into practice. The same applies to many men.

I now wish to proceed to examples, which will be brief since I have avoided the fatigue of reading every history book available, knowing that their authors, being men and jealous of women's noble deeds, have not recounted women's most worthy actions but have remained silent about them. I cite the words of the historians themselves, and I warn my readers that there may be many errors in their language, since they were not very careful with their words. Ariosto exposes the lies of these writers in *Orlando furioso*:

> And if by themselves they could have achieved undying reputation without having to beg it from authors whose hearts are gnawed by resentment and envy, so that the good which they could say is often passed over in silence, and the evil they do is heard by all, their name would rise to such an extent that perhaps masculine fame could not attain to such a level.

> It is not enough for many men to augment each others' reputations and make them glorious in the eyes of the world they also study ways to disclose any blemishes in women. They do not want to put women above them and do their best to keep them down; I speak of the men of old, as if women's honor would obscure their own like the mist the sun.

> But there was never a hand or tongue to give voice, or describe on paper (though it used every skill to inflate evil and belittle good) that could extinguish women's glory so that no part of it remains; some does, but not so much as approaches the mark nor yet draws near to it by a long way.

> Faithful, chaste, wise and strong women have existed, not only in Greece and Rome, but in every region where between the Indies and the Garden of the Hesperides the sun spreads its rays: their virtues are lost to fame so that from among a thousand hardly one is named; and this because in their day they had writers who were deceitful, envious and mean.[12]

---

ne disuguale; / O la ponesse fra l'armate squadre / Seco, o a imparar qualche arte liberale; / Ma perché in altri affar viene allevata, / Per l'education poco è stimata."

12. Ariosto, *Orlando furioso* 37:2–4,6: "E che per se medesime potuto / Avessin dar memoria alle lor lode / Non mendicar da gli scrittori aiuto / Ai quali astio, e invidia il cor si rode. / Che'l ben, che ne puon dir spesso è taciuto, / E'l mal quanto ne san, per tutto s'ode; / Tanto il lor nome sorgeria, che forse / Viril fama a tal grado unqua non sorse.

"Non basta a molti di prestarsi l'opra / In far l'un l'altro glorioso al mondo, / Ch'anco studian di far che si discuopra / Ciò che le donne hanno fra lor d'immondo. / Non le vorrian

How does this seem to you, brothers? You who do not wish to reveal the good works of the worthy and excellent female sex, and what is worse, constantly seek new ways to vituperate it so that it may remain oppressed and buried? And yet your mothers were women. And do you dare to reproach them? How inhuman of you. You are like new Neros, who seek to kill your own mothers' fame.[13] Your attempts will be fruitless because the truth, shining forth from these, my poorly written pages, will raise them to the skies in spite of you. I speak now about those men who do not recognize women's excellence, because there are not lacking, nor have there lacked (even if their numbers are small), writers who have not been envious of the female sex and who have praised them with all their powers, refuting those men who have offended the female sex, either by deed or word, as lacking in wit and humanity.

One of these was Cato the Elder, who held that those who offended their wives were worse than those who robbed the temple and offended the Gods. He esteemed far more highly a man who was a good husband than one who was an important member of the Senate, as Plutarch recounts in his *Life*, for he knew that man must love woman more than his life and prize her for her nobility among the things he holds most dear and honorable.[14] This is also affirmed by Orsato Giustiniano, the Venetian senator, in the following sonnet composed by him in praise of his wife, who was most faithful, chaste, and deserving of his love:

> He truly has a breast of iron and heart of stone who far from his faithful, dear wife can ever lead a peaceful, unclouded life; or without great sadness move his steps. I find myself that as the hours pass far from you, my rare and only hope, I can find no peace, and my life is bitter, stripped of every good and purposeless.[15]

---

lasciar venir disopra, / E quanto puon, fan per cacciarle al fondo: / Dico gli antiqui; quasi l'onor debbia / D'esse il lor oscurar, come il sol nebbia.

"Ma non ebbe e non ha mano né lingua, / Formando in voce o discrivendo in carte / (Quantunque il mal, quanto può, accresce e impingua / E minuendo il ben va con ogni arte), / Poter pero, che delle donne estingua / La gloria sì, che non ne resti parte; / Ma non già tal, che presso al segno giunga, / Né ch'anco se gli accosti di gran lunga.

"E di fedeli, e caste, e sagge, e forti / Stato ne son, non pur in Grecia e in Roma, / Ma in ogni parte, ove fra gl'Indi, e gli Orti / De l'Esperide il Sol spiega la chioma: / De le quai sono i pregi, agli onor morti, / Sì ch'a pena di mille una si noma; / E questo; Perché avuto hanno ai lor tempi / Gli scrittori bugiardi, invidi ed empi."

13. See 2.30.3 of this volume for the story of Nero and Agrippina.

14. Plutarch, *Life of Cato the Elder* 20.2 (347).

15. Orsatto Giustiniano, Sonnet in *Rime di Celio Magno et Orsatto Giustiniano*, p. 50 (Venice, 1600),: "Ben ha di ferro il petto, e'l cor di sasso, / Chi può lontan da fida sposa, e cara / Menar vita giamai tranquilla, e chiara; / O senz'alto dolor pur mover passo. / Provolo in me, che mentre

In another sonnet he demonstrates that she is the serene harbor of his good fortune:

> Benignly the heavens respond to your prayers, dear wife, and may the Gods be favorable to you. For you are always a tranquil harbor to my fortunes, and my sweet, fertile breeze.[16]

These two men have clearly recognized the illustrious and unclouded gifts of women. Let these two suffice for now, since if I wished to cite all those who have (with reason) praised women, I would take up so much time that I could not proceed to the examples. These will be divided by me into eleven [sub]sections which I will keep as brief as possible.

SECTION 1: OF LEARNED WOMEN AND THOSE WHO ARE ILLUSTRIOUS IN MANY ARTS

Some people, possessing little knowledge of history, believe that women who are skilled and learned in the arts and sciences have never existed and do not exist now. To them such a thing appears impossible; nor can they yet understand that they see and listen to these women every day. These people have persuaded themselves that Jove has bestowed wit and intellect only on men and left women deprived of even the smallest quantity.

But if women have the same reasoning souls as men, as I have clearly shown above, and souls that are still nobler, why should they not be even better than men at learning the same arts and sciences? Indeed the few women who are interested in learning become so skilled in the sciences that men envy them, as lesser people tend to envy greater ones.

In order not to waste time on this point that I have already proved in preceding chapters, I will move on to examples, the first of which will be Amphiclea, who was greatly praised by Porphyry in his *Life of Plotinus*. He tells how she achieved a marvellous success in philosophy as Plotinus's disciple.[17] Dicaearchus, also, writes of two extremely powerful women who abandoned their riches so that they could better follow the doctrines of the learned Plato.[18] Nicaula, Queen of Egypt, was a very learned woman with a

---

hor l'hore passo / Lungi da te mia speme, unica, e rara, / Pace non trovo: e m'è la vita amara, / D'ogni ben rimanendo igniudo, a casso."

16. Ibid., p. 50: "Benigno il cielo a tuoi preghi risponda / Cara moglie in favor ti sien li Dei. / Poi che ne le fortune ogn' or mi sei / Tranquillo porto, e dolce aura feconda."

17. Porphyry, *Life of Plotinus* 9. Amphiclea was a disciple of the third-century Neoplatonic philosopher Plotinus; she was also the daughter-in-law of Iamblichus.

18. Diogenes Laertius, *Lives of Eminent Philosophers* 3.46, on Lastheneia of Mantineia and Axiothea of Phlius, citing Dicaearchus as his authority.

great desire to understand secret matters who went to visit King Solomon in order to resolve a doubt over something difficult and obscure.[19] Battista, the honorable wife of the Duke of Urbino, excelled at composing speeches and letters. She went to Rome and prayed in the presence of Pope Pius II to everyone's amazement and wonder, and ruled the state most justly and to great acclaim for many years.[20] What should I say of Aspasia, so learned in philosophical study that she was worthy to teach that great Pericles who thundered and lightninged when he spoke?[21] What of Asfiotea, celebrated by Apuleius and Plutarch in the book of Plato's Dogma? She was a disciple of Plato and most accomplished in the study of philosophy, which is why she is placed among the illustrious and outstanding women.[22] Where should we place Cleobulina, daughter of one of the Seven Wise Men of Greece, whose beautiful writings were most highly praised in Suidas, Athenaeus, and several other great authors?[23] Where Barsine, wife of Alexander the Great, who composed beautiful hymns in praise of Neptune?[24] Where Cornelia, daughter of Scipio Africanus and mother of the Gracchi, who wrote letters demonstrating her great learning? Quintilian writes of her:

> We have heard that the mother, Cornelia, contributed much to the eloquence of the Gracchi, and her learned discourse is also handed down to posterity in her letters.[25]

Leontium, a young Greek girl, was very distinguished at philosophy and did not hesitate, much to her credit, from writing against the highly praised philosopher Theophrastus.[26] Another accomplished woman was Daphne, the daughter of Tiresias, who composed many books of poetry that, as

---

19. Queen of Sheba, I Kings 10:1–13. Also Boccaccio, *Concerning Famous Women* 41. Trans. Guido A. Guarino (New Brunswick, N.J.: Rutgers University Press, 1963).

20. Giuseppe Betussi, *Delle donne illustri* (including translation of Boccaccio's *Concerning Famous Women*), 18.176, on Battista, Duchess of Urbino (Venice, 1547).

21. Plutarch, *Life of Pericles* 24, on Aspasia.

22. Apuleius and Plutarch both wrote on Plato and his doctrine, but neither contains a reference to Asfiotea, nor can I find one to her in any other source.

23. Athenaeus, 4.171; 10.448, on Cleobulina. (Suidas. See note 42.)

24. Plutarch, *Life of Alexander* 21.4–5, on Barsine.

25. Quintilian, 1.1.6: "Nam Gracchorum eloquentiae multum contulisse accepimus Corneliam matrem, cuius doctissimus sermo in posteros quoque est epistolis traditus." One of the most highly reputed women in Roman history, Cornelia was the daughter of Scipio Africanus, who defeated Hannibal, and she was married in 169 B.C.E. to Tiberius Sempronius Gracchus. Widowed, she brought up and educated twelve children on her own, and was widely praised both for being highly educated herself and for the excellent education she bestowed on her children. Her sons Tiberius and Gaius became famous tribunes who campaigned on behalf of the Roman people.

26. Boccaccio, *Concerning Famous Women* 59, on Leontium. Also Diogenes Laertius, 10.4.

Diodorus Siculus affirms, Homer used in his learned poems.[27] Damone, the daughter of Pythagoras, achieved such good results at philosophy that her own father dedicated several commentaries to her. After his death she became a public lecturer in schools.[28] Damophyle was most skilled at poetry. She composed several amorous poems, and others in praise of the chaste Diana.[29] Does Phemonoe merit silence? She who was so illustrious and famous at letters that Eusebius of Caesarea, Lucan, Statius, Pliny, Strabo, and others mention her in their books?[30] Antisthenes states that she was the inventor of that great saying *Nosce te ipsum,* "know thyself."[31] Zenobia, Queen of Palmyra, was, as Trebellius Pollio relates, a great scholar of languages who produced an abridged version of the *History of Alexandria.*[32] Did not Hildegard of Germany write four most accomplished books on nature?[33] Did not Elena Flavia Augusta, daughter of Celius, King of Brittany, write books on Divine Providence and the immortality of the soul, as well as many others that I will leave out for the sake of brevity?[34] A noble lady of Brescia known as Laura wrote most elegant letters to Brother Girolamo Savonarola.[35] Nor do I wish to omit Aganice, whom Plutarch praises highly in his book of matrimonial precepts and who had an unusual knowledge of the science of astronomy.[36] But where is Deborah, who had a great knowledge of holy letters?[37] Where Catherine,

---

27. Diodorus Siculus, *The Historical Library* 4.66.5–6. Daphne was a mythical figure, the daughter of the blind seer Tiresias (who, among other things, appeared in Sophocles' tragedy *Oedipus Rex* to predict the fate of Oedipus). She was often known as Manto. Prophetess of the Ismenian Apollo at Thebes, after the fall of Thebes she was taken to Delphi, where it was discovered that she had the same prophetic powers as her father. According to this passage she also composed poetry, some of which inspired Homer.

28. Diogenes Laertius, *Lives of Eminent Philosophers* 8.42, on Damone, daughter of Pythagoras.

29. Philostratus, *Life of Apollonius* 30, on Damophyle.

30. Phemonoe is the name of a mythical Greek poetess from the pre-Homeric (i.e., prehistoric) age. She was the first priestess at Delphi, and is said to have been the daughter of the god Apollo. She is credited with the invention of hexameter verse. See Pliny the Elder, *Natural History* 7.57, Strabo *Geography* 9.3.5.

31. No works of Antisthenes survive. I have been unable to trace the source from which she might have taken her statement.

32. Trebellius Pollio, *The Thirty Tyrants* (in the *Scriptores Historiae Augustae*), on Zenobia.

33. St. Hildegarde of Bingen (1098–1179), wrote *Liber item Quatuor Hildegardis, De Elementorum, Fluminum, aliquor Germaniae, Metallorum, Leguminum, Fruticum, Herbarum, Arborum, Arbustorum, Piscium, Volatilium, et Animantium terrae naturis et operationibus* (Strasbourg, 1544).

34. Elena Flavia Augusta is also mentioned by C. Bronzino in *Dialogo della dignità e nobiltà delle donne* (Florence: Zanobi Pignoni, 1624), Day 4, p. 39. I can find no trace of her in earlier works.

35. The reference is to Laura Cereta (1469–99). Her letters have been translated by Diana Robin in a volume in this series. There are no extant letters from her to Savonarola.

36. Plutarch, *Matrimonial Precepts* (in *Moralia*) 145c–d, on Aganice.

37. Judges 4–5, on Deborah.

the wife of Henry VIII of England, who composed a book of meditations on the Psalms?[38] Where is Anyta, who wrote most noble poems, as Tatian relates in his book *To the Greeks*?[39] Where is Aretaphila, who became the wife of Nicocrates, tyrant of Cyrene, on account of her eloquence?[40] Where is Erinna of Telos, whose verses were so sweet and majestic that when she was thirteen, as Pliny, Stobaeus, and Eusebius confirm, they were equal to Homer's?[41] Theano was excellent at lyrical verse, and another Theano, of Metapontus or Cresca, wrote a commentary on the virtues of philosophy as well as many illustrious poems.[42] Hypatia of Alexandria, wife of the philosopher Isidorus, wrote several commentaries on astronomy. Hypatia, the daughter of Theon the great mathematician, became so successful at philosophy that she succeeded Plotinus in the same school and chair. Suidas writes that she was a scholar of science and astronomy, taught many arts and sciences in public, and had a great quantity of scholars at her lessons.[43] Was not Iambe the inventor of the verse named iambic?[44] Diotima was so expert at philosophy that Socrates did not blush to call her his teacher and attend her scholarly lessons, as Plato relates in the *Symposium*.[45] Laura Veronese, the daughter of Nicolò, wrote admirable Sapphic verses, epistles, and orations in Greek and Latin.[46]

Where is Sappho of Lesbos, the glory of poetry, who flourished at the time of the poets Alcaeus and Stephichorus? She wrote eleven books of lyric

38. Catherine Parr (1513–48), sixth wife of Henry VIII of England. Author of a collection of fifteen psalms followed by *Prayers or medytacions, wherein the mynd is stirred, paciently to suffre all afflictions here, to set at nought the vayne prosperitee of this worlde, and alwaie to longe for the everlastynge felicitee* (London, 1545).

39. Tatian, *To the Greeks*, chap. 33, on Anyta.

40. Plutarch, *Bravery of Women* 19 (255e–57e), on Aretaphila, wife of Nicocrates.

41. Pliny the Elder, *Natural History* 34.19.57–58, on Erinna of Telos.

42. The Suda (or Suidas, a lexicon that is really a historical encyclopedia, compiled ca. 1000 C.E. and published in five volumes edited by A. Adler [Teubner, 1928–38]) mentions two women called Theano, one of whom was a celebrated philosopher of the Pythagorean school, while the other wrote several philosophical works and poems.

43. Hypatia is referred to here as if she were two different people. Theon, a Platonic mathematician, and Isodorus of Gaza, a Neoplatonic philosopher, are both best known for their association with her striking story. Learned in both mathematics and philosophy, Hypatia is said to have presided over Plotinus's Neoplatonic school in Alexandria. A woman of great virtue, she was nevertheless torn to pieces (415 C.E.) by an enraged Christian mob, incited by their bishop Cyril (later sainted). The Suda (see note 42 above) writes of her that she married Isodorus and wrote on astronomy.

44. Iambe was a mythical figure, the daughter of Pan and Echo, and was associated with the goddess Demeter. Marinella's sources are probably Apollodorus 1.5.1 or Diodorus Siculus 5.4.

45. Plato, *Symposium* (201d), on Diotima.

46. Betussi, *Delle donne illustri* 21.181, on Laura Veronese.

poetry, as well as other epigrams and elegies, and was the inventor of Sapphic verse, which was named after her. So sweetly and so copiously did she sing that the heavens marvelled at her.[47] In her honor I will quote those most beautiful verses from *Meditations* entitled *Christi cruciatibus*, "Christ crucified," by Fabio Paolini, public lecturer of the Venetian Senate:

> Abilities to which the glories of Nestor's sweet eloquence yield, and father Linus himself yields, as does Orpheus himself and the one who built the Theban citadel with his singing. But these are nothing—even the heavens and the stars often used to marvel at her as she spoke; the sun, captivated by the amazing sweetness, stopped in his course, the winds ceased to rage, and the meandering rivers no longer urged on their headlong flow; often the birds came to a stop in the air above on motionless wings.[48]

What shall we say of the great wit and profound memory of the Damigella Trivulzia? She was a miracle of nature, who many times recited Latin orations composed by herself in the presence of popes. She learned Greek, and whenever she heard a speech recited by anyone she was able to memorize it word for word, even if she had only heard it once. If she read a book once or twice, she could recite it all.[49]

Marguerite, sister of the King of France and wife of the King of Navarre, was most learned at holy letters.[50] Marta Proba, Queen of Britanny, was highly skilled in the liberal arts.[51] Phintys wrote a book on the temperance of women.[52] Polla Argentaria, the wife of Lucan, was excellent at composing verses, and completed the verses begun by her husband with great

---

47. Boccaccio, *Concerning Famous Women* 45, on Sappho.

48. Fabio Paolini, *Meditations:* "Copia Nestorei, cui cedat gloria mellis / Cedat, et ipse pater Linus, concedat, et Orpheus / Et qui Thebanas cantando condidit arces. / Parva loquor, coeli hunc, et fidera saepe loquetem / Obstupuere, suum mira dulcedine captus / Sol tenuit cursum, tenuerunt Flaminia venti, / Nec vaga praecipites agitarunt flumina cursus. / Saepius immotis volucris super aere pennis. / Substitit."

Nestor was a legendary pre-Trojan king of Pylus renowned for eloquence and wisdom (see note 3 to Marinella's Introduction). Linus was a figure from Greek legend, the son of Apollo, god of music, and the teacher of Orpheus, who was himself a famous mythic singer of Thrace who charmed nature when he sang: he is the model for this passage.

49. Betussi, *Delle donne illustri* 31.194, on the Damigella Trivulzia.

50. Ibid., 37.209, on Marguerite of Navarre.

51. Boccaccio, *Concerning Famous Women* 95, describes Proba, the wife of Adelphus, who was skilled in liberal arts.

52. Phintys was the daughter of Callicrates, a Pythagorean philosopher, according to Stobaeus, *Floralia* 74.61.

elegance.[53] Themistocleia taught her brother Pythagoras many brilliant things, as Aristoxenus writes.[54] Theselides [Telesilla], a woman of Argos, was very skilled at poetry.[55] Cassandra Fedele was also most learned. She took part in public debates in Padua, wrote an elegant book on the order of the sciences, and beautiful lyric verses.[56]

The profound wisdom of Lucrezia d'Este, Duchess of Urbino, both in philosophy and poetry, is to be marvelled at. This can be seen by a sonnet written to her by Giulio Camillo:

> It is you, only you with your lofty mind surpassing reason in everything, who extracts nature's secrets from her. And as Apollo and his muses stand attentive to your learning and style, already glorious you surpass the philosophers and poets.[57]

Sosipatra was a soothsayer. She was so skilled at science that people thought some god must have been her master.[58] Passilla was very adept at composing epigrams. Many writers attest to this and speak in her honor.[59] Praxila was the poetess of Sicyon. In one of her poems Adonis is questioned in hell about what beautiful and worthy things he has left behind in the world. He replies the sun, cucumbers, and apples. He chooses the sun not because it seems beautiful to him but because it ripens apples and cucumbers with its sweet warmth.[60]

---

53. Polla Argentaria was the wife of the Roman poet Lucan (author of the epic poem *Pharsalia* and nephew of the philosopher Seneca), who was forced to commit suicide after being implicated in a plot to murder the emperor Nero in 65 C.E. After his death she is said to have edited his poems. Many years later the poets Martial and Statius were commissioned by her to write poems celebrating her dead husband's birthday: Statius, *Silvae* 2.7, and Martial *Epigrams* 7.21 and 7.23. All of these poems contain eulogies to her; for example, *Silvae* 2.7 is entitled "An Ode to Polla in Honor of Lucan's Birthday," and lines 81–87 write of their marriage, describing Polla as a learned poetess well suited to Lucan's genius and endowed with all the other appropriate graces.

54. Themistocleia (or Aristocleia) was a priestess at Delphi from whom Pythagoras claimed to have learned much (Porphyry 41). It is Diogenes Laertius (*Lives of the Philosophers* 8.6) who calls her Themistocleia.

55. Plutarch, *Bravery of Women* 4 (245c–f).

56. Betussi, *Delle donne illustri* 28.190, on Cassandra Fedele. Her complete works appear in this series.

57. Giulio Camillo Dalminio (1480–1544), *I fiori delle rime de' poeti illustri, nuovamente raccolti et ordinati da Girolamo Ruscelli,* p. 109 (Venice, Sessa, 1558): "Ben voi voi, sola con l'eccelsa mente / A le cagion passando in ogni cosa, / Levate a la natura i suoi secreti. / E stando Apollo, e le sue muse intente / Al vostro dotto, stil, già gloriosa / Avanzate i Filosofi e i Poeti."

58. Sosipatra taught philosophy in Pergamon in the first half of the fourth century. (Eunapius, *Lives of the Sophists,* 6.6–92.)

59. I cannot trace any person by this name.

60. Praxila (or Praxilla) of Sicyon was a lyric poetess writing around 450 B.C.E. She is one of the nine poetesses distinguished in Suda as the Lyric Muses. A few fragments of poems and ancient

Corinna of Thebes beat Pindar, the prince of lyric verse, in a poetry competition.[61] There was also another Corinna who was a great poet in Ovid's time.[62] I do not wish to omit Cornificia, who wrote most elegant epigrams and other beautiful works.[63] Nor should I leave out Lastheneia of Mantineia and Axiothea of Phlius, who, dressed as men, followed Plato in order to hear him speak, as Plutarch writes.[64] Thargelia had a wide knowledge of philosophy, as the same author relates in his *Life of Pericles*.[65]

Veronica Gambara was very learned at poetry, and most original, as can still be seen from her writings, and as Ariosto states in this verse:

Veronica Gambara is among them, the beloved of Phoebus and the holy Ionian choir.[66]

Vittoria Colonna was extremely accomplished, and composed many beautiful sonnets. Ariosto says of her:

She has not only made herself immortal with her sweet style, which I have never heard surpassed, but she can even raise from the tomb and immortalize whomsoever she speaks or writes about.[67]

Let us now mention Isotta Nogarola Veronese, who was learned at philosophy and led a philosophical life, contenting herself with little. She corresponded with Popes Nicholas and Pius, and always remained a virgin.[68]

---

references to poems are extant, and there is reference to a poem about Adonis (Zenobius, *Proverbs* 4.21).

61. Corinna of Thebes was a poetess writing at the beginning of the fifth century B.C.E., who is said to have instructed the poet Pindar. (Plutarch, *Athenian Glories* 4, 347f–48a.)

62. Corinna was the name given to the mistress, whether real or fictional, to whom Ovid addressed many of his love poems, or *Amores* (first century C.E.). There is no evidence that she was a poetess.

63. Cornificia, sister of the poet Cornificius (mentioned by Ovid in his *Tristia*), is said by Jerome (*Chronicle of Eusebius* 61.184.4) to have written excellent epigrams.

64. This incident cannot be traced in Plutarch. Lasthenia of Mantineia and Axiothea of Phlius are mentioned in Diogenes Laertius, *Lives of the Eminent Philosophers* 3.46 and 4.2.

65. Plutarch, *Life of Pericles* 24.3–4: Thargelia was a courtesan in ancient Ionia, whose fair person, sharp wit, and pleasant tongue brought her the acquaintance and friendship of the most powerful men of Greece. Again Marinella appears to be adjusting a reference to suit her own ends.

66. Ariosto, *Orlando furioso* 46:3: "Veronica da Gambara è con loro / Sì grata a Phebo, e al Santo Aonio choro."

67. Ibid, 37.16: "Questa una ha non pur sé fatta immortale / Con dolce stil de che 'l miglior non odo, / Ma può qualunque di cui parli, o scriva / Trar del sepolcro, e far ch'eterno viva."

68. Betussi, *Delle donne illustri* 13.169. For her biography, see M. L. King, "Isotta Nogarola," in *Italian Women Writers*, ed. Rinaldina Russell (Westport, Conn., 1994), 313–23. For a translation of her major work, see M. L. King and A. Rabil, eds., *Her Immaculate Hand* (Binghamton, N.Y., rev. ed., 1992), 57–67.

Cassandra, the daughter of Priam, was famous for her learning and for the accuracy of her prophecies.[69] I must not ignore Claudia, the wife of Statius Papinius, who was the marvel of her age because of her wide knowledge of the sciences.[70] Nor Nesstrina, Queen of the Scythians, who, as Herodotus writes, was completely fluent in Greek, and taught it to her son Silius.[71] Nor Myrtis of Anthedon who taught the great poet Pindar.[72] Nor Roswitha, the nun of Saxony, who wrote many books in prose and verse.[73] Hydra was a woman of such vast wisdom that not even Hercules had the spirit to resist or contradict her learned and quick-witted ripostes. The divine Plato praises her highly for this in one of his dialogues.[74]

Costanza, the wife of Alessandro Sforza, is celebrated among illustrious women. As a young girl she was most studious at philosophy and poetry, and was praised and celebrated by Poliziano.[75] Minerva, the daughter of Jove, is included among the gods by poets solely for the good arts that she invented.

69. Boccaccio, *Concerning Famous Women* 33, on Cassandra, daughter of King Priam of Troy.

70. Claudia was the wife of the Roman poet Statius (ca. 40–96 C.E. and see note 53 above), who wrote epic poems (the *Thebaid* and the unfinished *Achilleid*) and a collection of shorter poems, the *Silvae*, mostly written to celebrate specific occasions at the request of various patrons including the emperor Domitian. One of his *Silvae* (3.5) is addressed to Claudia and attempts to persuade her that they should retire together to the Bay of Naples. The poem is a tribute to her loyalty and support for him.

71. Neither Nesstrina nor her son Silius is mentioned in Herodotus. It is not clear where Marinella might have got such information.

72. Myrtis of Anthedon was said to have been first the teacher and then the poetic rival of the early Greek poet Pindar. She is mentioned in a surviving fragment of Corinna (see note 61), and the Suda calls her one of the nine Lyric Muses (different from the ten muses mentioned in note 77 below).

73. Roswitha of Saxony (c.932–1002) was a German Benedictine nun who wrote Latin poems and six Latin comedies in prose.

74. Plato, *Euthydemus* 297c: "Even Hercules could not fight against the Hydra, a she-sophist who had the wit to shoot up many new heads of argument when one of them was cut off." Plato is using the legendary monster as a metaphor for skillful argumentation, but as so often, Marinella appears deliberately to misunderstand and refers to Hydra as if she were an ordinary and extremely intelligent woman.

75. Costanza Varano (1426–47) married Alessandro Sforza in 1444; her native city of Camerino was returned to the Varano family at that time by the brother of Alessandro Sforza, Francesco, who controlled it. Costanza delivered an oration to Bianca Maria Visconti, the wife of Francesco Sforza, on the occasion of its return to her family (see *Her Immaculate Hand*, trans. and ed. M. King and A. Rabil [Binghamton, N.Y., rev. ed. 1992], 39–41). Angelo Poliziano (1454–94), Renaissance humanist, teacher, and poet, wrote various elegies, odes, and epigrams in Latin and Greek as well as poems in the vernacular. He did not write in praise of the youthful Costanza Varano—dead before he was born—but rather in praise of Cassandra Fedele. For his letter to Fedele, see *Her Immaculate Hand*, 126–27. Costanza is praised by Betussi, *Delle donne illustri* 17, p. 160. He notes that she was familiar with the works of Poliziano.

Her learning caused her to be named goddess of wisdom, science, prudence, study, maturity, judgment, law, and every virtue. Athena, the mother of studies, took her name from her because Athena means Minerva.[76] The nine muses are no more than nine young women, as Diodorus Siculus states, who excelled at every discipline, and especially the art of singing. Clio invented the satire. Euterpe invented the flute. Thalia was goddess of comedies, and Melpomene of tragedies. Polymnia ruled over warlike deeds and discovered rhetoric. Erato invented geometry, Terpsichore was goddess of poetry, and Calliope discovered literature.[77] Each of these young women was most adept at the art she had invented.

Clement of Alexandria writes of an Artemisia who was very learned in dialectic science and who named herself Dialectica.[78] Queen Amalasunta was very accomplished at Greek literature.[79] Both Clement and Didymus of Alexandria praise Anaxandra for her remarkable knowledge of painting.[80] I could speak of many others, such as Laura Terracina, who was most skilled at poetry;[81] Ginevra Veronese, who was illustrious at letters;[82] Manto, the daughter of Tiresias;[83] and many more whom I leave out for the sake of brevity. From these few mentioned by me (I say few by comparison to the many whom I have left out), it can easily be understood by everyone what good advantage women have taken of their education and of everything else to which they have devoted themselves.

---

76. Boccaccio, *Concerning Famous Women* 6, on Minerva.

77. In his *Historical Library*, book 4, section 7, Diodorus Siculus writes of the tradition of the ten Muses, said by most authorities to be the daughters of Zeus and Mnemosyne, who live on Mount Olympus with the gods and preside over various areas of the arts. They are commonly invoked by ancient poets as the inspiration of their work. Diodorus's own source for this version of their names and fields is Hesiod's *Theogony*. In Marinella's version, however, the Muses are credited with slightly different fields, and she omits to mention a couple of muses who are included by Diodorus. Traditionally, Clio is the inventor of history rather than satire; Euterpe of lyric poetry, although she is often portrayed with a flute; Polymnia of lyric poetry; Erato of erotic poetry and mime, rather than geometry; Terpsichore of choral song and dance; and Calliope of epic poetry.

78. Clement of Alexandria, *The Pedagogue* 2.72.3.

79. M. G. Tarcagnota, *Delle istorie del mondo* (Venice, 1585), 2.6, p. 237, on Queen Amalasunta of Italy.

80. Anaxandra, daughter of Nealcis, is mentioned in Clement of Alexandria's *Miscellanies* 4, where he cites the lost work of Didymus of Alexandria as his source.

81. Laura Terracina (c.1500–95) was a Neopolitan poetess whose first poem was published in 1550. Four editions of her poetry were published in Venice.

82. Betussi, *Delle donne illustri* 12.169, on Ginevra Gambara of Verona.

83. Boccaccio, *Concerning Famous Women* 28, on Manto, daughter of Tiresias. see also note 27 above.

Where is Saint Bridget who left us a noble book of her revelations?[84] Where is Saint Catherine of Siena, whose letters and dialogues show us the wisdom with which she was gifted? She even spoke most eloquently before Popes Gregory XI and Urban VI.[85] Eustochium and Fabiola received great praise in the epistles of St. Jerome for their rare knowledge of holy letters.[86] Anastasia, a disciple of Chrysostom, wrote many wondrous letters.[87] Hilda Erenica left many written premeditations and wrote a book attacking Agilbert the Parisian, bishop of Saxony.[88] Hildegarde, a virgin from the city of Mainz, composed several books. Saint Bernard, who lived at the same time as her, wrote her many letters.[89] Catherine, daughter of Cosroe, King of Alexandria, disputed with the learned philosophers who were trying to persuade her to idolatry, and she, with most true reasoning, converted them to Christianity, for she was well versed in the art of philosophy, which had interested her even as a young girl more than her needle and thread, as Marco Filippi, known as Il Funesto (The Woeful), says in her biography:

> But the learned disciplines that reach so high, and take with them our bitter, earthly senses, so that enclosed in our bodily veil we might then know about the earth and sky.[90]

84. St. Bridget of Sweden (1302–73) was a Swedish visionary whose *Revelationes Sanctae Brigittae,* written by her confessors, has passed through many editions.

85. St Catherine of Siena (1347–80) wrote devotional pieces, letters, and poems and prevailed on Pope Gregory XI to return from Avignon to Rome. See her biography by Marinella: *De' gesti heroici e della vita meravigliosa della serafica Santa Caterina da Siena* (Venice: Barezzo Barezzi, 1624).

86. Eustochium was a Roman lady of noble descent who devoted her life to prayer and study and with her mother, Paula, abandoned her wealthy home in 385 C.E. after Jerome's famous Epistle 22 on the subject of virginity, addressed to her, created so much controversy. They settled in Bethlehem, where together they founded several monasteries and convents that Eustochium directed after her mother Paula's death in 404. Fabiola was a Roman matron who, after the death of her second husband, devoted herself to charitable works and visited Jerome in Bethlehem in 394 C.E. in order to apply herself to the study of Scripture. He wrote two letters to her, Epistles 64 and 78. Most of the information about her life comes from his Epistle 77, written on the occasion of her death. See the *Oxford Dictionary of the Christian Church,* 3rd ed. (1977), 577, 594.

87. Anastasia was a Roman noblewoman who suffered under Diocletian's persecution of the Christians in 303 C.E. Two letters purporting to be written by her when she was in prison are preserved in the Suda.

88. Hilda Erenica appears to be St. Hilda (614–80). Her sister became a nun near Paris (perhaps accounting for the reference in the text to France) and though Hilda tried to join her she was recalled and made an abbess in England. She founded a monastery for both men and women at Whitby which became famous. At the Synod of Whitby (664) she defended Celtic customs over those of the Roman church against Wilfrid. See *Oxford Dictionary of the Christian Church,* 3rd ed. (1997), 770, 1741.

89. On Hildegarde of Mainz, see above, note 33.

90. Marco Filippi, *Vita di Santa Caterina in ottava rima* (Venice, 1592): "Ma le scienze, che tant'alto vanno, / E portan seco i sensi agri, e terrestri, / Che poi rinchiusi nel corporeo velo / Sappiamo come sta la terra, e il Cielo."

Joan of Anglia should not remain shrouded in silence. She was so learned in holy letters that there was no man in Rome to equal her![91] The Sibyls were all most literate women, and full of the prophetic spirit. They composed the Sibylline verses, which were held in great awe and reverence. The first was born in Persia and named Persica. She is described by Nicanor, who wrote the history of Alexander the Great. The second was from Libya and named Libyca, celebrated by Euripides. The third was from Delphi and named Delphica. The fourth was from Cumae in Italy and known as Cumana. The fifth was Eritrea, who predicted the ruin of Troy. Apollodorus of Erythraea boasts that she was born in his native land. The sixth was from Samos and named Samia, and it is said she lived at the same time as Romulus. The seventh was Amalthea; the eighth, Elespontica, who was born under Trojan rule at the time of Cyrus, and Heraclitus of Pontus wrote about her. The ninth was from Phrygia. The tenth was named Tiburtina because she was born at Tiburtis. As Lactantius relates, these women prophesied many worthy matters.[92]

SECTION 2: OF TEMPERATE AND CONTINENT WOMEN

Men are called continent and temperate when they use their reason to oppose the delights and pleasures of the senses—in particular, as we know from Aristotle, the senses of taste and touch. He explains this in the *Ethics*, where he states:

> He is temperate who does not grieve over the absence of pleasure, and in its presence abstains from it.[93]

But if by chance he should desire such pleasures, he will, in a moderate way, take advantage of the time and means and every convenient circumstance. In the same chapter Aristotle writes:

> He shall desire moderately and as he should the things which, being pleasant, make for health or good condition . . . this right reason prescribes.[94]

---

91. Boccaccio, *Concerning Famous Women* 99, on Joan of Anglia, the fictitious Pope Joan.

92. The Sibyls. Marinella paraphrases Lactantius, *The Divine Institutes* 1.6 (a Christian work written 304–313 C.E.) on the Sibyls. This is one of our earliest sources that contains a historical discussion of this sort on the Sibyls.

93. Aristotle, *Nicomachean Ethics* 3.11 (1118b31–32): "Temperatus est, qui absentia voluptatem non dolet, et presentibus se abstinet."

94. Ibid. (1119a16–20): "Cupid mediocriter ea, et sicut decet, et ea tantummodo iucunda, quae vel ad sanitatem, vel ad bonam habitudinem faciunt [. . .] recta enim ratio sic praescribit."

And thus, defining temperance, he says that it is moderation in the pleasures of taste and touch. This is also the definition given by Speusippus, who writes:

Temperance is moderation of the soul around natural desires.[95]

Or as Claudian states:

Be moderate, so that you may strive for purity.[96]

And Cicero in the *Tusculan Disputations*:

Let temperance control [all] the appetites and make them obey right reason.[97]

And so it was named by him as the moderator of all the frenzies of concupiscence.

It is a fact known to everyone that women are continent and temperate, for we never see or read about them getting drunk or spending all day in taverns, as dissolute men do, nor do they give themselves unrestrainedly to other pleasures. On the contrary, they are moderate and frugal in everything. Accordingly, I will bring various examples of this to the attention of my readers.

The first will be that of Zenobia, Queen of the Palmyrenes, who, after the death of her husband, Odenatus, restored the Empire of the Orient to much acclaim. In war she showed herself to be a most noble and valiant captain and a brave warrior. She possessed great beauty and was young and very modest, never lowering herself to lasciviousness or vanity. She earned the greatest praise for her constancy and firmness of spirit. She waged many wars. Finally, when fighting with Aurelian, Zenobia was triumphant, in terms of human bravery. Aurelian's forces started to flee, but while they were fleeing a god appeared to them and put new heart into them, so that returning to the battle they emerged victorious. It was not, then, because of their own valor that they conquered this heroic woman, but with the help of the god. This is related by Tarcagnota.[98] During her reign few people had the

---

95. "Temperentia est moderatio animi circa naturales concupiscentias." Speusippis was a disciple of Plato's at the Academy in Athens and is mentioned several times by his contemporary Aristotle as well as by other ancient writers, although none of his own writing survives. It is not clear where Marinella's quotation comes from, but it is almost certainly a reference found in a later author.

96. Claudian, *On Stilicho's Consulship* 2.107: "Temperies, ut casta petas." The Loeb translation is: "Temperance guides thee to chaste desires" (Claudian, 2, p. 11).

97. Cicero, *Tusculan Disputations*, 4.9.22. The Latin is misquoted. It should read: "Temperantia sedat [omnes] appetitiones, et efficit, ut eae rectae rationi pareant."

98. Tarcagnota, *Delle historie del mondo* 2.5, p. 159, on Zenobia.

courage to take up arms against her, and Petrarch writes of her thus in the
Triumphs:

> Zenobia, much more jealous of her honor, was beautiful and in the
> flower of youth. And all the more in beauty and in youth to cherish
> honor is to merit praise. In her female heart there was such constancy
> that with her beautiful face and armored locks she caused fear in those
> more used to feeling scorn. I speak of the Imperial might of Rome.[99]

I do not want the memory of Sophronia, that most noble Roman matron,
to be buried in silence. When Maxentius was emperor she was frequently
importuned by him, who, wishing to enjoy her favors, was so determined
that she saw clearly that if she did not consent of her own free will, he would
take her by force. She told her husband everything, and he, either from fear
or from baseness of soul, gave his consent to this shame. On knowing her
husband's will, she adorned herself with jewelry and gold and, accompanied
by a soldier, entered the emperor's chamber, where, in a long speech, she
excused herself before God for departing from this life on a day prior to the
one chosen by Him. She then took a knife and killed herself so that there
should be no stain on her body or the modesty of her soul.[100] Lucretia was
also chaste, as Petrarch states in his *Triumphs*:

> But I will speak of some at the pinnacle of truest honor, among them
> Lucretia on the right hand was the first.[101]

Monima of Miletus was such a friend to honesty that she would not
succumb to the desires of Mithridates, King of Armenia, even for the large
abundance of gold that he offered her.[102] When Thebes was razed to the
ground, the cruel Nicanor fell in love with a Theban virgin. He believed
that she would glory in such a lover and be grateful for the opportunity of
giving him pleasure, but although he made many attempts on her over a
long period, using both prayers and threats, he had no success. The virgin,

---

99. Petrarch, *Triumphs*, Fame, 2:108–114: "Zenobia del suo honore assai più scarsa / Bella era
nell'età fiorita, e fresca / Quanto in più gioventute, e 'n più bellezza / Tanto per c'honestà sua
laude accresca. / Nel cor femineo fu tanta fermezza, / Che col bel viso, e con l'armata coma /
Fece temer chi per natura sprezza: / Io parlo de l'Imperio alto di Roma."

100. Maxentius was Roman Emperor 306–12 C.E. He is described by all the historians as a
picture of lust, greed, and cruelty. The provenance of the story of Sophronia is uncertain.

101. Petrarch, *Triumphs*, Chastity, 1:130–33: "Ma d'alquante dirò, che'n sù la cima / Son di vera
honestate, in fra le quali / Lucretia da man destra era la prima."

102. Plutarch, *Life of Lucullus* 18.4–6. Mithridates, the conqueror of Monima's home city, Miletus,
tried to tempt her virtue with offers of money. She resisted, and held out until he offered her
marriage.

fearing that he would commit some outrage on her, killed herself in order to conserve her virtue.[103]

The chaste Penelope, wife of Ulysses, does not deserve silence. Homer tells us in the *Odyssey* that she was constantly importuned by suitors, all of whom competed with each other to make her their wife. She refused all of them and lived chastely and modestly awaiting her husband Ulysses. For this reason every time Homer refers to her, he describes her as chaste, prudent, or wise, the wise Penelope.[104] She waited twenty years for her husband, not knowing where he was. Petrarch celebrates the triumph of her chastity with the words:

> [On] the other [side is] Penelope: they have shattered Cupid's bow and arrows, and the quiver and plucked the shameless boy's wings.[105]

Ariosto, considering the importance of chastity, writes:

> Solely because she lived in chastity Penelope was not inferior to Ulysses.[106]

Great was the modesty of those fifty Spartan virgins who had been permitted to come to the city of Messene for some festival because of the accord between them. Some young men of Messene attempted to make love to them, and the modest maidens, in order to escape their violence, put honesty before life and killed themselves.[107] Although it may be true that one should not kill oneself for any reason, these maidens were nevertheless praised by the ancients, who were not illuminated by the light of true faith.

What should we say of Queen Dido? Her beloved husband, Sychaeus, having been killed by her brother Pygmalion, she lived in great grief and hatred toward her brother. When she saw that he sought to murder her as well, she pretended that her grief and hatred toward him had ceased, and she secretly made preparations to flee. In order to make her flight safer she pretended she wanted to go to her brother, having previously informed

---

103. Nicanor, son of Parmenio and a captain in the army of Alexander the Great, is mentioned by Tarcagnota, *Delle istorie del mondo* 1.19, p. 631, and 1.20, p. 663. However, there is no mention of the Theban virgin.

104. Penelope was the wife of Ulysses, legendary throughout antiquity for her faithfulness. She is often described by Homer in glowing terms, for example, *Odyssey* 17.492 or 17.498.

105. Petrarch, *Triumphs*, Chastity, 1:136: "L'altra Penelope queste gli strali / Et la pharetra, e l'arco hanno spezzato . . . / A quel protervo, e spennachiate l'ali."

106. Ariosto, *Orlando furioso* 13:60: "Sol perché casta visse / Penelope non fu minor d'Ulisse."

107. Tarcagnota, *Delle istorie del mondo* 1.7, p. 188, mentions an incident in which a number of Spartan virgins were sacrificed by the Messenians, thus bringing about the first Messenian war in 743 B.C.E. However, there is no mention of the virgins killing themselves.

many of her principal gentlemen of her plan, and many of them fled with her, because they hated the tyrant. After a long voyage Dido arrived in Africa, where she founded Carthage and, with much pleasantness, drew the local people to converse with her and soon filled the city with people. Many people from far and wide assembled there, so much so that the queen and her people took great pleasure in this.[108]

Then Iarbas, King of Mauritania, seeing how the Tyrians were prospering, and having already heard of Dido's great beauty, sent for ten of the principal Carthaginians to come to Mauritania and ordered them to do their best to make their queen his wife, threatening otherwise to wage a cruel war against them. They, knowing how far such an idea was from Dido's thoughts, were full of grief, but on their return to Carthage they informed her that Iarbas desired her and wished her for his wife, and that if she did not agree a cruel war awaited them. When she heard this she felt greatly troubled and began to cry and call on her dear Sychaeus. Then, turning to her people, she told them she would follow her destiny and that of her city. Four months later she had a pyre erected in the highest part of the city, as if to placate the soul of Sychaeus before going to her new husband. After offering many sacrifices, she mounted to the top of the pyre with a naked sword in her hand and announced that she wished to go and meet her husband as she had promised. She then slew herself in the presence of the whole population.[109] For as long as Carthage endured Dido was worshiped like a goddess, as Tarcagnota relates.[110] This truly was a most clear example of honesty and fidelity, even if Virgil pretends (and Passi follows him) that Dido killed herself for love of Aeneas, which is false.[111] Petrarch refutes this opinion with the words:

> Let the ignorant mob be silent, I say that Dido was led to seek death
> by her devotion to honor—not to Aeneas, as the masses believe.[112]

And what of Virginia, the daughter of Virginius, a Roman plebeian? He had promised his daughter to the tribune Lucius. But when he was away on an expedition with the other Romans, Claudius, one of the decemvirs who administered nearly half the Roman dominions, attempted several times by

---

108. Boccaccio, *Concerning Famous Women* 40, on Dido.

109. Ibid.

110. Tarcagnota, *Delle istorie del mondo* 1.1.5, p. 136, on Dido.

111. For this version of the story, see Virgil, *Aeneid* 4.

112. Petrarch, *Triumphs*, Chastity, 1:158: "Taccia il vulgo ignorante, e dico Dido / Cui studio d'honestade a morte spinse, / Non quei d'Enea, com'è publico grido."

flattery and gifts to induce Virginia to submit to his pleasure. All this was in vain because, being as wise and chaste as one can imagine, she would not consent to his wishes. The good Appius Claudius, having seen that he was not going to succeed with her, arranged with one of his men, an audacious freedman, to kidnap the young girl as she walked in the street. He was to say she was a fugitive slave and take her before the tribunal where she would be judged by him. The freedman did as Appius Claudius commanded him. Meeting Virginia one day, he seized her. She defended herself, and the women who were with her defended her, and thus a crowd of people flocked there, her husband among them. This dissension was announced to the judge, who said that he wished to pass sentence the following day.

Virginius, hearing the news, came immediately to Rome but was not in time to prevent Claudius from pronouncing sentence that she was the freedman's servant. The young girl's father, hearing this, begged Claudius to allow him to speak to his daughter and her nurse in the presence of the people. The perverse Claudius consented to this request. Virginius took Virginia aside and said: "My daughter, this is the only way at my disposal to restore your liberty," and in the presence of the judge he took out a knife and stabbed her in the chest, which she offered him without fear, consenting generously and voluntarily to her fate. Once the iniquity of Claudius was known, he was seized and put in prison where he died in misery.[113]

I also remember Orithya, daughter of Erectheus, King of Athens, who was one of the Amazons. She was praised by everyone for her chastity because she always conserved her virginity.[114] The daughters of Aristotimus, the tyrant of Elis, hanged themselves rather than submit to rape.[115] This was truly an example of real chastity.

I remember Isabella as well, who had her own head cut off, after having bathed her white neck with the juice of herbs. She did this in order to preserve her honesty, as was related truthfully by Brasilla da Durazzo, from whom Ariosto took the story.[116] Imagine, courteous reader if you can, this beautiful pretext for remaining chaste when confronted by the unbridled Rodomont. She gave him to understand that the herbal brew, if one bathed

113. Boccaccio, *Concerning Famous Women* 56, on Virginia.

114. Ibid. 18, on Orithya.

115. Plutarch, *Bravery of Women* 15 (253d–e), on the daughters of Aristotimus. Aristotimus was a brutal tyrant of Elis in the third century B.C.E., who was eventually overthrown and murdered. His daughters were allowed to commit suicide to preserve their chastity.

116. Ariosto, *Orlando furioso* 29:3–30.

oneself three times with it, hardened the body to such an extent that it was protected against fire and steel. Having boiled the herbs, she bathed her chaste neck and breast and offered them to the ferocious and careless Rodomont so that he should sever them from her body, as Ariosto relates in *Orlando furioso*:

> She bathed herself as she said, then joyfully offered her bare neck to the pagan, unwary, and perhaps befuddled by wine, against which helmet and shield are unavailing. The brute believed her, and used his hand and cruel sword so that her fair head, once the abode of love, was cut clean from her shoulders.
>
> Her head bounced three times, and from it could be clearly heard a voice pronouncing the name of Zerbin, to follow whom she had found so rare a way to escape from the hand of the Saracen. Spirit who preferred fidelity, and the name (virtually unknown, and alien in our day) of chastity, to your life and tender years.[117]

Something that was truly worthy of being remembered for ever.

According to Livy, Sulpicia was extremely virtuous. She was the patrician daughter of Sulpicius and the wife of Quintus Flavius Flaccus. She erected a temple to the goddess Venus and called her Verticordia, hoping she would turn lascivious souls to honesty and virtue, as Pliny writes.[118] She was no less famous for her chastity than Lucretia, and thus Petrarch writes of her:

---

117. Ibid., 29:25–26: "Bagnossi, come disse, e lieta porse / All'incauto pagano il collo ignudo, / Incauto, e vinto anco dal vino forse / Incontra a cui non vale elmo né scudo. / Quel uom bestial le prestò fede, e scorse / Sì con la mano sì col ferro crudo, / Che del bel capo, già d'Amore albergo, / Fe' tronco rimanere il petto e il tergo.

"Quel fe' tre salti; e funne udita chiara/ voce, ch'uscendo nominò Zerbino, / Per cui seguire ella trovò si rara / Via da fuggir di man del Saracino. / Alma, ch'avesti più la fede cara, / E'l nome quasi ignoto, e peregrino / Al nostro tempo, della castitade / Che la tua vita, e la tua verde etade."

118. Here Marinella confuses two different women called Sulpicia. The first, who is mentioned at Livy, *History of Rome* 39.11–13, was a *gravem feminam* (a "woman of good character"), who was instrumental in uncovering the Bacchanalian scandal of 186 B.C.E., when the Roman authorities uncovered and then suppressed the celebration of a secret and wild cult associated with the wine god Bacchus—which involved, among other transgressions, drunkenness and illicit sex. Dozens of apparently respectable upper-class Roman women were involved in the scandal and subsequently lost their lives. For the full story, see Livy, *History of Rome* 39.8–18. This Sulpicia's husband was Quintus Fulvius, not Flavius, in the original. The second Sulpicia was chosen in 113 B.C.E. as the most chaste matron in Rome to dedicate the statue of Venus Verticordia, or "Venus who changes hearts," which, it was hoped, would turn women's minds away from vice and toward virtue. The sources for this story are Valerius Maximus, *Memorable Deeds and Words* 8.15.12, and Pliny, *Natural History* 7.35.

Thus we reached the sovereign city first at the temple; that Sulpicia dedicated to extinguish the flame of madness from the mind.[119]

And what shall we say of the modest Princess of Taranto who was promised to Corsamonte? She was abducted by the Goths, and Corsamonte, in freeing her, was slain because of Burgenzo's deception. Despite Belisarius's entreaties, she would not take another husband and had herself locked up in a little room near Corsamonte's tomb in order to preserve her virginity. Trissino, in *Italia liberata dai Goti*, book XXIII, has her reply to Belisarius, who wished to find her another husband of Corsamonte's age:

Come my Lord, allow me to lock myself in a dark and polished chapel hidden to the world and lucid to life, where my virginity will remain intact, and I may purge those foolish wishes which were once in my heart to have a husband.[120]

Diana was so chaste that she was called the goddess of chastity. Shunning the company of men, she devoted herself to hunting, always in the company of virgin nymphs. Entering into a shining river or fountain one day with her nymphs, she was disturbed by Actaeon, who gazed at her. She blushed with honest shame as Ovid relates in book III of *Metamorphoses*,

As the clouds grow red at sunset, as the daybreak reddens, Diana blushed at being seen without clothes.[121]

She splashed him with water and turned him into a stag.

One of Diana's attendants, the nymph Arethusa, daughter of Nereus and Doris, bathed one day in the river Alpheus, which flows through Arcadia, in order to refresh herself. Alpheus, the god of the river, immediately fell in love with her and wanted to possess her. She, being a chaste virgin, fled from him and ran so far and sweated so much that she dissolved and turned into a fountain, as Ovid relates in book V of *Metamorphoses*. These verses, translated into the vernacular by Fabio Maretti, read thus:

An icy sweat in every part oppressed my besieged limbs on every side and it seemed that my whole body was dripping and the pale blue

---

119. Petrarch, *Triumphs*, Chastity, 1:178: "Così giungemmo alla Città soprana / Nel tempio pria; / che dedicò Sulpitia / Per spegner ne la mente fiamma insana."

120. Giangiorgio Trissino, *Italia liberata dai Goti* 23 (line 52): "Deh lasciate Signor, ch'io mi rinchiuda / In un oscuro, e lucido sacello / Oscuro al mondo, e lucido alla vita, / Ove la mia verginità si servi / Intatta, e purghi quei pensieri insulsi / Ch'eran già nel mio cor d'haver marito."

121. Ovid, *Metamorphoses* 3.183–85: "Qui color infectis adversi solis ab ictu / Nubibus esse solet, aut purpureae Aurorae / Is fuit in vultu visae sine veste Dianae."

drops fell to earth: and where I moved my feet the ground was wet and dew was falling from my loose hair and more quickly than I can tell you I dissolved and turned completely to water.[122]

I also recall the nymph Syrinx, who was famous among the Hamadryads, and who, for love of honesty and virginity, scorned the satyrs and gods who dwelt in the forests. It happened that she was seen one day by the god Pan, who wished to make her his wife. She rejected his advances and fled, entreating her chaste sisters to change her into some new form so that she might escape the god. Thus she was transformed into marsh reeds, as Ovid relates in book I of *Metamorphoses,*

> and when Pan thought that he had at last caught hold of Syrinx, he found that instead of the nymph's body he held a handful of marsh reeds.[123]

Daphne, a follower of Diana, always lived chastely and took pleasure in hunting. She asked her father if she might always remain a virgin, as Ovid writes in the same book:

> My dear, dear father, let me enjoy this state of maiden bliss forever! Diana's father granted her such a boon in days gone by.[124]

Apollo fell in love with her and chased her. She fled from him, and after a long time arrived at the river Peneus, whom she begged to relieve her of her beauty, and she was transformed into an evergreen laurel. Again, Ovid describes it:

> Her prayer was scarcely ended when a deep languor took hold on her limbs, her soft breast was enclosed in thin bark, her hair grew into leaves, her arms into branches, and her feet that were lately so swift were held fast by sluggish roots, while her face became the treetop. Nothing of her was left, except her shining loveliness.[125]

---

122. Fabio Maretti, *Le metamorfosi* (Venice, 1570): "Un gelido sudore in ogni parte / Mie membra assediate intorno oppresse / E par, che'l corpo mio tutto si stille / E'n terra caggian le cerulee stille / E dove mossi il piè 'l sito ho bagnato / E rugiada cadea dal crine sciolto / E ratto più, ch'io non ti narro il fatto / In acque tutta mi disfaccio, e volto."

123. Ovid, *Metamorphoses* 1:705–6: "Panaque, cum prensam sibi iam Siringa putaret / Corpore pro Nymphae calamos tenuisse, pallustres." (Translation by Mary Innes, Penguin ed., pp. 47–48)

124. Ovid, *Metamorphoses* 1:476–89: "Da mihi perpetua genitor carissime dixit, / Virginitate frui: dedit hoc pater ante Dianae." (Translation by Mary Innes [Harmondsworth, Eng.: Penguin, 1955], p. 42).

125. Ibid., 1:548–52: "Vix prece finita torpor gravis occupat artus, / Mollia cinguntur tenui precordia libro / In frondem crines, in ramos brachia crescunt, / Pes modo tam velox pigris

And what of the maidens of Lacedaemon? Of the Spartans, of the women of Miletus, of the Thebans? These maidens prized the ornament of their holy modesty more than kingdoms and more than their own lives. What of the Germans? They disfigured their faces with filth and with knives, and many of them drowned themselves in order to keep themselves chaste and spotless.[126] What of Hersilia and the other Sabines? After having been stolen away with her companions by the Romans she lived most chastely and faithfully, as did the others, with their husbands, as all Roman historians relate.[127] For this Petrarch praises them for their chastity in the *Triumph of Chastity*, saying:

> Then I saw Hersilia with her Sabine women, an array whose name fills every book.[128]

Nor should I omit Claudia, the Vestal Virgin. Many people doubted that she was chaste because she adorned herself, but you will hear how her uncorrupted chastity was discovered. An image of the great Mother Earth was brought by ship from Phrygia to Rome. When the ship arrived at the mouth of the Tiber, where most of the people of the city had gone to meet it, it stopped and could not be moved from that place, even though many people tried to pull it along the river. Claudia then prostrated herself on the bank of the river and held out her arms to the goddess. "You know, holy goddess," she said, "that I am held to be immodest by the people of my city, Rome. If this is true, I beg you to give them a sign, so that condemned by you, who know the innermost secrets of my heart, I may confess myself worthy of death. But if it is not true, may you who are chaste and pure give these people faith in my integrity by following my modest hand." This said, she took hold of a small rope, and pulled the ship at her pleasure, showing, to the great wonder of those who saw her, that the goddess followed her willingly. This was a sure sign of her purity.[129]

---

radicibus haeret / Ora cacumen habent, remanet nitor unus in illa." (Mary Innes's translation, p. 43).

126. It is not clear what specific reference is intended here.

127. The story of the rape of the Sabine women by Romulus and his men is one of Rome's founding myths. The earliest Romans were a collection of brigands and fugitives, among whom there were no women; to procure themselves wives, the Roman men seized the virgin daughters of one of the neighboring tribes, the Sabines, at a festival to which they had invited them. The Sabines and Romans subsequently went to war over this outrage, but the women, daughters of one side and wives of the other, intervened between the two armies and reconciled them. Hersilia, the kidnapped wife of Romulus, is said to have made a speech pleading with the two sides to make peace for the women's sake (Livy, *History of Rome* 1.9).

128. Petrarch, *Triumphs*, Chastity, 1:152: "Poi vidi Ersilia con le sue Sabine / Schiera, che del suo nome empie ogni libro."

129. Boccaccio, *Concerning Famous Women* 75, on Claudia. This Claudia was not a Vestal Virgin in the original.

No less worthy than Claudia was another Vestal Virgin who, as the judges were disputing in the temple about whether she had been falsely accepted into the order, entered the temple with a sieve filled with the waters of the Tiber, from which not even a tiny drop fell. This is related by Livy.[130] Thus all suspicion vanished from the minds of the judges. For this reason Petrarch writes these words about her in the *Triumph of Chastity*:

> Amongst others the pious Vestal Virgin who ran boldly to the Tiber and to exonerate herself from wicked blame brought water from the river to the temple in a sieve.[131]

How dear to Mica of Elis was her virginity! She fell into the hands of Lucius, one of Aristotimus's soldiers, and refused absolutely, in spite of gifts and threats, to give in to his wishes, even though her own father begged her to do so. Strong-willed in her chastity, she knelt at his feet and begged him not to permit this outrage, but the unbridled Lucius beat her cruelly in her father's arms and then cut off her head.[132]

Laura, as Petrarch writes, was a very chaste woman. As well as celebrating this throughout the *Canzoniere*, he also puts her in the *Triumph of Chastity*, saying:

> Here I pass over great and glorious things that I saw and dare not tell, and come now to my lady and her less worthy companions. She wore that day a white gown and held that shield which reflected Medusa. To a beautiful jasper pillar that was there with a chain once dipped in the Lethe, a chain of diamonds and topazes that women today no longer wear, I saw him [Cupid] fastened and chastised enough to wreak a thousand revenges, and for myself I was well content and satisfied.[133]

He describes her as dressed in white, in order to denote her chastity.

---

130. The Vestal Virgin Tuccia was accused of being unchaste. She appealed to Vesta for a sign to prove her innocence and was rewarded by being able to carry water in a sieve. This story is not found in Livy, but related in Valerius Maximus (first century C.E.), *Memorable Deeds and Words* 8.1.5.

131. Petrarch, *Triumphs*, Chastity, 1:148: "Fra l'altre la Vestal vergine pia / Che baldanzosamente corse al Tibro / Et per purgarsi d'ogni colpa ria / Portò dal fiume al tempio acqua col cribro."

132. Plutarch, *Bravery of Women* 15 (250f–51c). The story of Mica (Micca) is part of the same story as note 131 above.

133. Petrarch, *Triumphs*, Chastity, 1:115–126: "Passo qui cose gloriose, e magne / Ch'io vidi, e dir non oso, a la mia donna / Vengo, e a l'altre sue minor compagne / Ell'havea in dosso il dì candida gonna, / Lo scudo in man, che mal vide Medusa / D'un bel Diaspro era ivi una Colonna / Alla qual d'una in mezzo Lethe infusa / Catena di Diamanti, e di Topazio / Che al mondo fra le donne oggi non s'usa. / Legare il vidi, e farne quello stratio / Che bastò bene a mille altre vendette, / Et io per me ne fui contento, e satio."

Fiordiligi was also chaste, and a faithful wife to Brandimart. When he was killed she had a cell made inside his tomb and lived there in perpetual chastity, as Ariosto writes in the *Orlando furioso*:

> Since her tears were inexhaustible and her sighs could not be quenched, nor by constantly saying offices and masses could she ever satisfy her emotions, she conceived the wish never to leave this place until her soul left with her last breath: so in the tomb she had a cell built, in which she closeted herself for life.[134]

Even though begged by Orlando, it was never possible to move her from that place.

And what of Rosmonda, who was believed to be the daughter of the King of the Goths? Their queen begged her to adorn herself so that King Germodus of Sweden would take her for his wife. She told her it was a great thing to be queen of a magnanimous people. Rosmonda, despising the grandeur of such a life and loving only chastity, replied thus, as Tasso relates in his *Torrismondo*:

> Mother, I do not wish to deny that in my mind this thought is already decided and fixed to live a free and solitary life in chaste liberty, and to preserve intact the dear honor of my virginity, which I esteem more than the acquisition of crowns and sceptres.[135]

I do not wish to omit the chaste and modest nymph Oenone from this honorable company. Paris, the son of Priam, took her as his wife and then abandoned her, whereupon she lived in perpetual chastity.[136]

Virginia, daughter of the patrician Aulus, and wife of the consul Lucius Volumnius, a plebeian, erected a temple to Chastity inside her house. She invited all the matrons there and reassured them that just as men competed for valor, women should compete for chastity and modesty. This Virginia was as honest as can be imagined, as Livy attests.[137]

---

134. Ariosto, *Orlando furioso* 43:183: "E vedendo le lacrime indefesse, / Ed ostinati a uscir sempre i sospiri, / Né per far sempre dire uffici e messe, / Mai satisfar potendo a' suoi disiri; / Di non partirsi quindi in cor si messe, / Fin che del corpo l'anima non spiri: / E nel sepolcro fe' fare una cella, / E vi si chiuse, e fe' sua vita in quella."

135. Tasso, *Il re Torrismondo*, 2.4:83–88: "Madre io no'l vò negar, ne l'alta mente / Questo pensiero è già risposto, e fiso / Di viver vita solitaria, e sciolta / In casta libertade, e'l caro pregio / Di mia verginità serbarmi integro / Più stimo, che acquistar corone, e scettri."

136. Oenone was the nymph whom Paris abandoned after being awarded Helen of Troy by Aphrodite, according to ancient Greek legend.

137. In 296 B.C.E., Virginia was excluded from the Temple of Patrician Modesty, to which all patrician or upper-class Roman matrons belonged, because she had married a plebeian man.

SECTION 3: OF STRONG AND INTREPID WOMEN

Fortitude is a constancy of spirit that overrides the fear of death when it is for a worthy, honest cause or for valor. Speusippus describes it thus:

> The soul that is strong is constant against itself because it is accustomed to terror for the sake of valor.[138]

In *Ethics* III.6, Aristotle states that strong people do not fear death even though they may not desire it, since it is the most terrible and frightening thing in the world.

> Death is certainly the most terrible thing of all.[139]

In the same chapter he goes on to say that the goal of these people is always honor. This is what he writes:

> [The brave man is concerned with] the death that occurs in the noblest circumstances; that is, those that are met with in battle, clearly the greatest and most noble danger. And this corresponds to the way in which honors are bestowed by cities and by kings.[140]

Therefore strong people chose to place themselves in mortal danger if the enterprise had an honorable goal, and if they did not do so, they would reap reproach. He adds:

> And because of this the noble man chooses death and proceeds, since it is shameful not to do so, and the brave man fears shame more than death.[141]

It may reasonably be stated therefore that a strong man cannot be wretched, as Seneca writes:

In response she erected her own temple to Modesty for the plebeian matrons of Rome. (See Livy, *History of Rome* 10.23.)

138. "Est fortitudo animi costatia ad versus ea, quae terrere solent virtutis gratia." On Speusippus see above note 95. The provenance of this quotation is also unknown.

139. Aristotle, *Nicomachean Ethics* 3.6 (1115a27): "Mors enim maxime omnium terribilis est rerum."

140. Ibid. (1115a30–33): "Que mors in pulcherrinis rebus contingit, cuiusmodi sunt, que in bello oppetuntur in maximo silicit et pulcherrimo periculo, his consentiunt etiam honores, qui et a civitatibus, et a regibus instituti sunt." In other words, under all types of government bravery in battle and willingness to face death are particularly rewarded.

141. Ibid.: "Et ea de causa quia honestum est eligit, et sustinet; vel quia id non facere turpe est magis enim timet turpitudinem vir fortis, quam mortem." This precise sentiment is not found in Aristotle's discussion of bravery, but this is a summary of its sense.

Whenever you see a brave man, do not call him wretched.[142]

Now let us move on to the examples of those women who, holding their own lives in contempt, accomplished great and marvellous feats and caused no little envy and shame to men by, as Aristotle describes it, electing to brave every danger because their goal was an honest and good one. The first of these honorable ones are the women of Curzola, a new and recent example, who, scorning their own lives, opposed the formidable forces of Selim, the Turkish Emperor who sought to conquer Curzola. These women, dressed in armor with helmets on their heads and with pikes, fired at the artillery and, with the sound of drums and bugles, invited the other women who had not come to fight. They caused Vluzali, the Turkish captain, to abandon the attempted undertaking with little honor. What do you say of these strong and intrepid women who, shaming the captain, the soldiers, and their own men who had fled, succeeded in saving their country?[143]

In no way inferior to those glorious women was Martia Bronchia, who, armed with the weapons of her husband who had fled in fear, fought at the walls of Pisa. She succeeded in cutting a swathe through the enemy and liberating her country. As a consequence the people she had liberated honored her by erecting a statue of her.[144]

Let us also place the mother of Hyrcanus among this intrepid band of well-born women. She was seized by her enemies and tortured in the presence of Ptolemy's son so that Hyrcanus should lift his siege. In spite of being old, she bore the tortures and begged her son in a loud voice to continue the fight and not to relent—a true sign of a strong spirit.[145]

Let us not remain silent over the mother of Cleomenes, King of Sparta, who was taken hostage by Ptolemy in order that Cleomenes should keep faith with him and not make peace with his enemies without his consent. Cleomenes's mother, having understood that his enemies were offering him peace under honorable terms, wrote to him that on no condition did she wish him to reject the peace offer in order to save the life of an old woman,

---

142. Seneca the Younger, *Hercules furens* 464: "Quemcunquae fortem videris, miserum neges." The words are spoken by Amphitryon.

143. The corsair Vluzali and his campaigns in the service of Selim the Turkish Emperor are mentioned by both Mambrin Roseo and B. Dionigi da Fano in *Delle istorie del mondo.* In 1570 the Turkish fleet approached some rocks known as the Cruzolari near the castle of Lepanto and, after a long battle, were put to flight (5.1, p. 416). However, there is no mention of the women of Curzola.

144. I cannot trace this person.

145. Tarcagnota, *Delle istorie del mondo* 2.34, p. 529, on the mother of Hyrcanus.

since it was honest and useful for the country.[146] Let no one say that this lady did not possess a strong and invincible spirit, since she was prepared to scorn her own life for the sake of her country.

Great and wonderful were the deeds of the women of Argos under the guidance of Telesilla. King Cleomenes of Sparta, having killed a great number of Argives, took his army above Argos to sack the city. The women, having decided to defend it, made Telesilla their captain and presented themselves, armed, on the city walls to the astonishment of the enemy. They, having unsuccessfully attacked several times with great loss of life, were finally obliged to retreat. The same women drove out King Demaratus, who had occupied a part of Argos called Pamphylia. Thus, through the valor of the women, the city of Argos conserved its freedom.[147]

Enough now of women who put their lives at risk to save their countries. I shall deal with them at greater length in the chapter on women's love for their country. Let us turn now to examples of those valiant women who willingly took their own lives in order to escape servitude at the hands of their enemies when not to do so would have brought them great shame. As Aristotle states:

> Because it is shameful not to do this; the strong man fears shame more than death.[148]

The first of these women is Monima of Miletus, the wife of Mithridates. When she heard of the loss of the army and the flight of Mithridates, her husband, she decided to kill herself. Lifting the crown from her head, she fastened it round her neck and hanged herself. It broke, however, since it was not sufficiently strong as a noose to sustain the weight of her body. She said: "Oh cursed diadem that has not served me in this sad office," and, spitting on it scornfully, called immediately for Bacchides her eunuch to kill her. Plutarch writes of this, and Passi refers to it in his book as an act of despair, which Plutarch does not, knowing that "the strong man fears shame more than death" and that it was her royal strength that led her to escape servitude. Roxana and Statira, sisters of the above-mentioned Mithridates, took poison. They praised their brother highly for having warned them of their danger, thus enabling them to die and escape servitude to the enemy.[149]

---

146. Plutarch, *Life of Agis and Cleomenes* 22.3–7.

147. Plutarch, *Bravery of Women* 4 (245c–f), on Telesilla and women of Argos.

148. Aristotle, *Nicomachean Ethics* 3.6 (see above, note 141): "Quia id non facere turpe est; magis enim timet turpitudinem vir fortis, quam mortem." See above note 141.

149. Plutarch, *Life of Lucullus* 18.4–6. According to Plutarch's story, the eunuch Bacchides was sent by Mithridates to tell his wives and sisters that they should kill themselves to save

I should also mention Zenobia the Queen of Armenia, who, fleeing from the Armenians with her husband and unable to bear the torment of the flight because she was pregnant, heartily begged her husband Rhadamistus to kill her so that she should not remain a captive. He, after many tears, cut her throat and threw her in the river Araxes.[150]

Cleopatra, the daughter of Ptolemy Auletes, King of Egypt, feared shame far more than she loved life. Being certain that she would be led in triumph by Caesar Augustus, and having had every means of killing herself taken away from her, she had some leafy figs brought to her, among which was an asp. Having removed the figs, she joyfully offered her white breast to the poisonous teeth of the cold asp in order to escape subjection to a foreigner. Thus in a few hours her life ended, depriving Caesar Augustus, who had believed he was going to lead her to Rome in triumph, of a great joy.[151]

A shining example of strength was the wife of Straton, Prince of Sidon. She could not bear the shame and indignity of being under siege and close to being seized by the enemy, and so she killed her husband and, with the same sword, pierced her own breast, the seat of eternal valor.[152] I also recall a most noble lady called Dugna who drowned herself in order to escape servitude and to avoid falling into the hands of the soldiers of Attila, King of the Huns.[153] Consider, if you please, the generous strength of the Phocian women who resolved to die by fire if Daiphantus's army lost, and prepared the stake in readiness so they would not fall into the hands of the enemy.[154]

Nor do I wish to omit the illustrious example of Panteus's wife. Ptolemy, having flayed the body of his enemy Cleomenes, desired that Cretesiclea, Cleomenes's mother, and his children should kill themselves together with

---

their honor because he was in trouble. In this account it was only his sister Statira who generously praised Mithridates for giving them warning of his fall and thus allowing them to die untouched, whereas Roxana died cursing him for bringing such an end upon her. See note 102 above.

150. Tacitus, *Annals* 12.51, on Zenobia, wife of Rhadamistus of Armenia.

151. Boccaccio, *Concerning Famous Women* 86, on Cleopatra.

152. This story is told by Battista Fulgosio in *Dictorum factorumque memorabilium: Exempla virtutum et vitiorum*, book 4, chapter 5, p. 825 (Basel, 1555). See part II, chapter 4, note 10 of this volume.

153. Many of the atrocities committed by King Attila of the Huns are listed by Tarcagnota, *Delle istorie del mondo* 3.6, pp. 212–18, but there is no mention of the noble lady Dugna.

154. Plutarch, *Bravery of Women* 2 (244b–e). The Phocians, at war with the Thessalians, built a huge pyre on which they planned to burn all their women and children should they lose the battle, to prevent them falling into enemy hands. In fact their army won, but the women's readiness to die in such a way was greatly admired.

Panteus's wife, a most beautiful woman of strong and valorous spirit. She had followed her husband into exile and borne up constantly under the reverses and trials of fortune. While the others were being led to their deaths she comforted Cleomenes's mother with sweet and loving words so that she went happily, in order to escape from servitude. When they arrived at the place where criminals were put to death, the unfortunate children of Cleomenes were killed first, before the eyes of the courageous women; then, after the children, they put Cretesiclea to death, and as she was dying Panteus's wife arranged her garments for her and comforted her. Panteus's wife remained alone, and being of a strong and intrepid spirit this most chaste woman presented herself for death without a sigh or a tear, not allowing anyone to approach her except the man who was to kill her, and making a death worthy of such a woman to the amazement and wonder of the cruel tyrant.[155]

Hasdrubal's wife does not deserve silence. Having learned of the cruel loss of her husband and fearing servitude, she threw herself into a blazing fire with her three young children.[156] And what should I say of Sophonisba, Hasdrubal's daughter and the wife of Syphax? Having heard that her husband was a prisoner and the field destroyed, she determined to die free rather than live in servitude, as Trissino has her say in his tragedy in these words:

> Shall it be that I leave my royal apartments, and my sweet, native land; that I cross the sea, and am obliged to stay in servitude under the proud restraint of a harsh and insolent people, the natural enemies of my country. Let not, let not such things be said of me; I would rather die than live as a slave.[157]

And note these beautiful lines that she utters a little later, undoubtedly worthy of a strong and generous spirit:

155. Plutarch, *Life of Agis and Cleomenes* 38. Cleomenes was the thirty-first king of Sparta, and these events took place around 220 B.C.E. See above, notes 146 and 147.

156. Hasdrubal was general of the Carthaginians in the Third Punic War against Rome. The Roman army besieged Carthage in 147–46 B.C.E., and the city eventually surrendered. Hasdrubal fled with his wife and children, but he later surrendered secretly to the Roman leader Scipio. His wife was disgusted by this display of weakness, and after berating him is said to have thrown herself and her children into the flames of a burning temple. Appian, *Roman History: Punic Wars* 131. (Marinella alters the details slightly.)

157. Giangiorgio Trissino, *Sophonisba* 3 (lines 97–105): "Sarà ch'io lasci la regale stanza, / E lo nativo mio dolce terreno; / E ch'io trapassi il mare, / E mi convegna stare / In servitù sotto il superbo freno, / Di gente aspra, e proterva, / Nemica natural del mio paese. / Non sien di me, non sien tai cose intese; / Più tosto vo morir, che viver serva."

Our life is like a beautiful treasure that must not be spent on vile things nor withheld in honorable undertakings, since a beautiful and glorious death gives splendor to all of one's past life.[158]

When the valiant lady saw Masinissa, King of Massala, she went to meet him and asked him to grant her the favor of not allowing her to be made a slave of the Romans. These are her words:

And if every way is closed to you of saving me from their power, remove me from your heart by granting me death. This I ask of you as your last gift.[159]

When Masinissa, not having been able to defend her, sent her poison, she accepted it willingly and took it without tears or sighs and without changing color, as the same author has a servant recount:

Where without delay she took the poison, and drank it all surely right to the bottom of the shining vessel, but that which seemed most marvellous to me was that she did all this without a tear or sigh; and without even changing color.[160]

This woman was surely worthy of every praise, and in the end she died unconquered and with glory.

What should I say of Sophronia, who, when Sultan Aladine wished to kill and burn the unfortunate Christians, thought she could save the others' lives by her own death? Tasso describes it in his *Gerusalemme liberata*:

To her, who is as generous as she is honest, comes an idea of how she can save them. Courage sets her grand idea in motion, then it is stopped by modesty and maidenly decorum; courage wins, or rather it comes to an understanding and makes itself modest and modesty courageous.[161]

---

158. Ibid. 3 (lines 112–16): "La vita nostra è come un bel tesoro, / Che spender non si deve in cosa vile / Ne risparmiar ne l'honorate imprese, / Perché una bella e gloriosa morte / Illustra tutta la passata vita."

159. Ibid. 5 (lines 107–10): "E se ciascuna via pur vi sia chiusa / Da tormi da l'arbitrio di costoro, / Toglietemi dal cor con darmi morte. / Questa per gratia estrema vi domando."

160. Ibid. 14 (lines 157–63): "Ove senza tardar prese il veneno, / E tutto lo bevè sicuramente / Infino al fondo del lucente vaso, / Ma quel che più mi par meraviglioso, / E ch'ella fece tutte queste cose / Senza gittarne lagrime, o sospiro; / E senza pur mutarsi di colore."

161. Tasso, *Gerusalemme liberata* 2:17: "A lei, che generosa è quanto onesta, / Viene in pensier come salvar costoro. / Move fortezza il gran pensier, l'arresta / Poi la vergogna e 'l verginal decoro; / Vince fortezza, anzi s'accorda e face / Sé vergognosa e la vergogna audace." From edition by Claudio Varese and Guido Arbizzoni (Milan, 1972).

Tasso, almost marvelling at such courage, goes on in canto II, stanza 22, to describe her behavior after approaching the tyrant Aladine and announcing that she herself has stolen the image:

> So she offered her proud head against the general doom and meant to gather it against herself alone: o noble lie, now when is the truth so beautiful that it can be preferred to you?[162]

And when in stanza 30 she sees the unfortunate Olindo approaching to offer himself for the same punishment in order to save her she asks:

> Am I therefore unable without you to bear what the wrath of a single man can do? I have yet a heart that thinks itself alone sufficient for one death, and asks no company.[163]

Clorinda, arriving and seeing them, draws near and watches them and sees Olindo moan while Sophronia remains silent:

> The crowds give way, and she draws up to look closely at the two who are bound together. She sees that one is silent and the other moans and the weaker sex is showing the greater strength.[164]

But if she showed greater strength she was not weaker but stronger, as can clearly be seen in many written examples by historians and poets.

I do not wish to omit Polyxena, the daughter of King Priam, who remained strong in the face of misfortune and death. When still a young girl she was taken to Achilles's tomb where, recalling her royal state, she willingly allowed herself to be killed rather than live as a servant to the Argives. Ovid describes her death and manner of dying in *Metamorphoses* XIII:

> Brave in spite of her misery, showing more than a woman's courage, she was led to the tomb, and offered as a sacrifice on that grim pyre. As she stood before the cruel altar, and realized that the barbarous rites were being prepared for her, she did not forget herself. Seeing Neoptolemus standing sword in hand, his eyes fixed on her face, she said: "Be quick, and shed my noble blood. I do not hinder you. Bury your sword in my throat or in my breast!" And she uncovered her breast

---

162. Ibid. 2:22: "Così al publico fato il capo altero / Offerse, e'l volse in sé stessa raccorre: / Magnanima menzogna, or quand'è il vero / Sì bello, che si possa a te preporre?"

163. Ibid. 2:30: 'Non son io dunque senza te possente / A sostener ciò che d'un uom può l'ira? / Ho petto anch'io, ch'ad una morte crede / Di bastar solo, e compagnia non chiede."

164. Ibid. 2:42: "Cedon le turbe, e i duo legati insieme / Ella si ferma a riguardar da presso. / Mira che l'una tace e l'altro geme / E più vigor mostra il men forte sesso."

and her throat together. "Assuredly, Polyxena would not wish to be slave to any man! But you will not appease the wrath of any god by such a sacrifice as this. My only wish is that my death could be concealed from my mother: she troubles me, and lessens my delight in dying, though indeed it is not my death but her own life she has to fear. But if there is justice in my plea, attendants, stand aside, and do not lay male hands upon a maiden's body. Let me go to the Stygian shades a free woman. Whoever it is you seek to placate by slaying me, he will welcome more gladly the blood of one who is free. Yet, if the last words I speak move any of you—it is King Priam's daughter, not a slave, who makes this request—give back my body without ransom to my mother. Let her buy the sad right to bury me, not with gold, but with her tears: when she could, she paid in gold as well." Polyxena finished speaking. The tears that she herself restrained were shed for her by the people. Even the priest himself was weeping, and with unwilling hands drove home the knife, piercing the breast she offered him. Her knees gave way, and she fell to the ground: but her face retained its look of fearless courage to the end. Even when she was falling, she took care to cover the parts of the body that should be covered, and to preserve what was proper for a modest girl.[165]

What do you think of this most courageous young girl, truly worthy of eternal praise (and indeed there are so many others whom I have not included).

Euripides, in his tragedy *Hecuba*, describes Polyxena's same intrepidness and fortitude. For the sake of brevity, I will quote only a couple of lines that Polyxena herself addresses to the man who has come to wound her. These clearly demonstrate her courageous spirit:

---

165. Ovid, *Metamorphoses* 13.451–80: "Fortis, et infelix, et plus quam femina virgo / Ducitur ad tumulum: diroque fit hostia busto. / Quae memor ipsa sui, postquam crudelibus aris / Admota est sensitque sibi fera sacra parari, / Utque Neoptolemum stantem, ferrumque tenentem, / Inque suo vidit figentem lumina vultu, / "Utere iamdudum generoso sanguine," dixit. / "Nulla mora est: aut tu iugulo, vel pectore telum / Conde meo;" iugulumque simul pectusque retexit. / Scilicet haud ulli servire Polyxena vellet! / "Haud per tale sacrum numen placabitis ullum. / Mors tantum vellem matrem mea fallere posset; / Mater obest; minuitque necis mihi gaudia: quamvis / Non mea mors illi, verum sua vita tremenda est, / Vos modo, ne Stygios adeam non libera manes, / Ite procul, si iusta peto, tactuque viriles / Virgineo removete manus! acceptior illi, / Quisquis is est, quem caede mea placare paratis; / Liber erit sanguis, siquos tamen ultima nostri / Verba movent oris, Priami vos filia regis / Non captiva rogat, genetrici corpus inemptum / Reddite, neve auro redimat ius triste sepulcri, / Sed lachrimis! tunc, cum poterat redimebat, et auro." / Dixerat at populus lachrimas, quas illa tenebat, / Non tenet, ipse etiam flens, invitusque sacerdos / Praebita coniecto rupit praecordia ferro. / Illa super terram defecto poplite labens, / Pertulit intrepidos ad fata novissima vultus; / Tunc quoque cura fuit partes velare tegendas: / Cum caderet; castique decus servare pudoris." (Mary Innes's translation, 297–98.)

Here young man, if it is my breast you want strike here, or if it is my neck, here is my neck ready.[166]

But now I must write of another story that Plutarch narrates about the Cimbrian women. When they learned of the defeat and flight of their men they dressed themselves in mourning, climbed into carts, and set up camp near the battlefield. As the Cimbrians fled the Romans, the women killed them. Some of them strangled their own husbands, fathers, and brothers. Others killed their sons with their own hands, throwing them on the ground between the horses' legs or under the cart wheels, and then they turned their swords on themselves in order to escape servitude to the Romans. He also speaks of a woman who hanged herself to the end of a cart ladder, having hanged her children to her heels with a noose, and she ended her life in this manner.[167]

Philip of Macedonia, having killed many noblemen, decided for his own safety to imprison the children of those he had unjustly slain. He had recently killed a man called Herodianus, a Thessalonian leader, as well as two of his sons-in-law, thus leaving his daughters fatherless widows. One of them was called Theoxena, the other Archo. Many men asked for Theoxena's hand in marriage, but she always refused them. Archo married and had many children, then died. Theoxena then married Poris, her sister Archo's husband and the father of her children, because she loved them so much that she wanted to bring them up herself. She fed them and taught them with as much care as if she had given birth to them, and also had a child herself, who was very young at the time when Philip issued his proclamation about imprisoning the children of those who had been slain by his commandment.

When Theoxena, who was a woman of great spirit, heard this, she determined for the sake of the love she bore them not to allow them to enter into servitude to Philip. She therefore resolved to kill them. But Poris, loathing the idea of such cruelty, said he would take them safely to some friends of his in Athens. That night, when the silence of the nocturnal shades quietened their troubled hearts, Theoxena and Poris went on board ship with their children. But because fortune nearly always pursues men, they were unable, in spite of strenuous attempts, to set sail because the wind was against them. When the sun left its maternal seat and brought light to the human race, the guardians of the king's port became aware that they were

---

166. Euripides, *Hecuba* (lines 563–65): "En iuvenis, hoc si pectus ense mavoles / Promptum ferire, ferito: sin cervicem, adest / Exprompta cervix."
167. Plutarch, *Life of Caius Marius* 28 (421e).

fleeing and sent many armed men after the ship, commanding them not to return without it. Poris urged the sailors on and prayed to the gods to lend them their help while his generous lady, knowing that escape was impossible, placed a container full of poison and a naked dagger before the children and said to them: "My dearest children, these are your means to freedom, and these two objects are your means to death. Choose which of them you please in order to escape servitude and royal pride. Come now," she went on, "those of you who are youths choose the steel, and those of you who are children take the poison if you prefer to die more slowly." The enemy were near, so she hastened them, some with poison and some with the dagger, to their deaths and while they were still half alive threw them into the sea. She then embraced her husband, her faithful companion through her sorrows, and threw herself after them. And so this lady, worthy of eternal memory as Livy recounts, escaped servitude.[168]

Nor should the brave and illustrious deed of a Greek matron go untold. For this reason I will relate how, after the Turks had taken Nicosia, a very famous and rich city on the island of Cyprus, by force, they loaded the noblest spoils and most precious objects of this unhappy city onto three ships. One of these three was a galleon in which they had placed the highest-born ladies in order to send them as slaves to the great ruler of Constantinople. This valiant lady of Cyprus, scorning the idea of servitude to a barbarian, set fire to the munitions, so that in a brief space of time all the ladies and men were burned [to death], apart from a few who saved themselves by swimming away.[169] Nobody of an impassioned spirit (believe me) will deny that this act was worthy of eternal praise or that for as long as the sky revolves, this noble cry from her strong breast will be heard by everyone as that of an enemy of tyranny and servitude. Certainly all those other gentlewomen who abhorred such cruel and barbarous servitude must naturally have been obliged to her for her deed that conserved them, Christian and chaste, for the next world.

SECTION 4: OF PRUDENT WOMEN AND THOSE EXPERT AT GIVING ADVICE

Of all the soul's virtues it would seem that prudence is regarded by everyone as the most noble. It is the quality by means of which people determine and advise what they can best achieve in difficult and important matters and

---

168. Livy, *History of Rome* 40.4, on Theoxena. In Livy's account, Theoxena is described as *ferox* (savage), rather than generous. As usual Marinella has adapted the original to suit her own ends.

169. Mambrin Roseo recounts this incident in Tarcagnota, *Delle istorie del mondo* 5.13, p. 367.

which enables them to choose the best course. For this reason Aristotle states in book VI, chapter 6, of the *Ethics*:

> It is the mark of a prudent person to be able to deliberate well.[170]

And in book VII, chapter 3, where his aim is to determine what is right, he demonstrates it with these words:

> No one would say that the intelligent person is the sort to do the worst actions willingly.[171]

And in book VI, chapter 9:

> They seek for themselves what is good, and they think that this is what should be done.[172]

It is true that we discover the subtlety and liveliness of our wits when we determine whether or not we should do something in a difficult situation. For prudence does not always consist in acting, but sometimes in not acting, when it is more useful and honorable not to do so. This can be better understood through examples.

Artemisia, Queen of Caria, was extremely prudent. She went with many ships to aid Xerxes, and advised him with spirited reasoning not to fight with desperate men but to draw matters out, because his enemies lacked provisions. She told him to remember always that she did not say this out of fear but from practicality and for the sake of Xerxes's honor. Xerxes, having fought other naval wars, did not want to take the Queen's shrewd advice, and went into battle and lost, as Trogus relates.[173] But what can I say of Joan, a young woman of Lothoringa? She acted with such prudence in war that she won back many of King Charles's lands for him. On her advice he proceeded to Rheims and was crowned there, as Tarcagnota relates.[174]

Semiramis was so wise and prudent that Ninus, knowing of her virtue, never acted without her advice.[175] Cyrus did the same with Aspasia, and involved her in thousands of enterprises. All his dealings turned out well and happily during the period in which he took her advice.[176] Julius Caesar related

---

170. Aristotle, *Nicomachean Ethics* 6.5 (1140a25): "Prudentis est bene consulere, et in angendo versatur."

171. Ibid. 7.2 (1146a6–7): "Prudentis non est sponte agere, quae sunt prava."

172. Ibid. 6.8 (1142a7): "Quaerunt sibi quod bonum, idque agendum esse existimant."

173. Trogus was an historian from the Augustan age whose work we know only through Justin's later epitome of it. The Artemisia story is originally found in books 7 and 8 of Herodotus.

174. Tarcagnota, *Delle istorie del mondo* 2.18, p. 725, on Joan of Arc.

175. Boccaccio, *Concerning Famous Women* 2, on Semiramis.

176. Plutarch, *Life of Pericles* 24.5–12. Aspasia was a Phocaean woman who was carried away by Cyrus the Younger to be part of his harem partly on account of her great beauty, but primarily

that the Gauls never made any decision without consulting their women.[177] They continue to do so to this day, knowing well how astute their women are. Augustus conferred with his wife and took her wise, mature advice on important affairs of state. He also lost a certain rustic severity of his and became both meek and mild.[178]

Was not Portia most prudent?[179] Was not Cornelia, the mother of Tiberius and Caius Gracchus, prudent, wise, and eloquent?[180] Emperor Justinian always consulted with his faithful wife on important matters concerning his empire and, because of her wise advice, their endeavors always had a most happy outcome.[181] It was for this reason that Aurelius Victor stated in his *Life of Emperor Julian*:

> The teachings of women assist their husbands.[182]

And for this reason, Tacitus states, the Germans, being aware of this maxim, never took up arms without the advice of their women, knowing with how much valor they were endowed. From this it can be understood that women are the honor and glory of the male sex.[183]

And what of Pompeia Plotina, who augmented Trajan's glory with her prudence?[184] As Paulus Diaconus states in book XIII of *History of Rome*:

> The wise Lacedaemonians took advice from their wives and attempted nothing without telling them about it.[185]

The Athenians, knowing the prudence of women, wanted them to vote on all the matters and resolutions taken in the senate like the best senators. Aristotle in *Politics* II, chapter 7, says of them:

---

because of her wisdom. She proceeded to advise him well throughout his life and became his favorite wife.

177. Caesar, *The Gallic War* 6.

178. Dio Cassius devotes several pages to a dialogue between Livia and her husband, the emperor Augustus, in which she advises him on matters of state (*Roman History* 55.14–22).

179. Boccaccio, *Concerning Famous Women* 80, on Portia.

180. On Cornelia see above, note 25.

181. Justinian was emperor of Rome and Constantinople 527–65. His wife Theodora was originally an actress, and their marriage caused a scandal. When Justinian became emperor he insisted that she be declared empress and have an equal role in the ruling of his empire. All officials had to swear oaths in both of their names.

182. Aurelius Victor, *Life of Emperor Julian*: "Feminarum precepta iuvant maritos."

183. Tacitus, *Germania* 8.2–3: "They believe that their women have an innate gift of divinely inspired foresight, and they don't scorn their advice or fail to heed their answers."

184. Pliny the Younger, *Panegyric* 83.4, for praise of Trajan's wife, Pompeia Plotina.

185. Paulus Diaconus, *History of Rome* 13.

In the state of Sparta many things were administered by women.[186]

Socrates, though a great philosopher, confessed to having learned many things from Diotima, a woman of wisdom and prudence.[187] The illustrious writer Plutarch mentions in his book of noble women that the ancient Gauls, after they had reached agreement and made peace with Hannibal, made a decree in which it was stated that if any Carthaginian received some injury or injustice from one of them, the Gallic women should judge the case.[188]

Placidia was so successful at giving sound advice that she prevented King Adolphus of the Goths from demolishing the great city of Rome, which he had threatened with barbaric fury and proud threats. Instead, because of her prudence, he restored it.[189] Another lady who was most prudent in her counsel was Catherine, mother of the King of France.[190] Ginevra Malatesta was praised for her great prudence by Ariosto in *Orlando furioso*:

> Had she been at that time in Rimini, when, proud of his conquest of Gaul, Caesar was debating whether to cross the river and antagonize Rome, I believe that he would have furled all his banners and divested himself of his rich trophies, accepted laws and covenants at her insistence, and perhaps he never would have become the oppressor of liberty.[191]

The Lady Regent of the city of Brussels also showed great prudence in forgiving those who had risen against her. They had assembled a large army against her, but she pardoned them in spite of this with royal clemency.[192]

---

186. Aristotle, *Politics* 2.9 (1269b32): "Multa in Lacaedemoniorum principatu a mulieribus administrabantur." Aristotle is using this as an example of licentious and bad political practice!

187. On Diotima, see above note 45.

188. Plutarch, *Bravery of Women* 6 (246c).

189. Galla Placidia, born about 390 C.E., was daughter of Theodosius the Great. Captured by Alaric in 400, she was kept as a hostage but treated well. On Alaric's death she became the wife of his successor Ataulphus or Adolphus, and was one of his advisers.

190. Catherine de' Medici (1519–89), wife of one king of France and mother of three. On the accession of her eldest son, Francis II in 1559, she found some scope for her ambition and on the accession of her second son, Charles IX in 1560, the government fell entirely into her hands.

191. Ariosto, *Orlando furioso* 46:6: "S'a quella etade in Arminio era, / Quando superbo de la Gallia doma / Cesar fu in dubbio, s'oltre a la riviera / Dovea passando inimicarsi Roma; / Crederò che piegata ogni bandiera / E scarca di trofei la ricca soma / Tolto avria leggi, e patti a voglia d'essa, / Né forse mai la libertade oppressa."

192. Margaret of Austria (1480–1530), daughter of Maximilian I, married first the Infante Juan, then Philibert II of Savoy. From 1507 she proved a wise regent of the Netherlands. On her, see *Contemporaries of Erasmus*, ed. P. G. Bietenholz and T. B. Deutscher (Toronto: University of Toronto Press, 1985–87), 3 vols., 2.388–89, and sources cited.

I will not omit to mention the great prudence of Periaconconau, who, when her brother Ismael died, kept the fact secret and sent for seven of the principal men of the realm to come to the palace. There, with inestimable courage and prudence, she sought to dispel the hatred between them in order to conserve the Persian Empire, which now needed more than ever for its sultans to be united. She explained to them that she was in dire need because of the death of Ismael and because Cudabende, his rightful successor, was far away. She realized that she was courting danger by divulging the death of the King, but if they continued in their hostilities the kingdom would go to ruin, and the sultans, as a result of their disagreements, would be forced to live subject to their enemies the Turks and Tartars. As a result of this great lady's prudence they put aside their enmity and, uniting with her, dealt with the discords of the kingdom. This story is related by Mambrin Roseo.[193]

And what of Semiramis? She was sent for by her husband Menones and no sooner had she joined him in camp than, being a most prudent woman, she showed him how he might take the enemy fortress. This caused Ninus, King of Assyria, to marvel greatly at her intelligence, as Tarcagnota relates.[194]

It was because of Tanaquil's prudence that Servius Tullius was accepted as king after the death of Tarquin.[195] But the prudence of women can be observed every day. Not just that of queens and great ladies, but of every lowly woman who organizes her household and family, who administers the possessions and wealth acquired by men and distributes it with great foresight according to need and to the times. Unhappy the men, and particularly those of France and Germany, if their women should cease to manage their wealth, for they would immediately lose their riches and become beggars. But they recognize women's prudence and allow themselves to be governed by women. The French never handle a single coin without asking their wives' permission. I pass over the fact that in the same countries women attend to business with a diligence that is unsurpassed by the foremost merchant in all of Italy—a sign of the highest intelligence.

193. Tarcagnota, *Delle istorie del mondo* 3.2, p. 497. The story of Periaconconau is in fact to be found in Bartolomeo Dionigi da Fano's *Aggiunta alla terza parte.*

194. Tarcagnota, *Delle istorie del mondo* 1.1, pp. 12–15, on Semiramis.

195. Tanaquil was the wife of Tarquinius Priscus, the fifth king of Rome. According to Roman legend, she correctly interpreted the ring of flame that appeared above the head of Servius Tullius (a slave boy). Understanding it to mean that he should be the next king of Rome, she took him into her own family and educated him for the role. Sources for the story are Valerius Maximus, *Memorable Deeds and Words* 1.6.1, and Livy, *History of Rome*, book 1.

VI

A REPLY TO THE FLIPPANT AND VAIN REASONING ADOPTED BY MEN IN THEIR OWN FAVOR

It seems to me that I have clearly shown that women are far nobler and more excellent than men. Now it remains for me to reply to the false objections of our slanderers. These are of two sorts, some founded on specious reasonings and others solely on authorities and their opinions. Commencing with the latter, I maintain that I am not obliged to reply to them at all. If I should affirm that the element of air does not exist, I would not be obliged to reply to the authority of Aristotle or of other writers who say that it does.

I do not, however, wish to wrong famous men in denying their conclusions, since certain obstinate people would regard this as being unjust. I say, therefore, that various reasons drove certain wise and learned men to reprove and vituperate women. They included anger, self-love, envy, and insufficient intelligence. It can be stated therefore that when Aristotle or some other man reproved women, the reason for it was either anger, envy, or too much self-love.

It is clear to everyone that anger is the origin of indecent accusations against women. When a man wishes to fulfil his unbridled desires and is unable to because of the temperance and continence of a woman, he immediately becomes angry and disdainful and in his rage says every bad thing he can think of, as if the woman were something evil and hateful. The same can be said of the envious man, who when he sees someone worthy of praise can only look at them with a distorted view. And thus when a man sees that a woman is superior to him, both in virtue and in beauty, and that she is justly honored and loved even by him, he tortures himself and is consumed with envy. Not being able to give vent to his emotions in any other way, he resorts with sharp and biting tongue to false and specious vituperation and reproof. The same occurs as a result of the too great love that men bear for themselves, which causes them to believe that they are more outstanding in wit and 119 intelligence and by nature superior to women—an exaggerated arrogance and over-inflated and haughty pride. But if with a subtle intelligence they should consider their own imperfections, oh how humble and low they would become! Perhaps one day, God willing, they will perceive it.

All these reasons therefore induced the good Aristotle to blame women —the principal among them, I believe, being the envy he bore them. For three years, as Diogenes Laertius relates, he had been in love with a lady concubine of Hermias, who, knowing of his great and mad love for her, gave her to him as his wife. He, arrogant with joy, made sacrifices in honor of his new lady and goddess—as it was the custom in those times to make to Ceres of Eleusis—and also to Hermias who had given her to him. Pondering then on all those worthy and memorable matters, he became envious of his wife and jealous of her state, since, not being worshiped like a god by anyone, he could not equal it.[1] Thus he turned to reviling women even though he knew they were worthy of every praise.

It can also be added that, like a man of small intelligence (pardon me you Aristotelians who are reading this; Timon also called him foolish),[2] he attributed the reasons for his long error to Hermias's lady, and not to his own unwise intellect, and proceeded to utter shameful and dishonorable words in order to cover up the error he had committed and to lower the female sex, which was an unreasonable thing to do.

To these two motives can also be added self-love, since he judged himself to be a miracle of nature and grew so excessively conceited that he reputed every other person in the world to be unworthy of his love. Therefore, whenever he remembered the time when he had been subservient to women and was secretly ashamed of it, he sought to cover up his failing by speaking badly of them.

The fact that it was disdain against certain women that induced him to injure the female sex is something that must of necessity be believed. He had been a lover, and as I have shown above, an unbridled lover. These were the reasons that induced poor Aristotle to say that women were more dishonest and given to gossiping than men, and more envious and slanderous. He did not see that in calling them slanderous, he too was joining the ranks of the slanderers.

In *History of Animals*, book IX, and in other places, he says that women are composed of matter, imperfect, weak, deficient and poor-spirited—things

1. This story comes from Diogenes Laertius's "Life of Aristotle" (see above, note 4 of Marinella's Introduction). Hermias, a eunuch, was tyrant of Atarneus, and Aristotle was said to have spent some years living with and advising him.

2. See note 1. This attribution to Timon comes from the same passage of Diogenes. The line of Timon's quoted there is "no, nor yet Aristotle's painful futility."

we have discussed in the third argument.[3] It could also be thoughtlessness that caused him to deceive himself about the nature and essence of women. Perhaps a mature consideration of their nobility and excellence would have proved too great a burden for his shoulders. As we know, there are many people who believe that the earth moves and the sky remains still,[4] others that there are infinite worlds,[5] still others that there is only one, and some that the fly is nobler than the heavens. Each and every person defends his or her opinion obstinately and with infinite arguments, and these are the replies that we give to those who vituperate the female sex.

There have also been some men who, on discovering a woman who was not very good, have bitingly and slanderously stated that all women are bad and wicked. They have made the grave error of basing a universal criticism on one particular case. It is true, however, that, having realised their error, they have then astutely praised good women. One reply is sufficient for the moral philosophers and poets who, when they criticize women are merely criticizing the worst ones, such as when Hesiod says that there is nothing worse than a wicked wife and then Theognis affirms that there is nothing dearer than a good one.[6] Plautus writes:

If one has bought an evil and hostile wife, one has paid dearly.[7]

From this we can see that each of these judgments contains its own reply since they speak honorably of good women and condemn bad ones.

In Guarini's *Pastor fido*, act I, the Satyr speaks thus in reproof of women:

O perfidious woman, it is to you I impute every cause of love's infamy. All that is cruel and wicked in him is derived from you alone and not from him.[8]

Later he condemns women's falsity in these words:

3. Aristotle, *History of Animals* 9.1. See above, chapters 3 and 4.

4. The reference is to Copernicus and his followers. Copernicanism was not proved until the publication (1609) of Johannes Kepler's calculations of the orbit of Mars, and was not known to have been proved until many years thereafter (Galileo, who died in 1642, never seems to have known that Kepler had solved the problem of planetary motion).

5. Giordano Bruno (1548–1600) was burned at the stake in Rome during the year Marinella's treatise initially appeared, for suggesting, among other things, the possibility of multiple inhabited worlds in the universe.

6. Hesiod, *Works and Days* (lines 702–4): "For a man wins nothing better than a good wife, and nothing worse than a bad one." Theognis, *Elegies* 1225–26, quoted in Stobaeus's anthology: "Nothing, Cyrnus, is more delightful than a good wife."

7. Plautus, *Miles gloriosus* (*The Braggart Warrior*), line 673: "In mala uxore, atque inimico si quid sumatur, sumptus est."

8. Guarini, *Pastor fido* 1.5 (lines 29–32): "O femenil perfidia, a te si rechi / La cagion pur d'ogni amorosa infamia; / Da te sola deriva, e non da lui, / Quant'ha di crudo, e di malvagio amore."

What do you have that is not completely false? If you open your mouth you lie, if you sigh your sighs are false, if you roll your eyes, your look is counterfeit, in fact every act etc.[9]

But in the second act, acknowledging his error at having generalized, he corrects himself and criticizes only the bad and wicked women like Corisca, saying:

Accursed Corisca and, I almost said, every female in the world.[10]

From these words, "I almost said," we see that he does not wish to condemn all women. Later he confirms that he is only speaking of the worst kind of woman:

Now she will be set aflame, and I'd like to see every wicked woman burnt and destroyed in the one same fire.[11]

Can it not be seen that he is only speaking of bad women?

Even though Petrarch says "Woman is fickle by nature,"[12] and Jacopo Sannazaro, in the *Arcadia*, introduces a wretched lover who says:

The man who places any trust in a woman's heart is ploughing the waves and sowing in the sands and hoping to ensnare the fleeting wind in his net.[13]

They are not, however, speaking of good women, as can be seen from Petrarch's *Triumph of Chastity*, where he praises many women for their constancy.[14] It can also be said that Sannazaro was speaking from passion or disdain.[15]

Giovanni della Casa echoes this in his verses against women because the lady he loved had turned her affections toward another lover. For this

9. Ibid. 1.5 (lines 66–69): "Qual cosa hai tu che non sia tutta finta? / S'apri la bocca menti, se sospiri, / Son mentiti i sospir, se movi gli occhi, / È simulato il guardo, in somma ogni atto, etc."

10. Ibid. 3.9 (lines 46–47): "Maledetta Corisca, e quasi dissi / Quante femmine ha il mondo."

11. Ibid. 3.9 (lines 56–58): "Hor le si darà il fuoco, ov'io vorrei / Veder quante son femine malvagie / In un incendio solo, arse, e distrutte."

12. Petrarch, *Canzoniere* 183:12: "Femina è cosa mobile per natura."

13. Jacopo Sannazaro, *Arcadia*, Eclogue 8 (lines 10–12): "Né l'onde solca, e né l'arena semina, / E 'l vago vento spera in rete accogliere, / Chi sua speranza fonda in cor di femina."

14. Petrarch, *Triumphs*, Chastity.

15. Jacopo Sannazaro (1456–1530), Renaissance humanist and writer of pastoral who lived virtually his entire life in Naples, was supposed to have suffered an unhappy love for one Carmosina Bonifaccio, ended by her untimely death. The character of the unhappy lover, Sincero, in his *Arcadia* is supposed to represent the author, who remained unmarried.

reason, upset, he turned to reproaching all women since he was not able to separate the true from the false. He shows that this is his motive when he says:

> If I could show you the words, and the countenance and express the habits and manners, of he whom in my place the wise lady who was once mine has chosen as her Narcissus, I do not know if astonishment, or laughter, or pity would move our hearts more. Indeed I know that you would feel anger and sorrow that I should regret such an advantageous loss.[16]

Oh how the poor man allows himself to be so carried away by spite that he speaks badly of all women, while all the time pretending to be unmoved. But he did not find anybody who would believe him and says at the beginning of his verses:

> Do not believe, however, that my pain and tears are because she left me; indeed I grieve and weep over the time that I was another's servant in the cage of love: great as my ardor and desire once were, now greater are my scorn and anger. Once I sang of her and now I regret having wasted my words on a subject so vile: but that which grieves and torments me is that she promises me and wants me to believe her and swears she loves me, and in a moment I see her submit herself to a stranger. Therefore how can the faith and vows of women be esteemed and believed by any man, for it will be like acquiring pearls, gold and purple cloths that she will then use to make herself the servant of a monster?[17]

It seems that even Vafrine, the great spy and receiver of smuggled goods, scorned women, as we read in Tasso's *Goffredo*, canto XIX, where Erminia tells him that she wishes to disclose a conspiracy. The words are:

16. Giovanni della Casa, archbishop of Benevento, 1503–56, Stanza in *Opere di Monsignor Giovanni della Casa*, vol. 1, p. 206 (Florence, 1707): "Che s'io potessi le parole, e 'l viso / Farvi, e i costumi, e le maniere espresse, / Di quel che in luogo mio per suo Narciso, / La saggia donna, che fu mia, s'elesse, / Non so, se più la meraviglia, o'l riso, / O la pietà, ne nostri cor potesse, / Anzi so, che n'avresti ira, e cordoglio, / Che di tant'util perdita mi doglio."

17. Ibid., p. 200: "Ne crediate però, che'l dolor mio, / E'l pianto sia perche lasciato m'habbia, / Anzi mi dolgo, e piango il tempo, ch'io / Fui servo altrui ne l'amorosa gabbia: / Già fu grande l'ardor, grande il desio, / Hor'è maggior lo sdegno, e più la rabbia; / Già ne cantai, e hor perder mi duole / In soggetto sì vil queste parole; / Ma quel di ch'io m'affligo, e mi tormento / E, che mi dà la fede, e vuol, ch'io creda / Giurando ella, che m'ami, e in un momento / La veggio darsi ad uno strano in preda, / Quanto possa la fede, e 'l giuramento / In donna quindi ogn'huomo stimi, e creda, / Che farà in acquistar perle, oro, e ostro, / Se così l'usa in farsi serva a un mostro?"

Thus she speaks to him and meanwhile he watches and is silent. He thinks on the example of the false Armida. Woman is a deceitful and talkative creature. She will and she will not. Man is a fool if he puts his faith in her.[18]

He does not consider himself a traitor for using every art to deceive the pagan army, but he reproves Armida's falsity, if it can be called falsity, for doing the same to the Christian one. Nor would I truly call Vafrine a genuine traitor, for the poor man did later see his own error and, realizing that there are many women who are both good and true, he replied to Erminia that he would lead her where she desired. This is the fickleness of the cunning man!

And now enough of the varying opinions of poets and, similarly, of our replies to them. Let us conclude that among women the virtuous far outnumber the bad and that men, moved by anger or other motives toward particular women, are quick to pass sentence on them and condemn them all, as the good Rodomont did who, out of his mind after having been scorned by Doralice, proceeded to condemn the entire female sex in biting language. Ariosto points out that he spoke like an angry and foolish man in canto XXIX of the *Orlando furioso*, when he says:

But that he spoke like an ignorant fool is clearly shown by experience: he brandished the dagger of his anger against all women without differentiating between them. Then one glance of Isabella's so touched him that he immediately changed his mind. Already he desired her and not the other, though he had only just seen her and did not yet know who she was.[19]

What do you say of this Mars who was so consistent in his curses? Does it seem to you that he stood firm? Ariosto knew that good women far outnumber bad and wicked ones, and that anger leads men to speak badly of women without any reason. He shows that the majority of women are good in these words:

With these complaints, and many others besides, the king of Sarza went on his way, now muttering to himself, now speaking in tones

18. Tasso, *Goffredo* (later published in its entirety as *Gerusalemme liberata*), 19:84: "Così li parla intanto, ei mira e tace / Pensa a l'essempio de la falsa Armida / Femina è cosa garrula e loquace, / Vuole e disvuole, è folle uom, che se'n fida."

19. Ariosto, *Orlando furioso* 29:3: "Ma che parlò, come ignorante, e sciocco / Ve lo dimostra chiara esperienza: / Già contra tutte trasse fuor lo stocco / De l'ira senza farvi differenza. / Poi d'Isabella un guardo sì l'ha toccò, / Che subito li far mutar sentenza: / Già in cambio di quell'altra la desia, / L'ha vista a pena, e non sa anchor chi sia."

that could be heard from far away to shame and revile the female sex. Of course he was not being reasonable, since for every one or two women to be held at fault, we must believe that a hundred are to be accounted virtuous.[20]

And a little later he writes:

But my fortune dictates that if there is one wicked one in a hundred, I will fall prey to her.[21]

What do you think of Ariosto? Does it seem to you that when he leaves scorn aside he is speaking the truth? I, for my part, am certain of it. Nor does he content himself with the statement that among a hundred women only one is bad. He goes on to say that it is because of Rodomont's scorn and anger that he slanders even that one. For this reason in the last lines of canto XXX, 1, he writes:

Alas, in vain I regret and curse myself for what I said in anger at the end of the last Canto.[22]

He then goes on to praise good women:

I am hoping, ladies, that in your courtesy you will pardon me, as I request. You must excuse me if in my frenzy, overwhelmed by bitter passion I rave; put the blame on my enemy, who has placed me in this abject position, and makes me say things that I regret. God knows that she is at fault, and that I love her.[23]

Can anyone speak more clearly in praise of women? Let this silence those who read only one stanza and then say that Ariosto speaks badly of them, which is ridiculous. What more can be said, since our enemies, in spite of themselves, are our friends?

Angelo Ingegnieri was also driven by scorn to slander women in his translation of Ovid's *Amores*, rendered by him in *ottava rima*. In these verses it is evident that he was moved by scorn :

---

20. Ibid. 27:122: "Con queste e molte altre infinite appresso / Querele il re di Sarza se ne giva / Or ragionando in un parlar sommesso / Quando in un suon che di lontan s'udiva / In onta e in biasmo del femineo sesso: / E certo da ragion si dipartiva; / Che per una o per due che trovi ree, / Che cento buone sien creder si dee."

21. Ibid. 27:123: "Ma mia fortuna vuol che s'una ria, / Ne sia tra cento, io di lei preda sia."

22. Ibid. 30:1: "Lasso, mi dolgo e affligo in van di quanto / Dissi per ira al fin dell'altro Canto."

23. Ibid. 30:3: "Ben spero donne in vostra cortesia / Haver da voi perdon, poi ch'io ve 'l chieggio, / Voi scuserete, che per frenesia / Vinto da l'aspra passion vaneggio; / Date la colpa a la nemica mia, / Che mi fa star, ch'io non potria star peggio, / E mi far dir quel di ch'io son poi gramo, / Sallo Dio, s'ella ha torto, e sa s'io l'amo."

You who now with sharp injuries now with bitter scorn for a long time have harmed me, for which scorn my brightest days have often turned into dark and woeful nights. Cruel woman, so that I do not return unworthy to the fire where you burned my vain heart, and so that I may still follow this worthy undertaking, be now every hour more incensed with rage against me.[24]

See how he was driven by anger, always wishing her to be cruel toward him in order to have an excuse for vituperating women. Later however, seeing the error he had committed in slandering them, he asks their pardon in a chapter written in *terza rima*, in these words:

Courteous ladies, your good judgment, if it yet retains its natural enlightenment, cannot condemn the ink I have used here, for wrongly do you see my style as having sought till now to harm you, since I always meant to praise you; on the contrary, anyone who will examine it will see that it is directed toward your well-being, without at all seeking advantages among men. If one lady or another refuses me, or if the whole crowd despises me, still you will not see me change my mind.[25]

Even Passi, our most cruel enemy, admits that it was anger that led him to blame women, saying in his letter to his readers:

Nevertheless I am not so arrogant, nor such a harsh and cruel enemy of the female sex, that I can detract from the authority of so many excellent writers who have praised the virtues and glorious deeds of famous and honored women, whose names live on and will continue to live for as long as the sun gives light to the world. But I was led to this only by anger against those women who, caring little for their honor, have been the cause of innumerable ills.[26]

24. Angelo Ingegnieri, *De rimedi contra l'amore*, book 1, canto II (Avignon, 1576): "Voi, c'hor d'acerbe ingiurie hor d'aspri scorni / Danno sentir lunga stagion mi feste, / Per lo cui sdegno i miei più chiari giorni / Spesso cangiarsi in notti atre, e funeste / Donna crudele, perch'io non ritorni / Al foco indegno, ond'il cor vano ardeste, / E perch'io segua pur la bella impresa, / Siate ogn'hor più ver me di rabbia accesa."

25. Ibid., closing *capitolo*, written in *terza rima* and dedicated to *Amorose donne*: "Cortesi donne, il bel giudicio vostro, / Se pur ritiene il natural suo lume, / Non può dannar il mio qui speso inchiostro, / Che del mio stile a torto si presume, / Ch'unqua si volga a procurarvi oltraggio / Poi che d'ogn'hor lodarvi hebbi costume; / Anzi vedrà, chi ben ne fara il saggio, / Rivolto pur a la vostra salute, / Senza punto de gli huomini vantaggio. / Non perch'una, e un'altra mi rifiute, / Non che mi sprezzi ben tutto lo stuolo, / Verrà giamai, che di pensier mi mute."

26. Giuseppe Passi, *Dei donneschi difetti* (Venice, 1599). Author's introduction, p. 1: "Nondimeno non sono così arrogante né meno così acerbo, e crudele inimico del sesso feminile, che io pensi

What do you say, readers? Does it seem to you that he is beaten? And yet earlier, in his first chapter, he generalizes by saying "There is not a single good woman,"[27] and thus gives them all a bad name. It is most reprehensible of him to jump from the particular to the universal, and therefore the inscription to the book would have been more appropriate if it had read: "the defects of wicked women."[28] But the motive behind this is his anger against the lady he loves rather than against women in general. The truth of this is confirmed by Morigi's sonnet in the last six lines:

> But, Joseph, what is the use (even though it gives you the comfort of revenge) if at the end it does not give you what you desire, what can it achieve? Iniquitous love, if only you had enlightened him, for then he would never have had such a troublesome task as he is now undertaking.[29]

Do we not know exactly what kind of anger toward a particular woman motivated him? Yes. Undoubtedly. And may he be forgiven, because he will amend his fault and recognize the nobility of women.

This is how we reply to those capable of reasoning. It is not worth the effort of replying to the opinions of vulgar, ignorant men who speak obstinately and without any basis or cause. This is why Ariosto, relating the tale narrated by the innkeeper in *Orlando furioso*, canto XXVIII, begs women not to lend their ears to the ignorant masses:

> Ladies, and you who hold ladies in esteem, for God's sake disregard this tale, which the innkeeper is preparing to tell to your disparagement, infamy and censure. Even though no tongue as vile as his can either sully or embellish your image it is the custom for the vulgar ignoramus to find fault with everyone, and the less he understands, the more he speaks.[30]

---

voler derogar all'autorità di tanti Eccellenti, e illustri autori, c'hanno celebrate fino al cielo le virtù, e gesti gloriosi di famose, e honorate Donne; i nomi delle quali vivono, e viveranno, mentre il Sole darà luce al mondo; ma solo sdegno m'indusse contra di quelle, che amando poco il loro honore, e men quello del suo sangue, sono, e sono state cagione d'innumerabili mali."

27. Ibid.: "Nulla mulier bona."

28. Ibid., p. 1: "gl'infiniti mali delle malvaggie Donne."

29. Giulio Morigi, Sonnet to Giuseppe Passi, in *Dei donneschi difetti*: "Ma Gioseppe, che pro (benche conforto / Di vendetta vi dia) s'al fin non rende / Quel che bramaste, e ch'ottener dovreste? / Iniquo amor, meglio era, pur ch'accorto / Fessi da prima lui; che sì moleste / Cure mai non havria; com'hora imprende."

30. Ariosto, *Orlando furioso* 28:1: "Donne, e voi che le donne avete in pregio, / Per Dio non date a questa istoria orecchia, / A questa, che l'ostier dire in dispregio, / E in vostra infamia, e biasmo

In canto XXIX he says that he would have done better to remain silent:

> I shall so exert myself with pen and ink, that it will be plain to everyone
> how much better it would have been to have remained silent and even
> bitten one's tongue first rather than to have spoken badly of you.[31]

I have replied to the opinions of certain obstinate little men out of
courtesy rather than duty, and I have demonstrated that there are many
writers who are held at first sight to be slanderers and censurers of women
though they in fact speak very well of them. As well as this you should
know—and I beg you to keep it in your memory—that almost every bad
deed that has been, is, or will be done by women had, has, or will have its
origin in the evil nature of many men. This happens in two ways. The first
is when the villainous and wicked example set by many men corrupts some
pure, innocent creature. The second is when with persuasion, obstinacy,
insolence, insinuation, and promises, men induce pious women to commit
cruel and wicked or else dishonest and lascivious deeds.

That man rather than woman is the cause of all the evils of wantonness
is clearly shown in an ancient story entitled *Aurelio and Isabella*, in which there
is a dispute, in the presence of the King of Scotland, as to whether man gives
woman greater cause to sin, or woman man. The conclusion is that man is
the origin of all women's sins.[32] It remains for me to reply to the frivolous
reasoning of certain men.

As for the main one, some men of small weight state that Helen brought
about the ruin of Troy, which is altogether false. Among them is our good
comrade Caporali, who is perhaps moved more by popular opinion than by
his own, being a truthful man in his compositions. His words are:

> Such beauties as these are always combined with scandal. Helen, she
> who radiated so many amorous darts, was with all her beauties so
> damaging to Troy, to Greece, to the whole world that still today she
> is talked about by everyone.[33]

They say that the Sabine women almost brought about the ruin of Rome—
something that is enough to make a dead man laugh. Tell me if you please

---

s'apparecchia; / Benché, né macchia vi può dar, ne fregio / Lingua sì vile, e sia l'usanza vecchia, /
Che'l volgare ignorante ogn'un riprenda, / E parli più di quel, che meno intenda."

31. Ibid. 29:2: "Io farò sì con penna, e con inchiostro, / Ch'ognun vedrà, che gli era utile, e
buono / Aver taciuto, e mordersi anco poi / Prima la lingua, che dir mal di voi."

32. The story of Aurelio and Isabella is a fifteenth-century Spanish epic by Juan de Flores,
translated into Italian by Lelio Aletiphilo as the *Historia di Aurelio e Isabella* (Venice, 1521).

33. Giovanni Battista Caporali (1475–1555): "Queste tante bellezze ogn'or congiunte / Con
lo scandalo stanno, Elena quella / Onde uscir già tante amorose punte, / Fu con le sue bellezze
così fella / A Troia, a Grecia, a tutto il mondo, ch'anco / Da ciascuno oggidì se ne favella."

who was the first to fall in love? Was it Paris with Helen or Helen with Paris? It was undoubtedly Paris with Helen, as can be seen from the letter he sent her, as Ovid tells, and which, translated into the vernacular by Remigio Fiorentino, reads like this:

> This is written to you, o esteemed daughter of Jove and of gentle Leda, by the pilgrim Trojan, who, burning with love, awaits his help only from you, his sweet beloved.[34]

Later he describes the long and difficult journey he underwent to arrive in Greece:

> Nor had she promised you to me for my wife in vain, the beautiful mother of Love, there in the valley of Ida, for which reason I took such a long road and made so many long and dangerous wanderings among Syrians and rocks and tempests so that I could return the Trojan sails and spars from Greece to the arenas of the Blessed.[35]

He then persuaded her to leave with him by criticizing the ugly features and bad manners of her husband. He exerted himself to such an extent that, overcome by the importunings of her lover, she went with him. It was Paris, therefore, who brought about the ruin of Troy, because he himself says that he passed through so many ordeals and traveled such a long way only for her. Just see how thoughtless he was for refusing the wisdom that Minerva offered him or the riches promised him by Juno, and not only was he thoughtless but unbridled and lascivious.

For this reason Laodamia, writing to Protesilaus, shows that Paris was the ruin of Troy, as Ovid writes in his *Epistles*, saying:

> O evil shepherd, o evil Trojan lover, whose beauty has brought about the destruction of your beautiful kingdom. If God consents to it, your cowardice as a warrior and laziness as an enemy and defender

34. From Ovid, *Heriodes*, a series of elegiac poems written in the form of letters between mythological lovers, whose stories form part of the cycle of myths about the Trojan war. Paris, a Trojan prince, was called upon by three goddesses to judge which of them was the most beautiful. Each offered him an outstanding reward if he should choose her, but Aphrodite's bribe of Helen, the most beautiful mortal woman in the world, was the one he found most tempting. Unfortunately, she was already married to Menelaus, the Greek king of Sparta, and the efforts of her husband and his allies to retrieve her became the Trojan war. Remigio Fiorentino has loosely translated Ovid's poems. This first quotation is from the opening lines of Poem 16, written as from Paris to Helen: "Questo ti scrive, o de l'eterno Giove / E di Leda gentil pregiata figlia / Il peregrin Troian, ch'ardendo aita / Sola da te dolce suo bene attende."

35. These lines of Fiorentino are a paraphrase of part of Ovid, *Heroides* 16: "Né promessa mi t'habbia in van la bella / Madre d'Amor là nella valle Idea / Per mia consorte, ond io sì lunga via / E così lunghi, e perigliosi errori / Tra Sirti e scogli, e tra procelle ho preso / Perch'io le vele e le Troiane antenne / Di Grecia torni a le Beate arene."

of Troy match your wickedness when you were a foreign visitor to the great Greek, whose courteous affection proved so harmful to him and destroyed his peace.[36]

This also occurred with the Sabine women, who did not rape the Romans but were violently raped by them. These good men proclaimed a festival to which the women were invited and then insolently seized them, as Livy relates.[37] What do you think of this wicked and iniquitous fraud, gallant gentlemen? Good God, what motives can be found more obscene and nonsensical than these?

Others, like the good Aristotle, state that women are less hot than men and therefore more imperfect and less noble.[38] Oh what irrefutable and powerful reasoning! I now believe that Aristotle did not consider the workings of heat with a mature mind, nor what it signifies to be more or less hot, nor what good and bad effects derive from this. If he had considered properly how many bad deeds are derived from [men's] heat, which exceeds women's, he would not have said a word about it. But the rascal proceeded blindly, and thus committed a thousand errors.

There is no doubt, as Plutarch writes, that heat is an instrument of the soul.[39] But it can be good and yet not wholly fit for the soul's operations, since one looks for a certain medium in heat between too little and too much. This is because little and failing heat, as in old people, is powerless for the soul's operations, while a lot of or excessive heat makes souls precipitous and unbridled. Therefore not every kind of heat is good, or able to assist in the workings of the soul, as Marsilio Ficino writes.[40] However, a certain level and proportion of it, such as women possess, is useful. Aristotle's reasoning that men are hotter and consequently nobler than women is not, therefore, valid.[41] Furthermore, young men are not reputed nobler than mature, virile men, and yet they are hotter.

---

36. The letter of Laodamia to Protesilaus is *Heroides* 13. Again Fiorentino has adapted the poem rather than made a translation of it. Here Laodamia is lamenting Paris as the cause of the Trojan war: "O mal Pastore, o mal Troiano amante, / La cui beltade al tuo bel Regno arreca / Gli ultimi stridi, almen consenta Dio, / Che tanto vil tu sia guerriero, e tanto / Pigro nemico, e difensor di Troia / Quanto empio fosti habitatore strano / Al maggior Greco, il cui cortese affetto / Li nocque tanto, e li turbò sua pace."

37. Livy, *History of Rome* 1.9.

38. *Generation of Animals* 4.6 (775a5–15).

39. I have not been able to trace the particular passage from Plutarch intended by this reference.

40. I have not been able to trace the particular passage from Ficino intended by this reference.

41. See above, note 38.

Besides, are there not many women who are by nature hotter than men? For this reason we cannot even concede that Aristotle's judgment is true for all women. There are many regions, not to mention towns and citadels, where women are hotter by nature than men from another region. Spanish and African women, for example, are hotter than men who live in the cold north, or in Germany. And should we not believe that there were and are many people with natures hotter than Aristotle's and Plato's? And are their spirits therefore nobler? Indeed! Let us therefore say this, that women are cooler than men and thus nobler, and that if a man performs excellent deeds it is because his nature is similar to a woman's, possessing temperate but not excessive heat, and because his years of virile maturity have tempered the fervor of that heat he possessed in his youth and made his nature more feminine so that it operates with greater wisdom and maturity.

There is no lack of others, Aristotle among them, who say that men are stronger and more robust, and therefore better at bearing weights and burdens than women are.[42] Note what a great advantage! To these I reply that women who are practiced at hard work surpass and beat men, but, truthfully, that this strength would be out of place in creatures who are gentle and delicate. Is it not true that kings, princes, and great men do not work as hard as porters? Nor do I believe that Aristotle, who describes women as languid and similar to the left hand,[43] was as strong as a male peasant, or indeed as many female ones. Was he therefore less noble than these rough men and women? If so, blacksmiths would be nobler than kings and learned men of science, which cannot reasonably be true.

If it were true, one could say that the Roman soldiers, who many times forced the prudent senators to elect emperors according to their wishes, were nobler and more excellent than the senators, which is patently false. This occurred because the army possessed strength, not right or reason, which is why that gallant man said "Strength lies in arms,"[44] and this is why it happens that a murderous but strong brother occupies the throne and title of another brother who is delicate and gentle. This is why the female sex, which is more delicate than the male one and less strong, being less accustomed to heavy work, is tyrannized and trampled upon by insolent and unfair men. But if women, as I hope, wake themselves from the long sleep

42. Aristotle, *Economics* 3 (1343b29–30): "Nature has made one sex stronger, the other weaker . . ."

43. See Aristotle, *History of Animals* 9.1 (608a15–b18), where some of the differences between male and female are set out. The left hand was associated with inferiority and hence with femininity in ancient Greek thought.

44. "vis erat in armis." The origin of this saying is obscure.

that oppresses them, how meek and humble will those proud and ungrateful men become.

There is no doubt that the replies which I have so far made to the authorities and reasoning of poets, learned doctors, philosophers, and Aristotle (not to mention Passi, whose examples are simple and few in number) are sufficient to answer all those who have in some way criticized the female sex. Nevertheless, in order to remove every reason for doubt, I am forced to reply specifically to many of them, including Boccaccio, who wrote the *Labirinto d'amore*; Ercole Tasso, who composed a declamation against marriage; Monsieur Arrigo di Namur, who in 1428 published his *Malvagità delle donne*; Speroni, who, naming one of his dialogues *La dignità o la nobiltà delle donne*, proceeded to reproach women, as did Torquato Tasso in his *Libretto della virtù feminile e donnesca*. Firstly, therefore, I will cite their opinions and then I will refute them.

1. OPINIONS OF ERCOLE TASSO AND OF
MONSIGNOR ARRIGO DI NAMUR NARRATED AND REFUTED

Ercole Tasso wrote a discourse, or rather a declamation, against taking a wife (something that Monsignor Arrigo di Namur had already done many years before, using almost the same reasoning).[45] In his favor he cites many authorities of philosophers and men reputed to be wise, such as Thales of Miletus, Prieneus, Bion of Borysthenes, and Antisthenes of Athens, who did, in fact, criticize marriage, and Sopharionus, who judged that it was wicked to get married but did not completely forbid it. He also cites Metellus Numidicus the censor and Cato, who said that if the world could exist without wives, we would not be without the Gods among us. He goes on to cite Diogenes the Cynic, Thales of Miletus, Menander, Arrius, Hesiod, and Achilles Tacitus of Alexandria. He also relates that the Jewish philosophers, the Essenes, abhorred the act of marriage.

After citing the authorities he passes on to their reasons. One of these is the unworthiness and wickedness of the female sex, another the evil effects of wives on their husbands. The reasons are nine in all. The first is that man is the act and form and has his being from what is good and that therefore woman has her being from what is evil. The second is that all things which do not have an end in themselves but which are created for someone else

---

45. Ercole Tasso, *Dello ammogliarsi. Contesa fra i due Tasso, Hercole e Torquato* (Bergamo, 1595). There also exists an English translation of this work by R. Tofte, *Of marriage and wiving. An excellent, pleasant and Philosophicall Controversie betweene the two famous Tassi now living, the one Hercules the Philosopher, the other Torquato the Poet* (London, 1599).

are vile, as is woman, who was created for man. The third reason is that something which does not contain its being within itself is false and a non-being, and that woman has no being apart from that which was given her by man's rib and therefore she clearly falls into the shameful category of non-being. The fourth is that everything which is born by chance, against the intention of nature, is flawed and monstrous. Woman was born thus, therefore woman is a monster. The fifth is that woman is born because of a defect in the working power of nature, like monsters who are born through a defect or superabundance of matter, therefore she is born by accident. The sixth states that every woman would wish to be a man, just as every deformed person would wish to be beautiful and every idiot learned. The seventh is that every woman is under the particular influence of the moon. The eighth is that women are habitually cold and moist, which is apparent from the softness of their flesh and the fullness of their breasts. The ninth and last is that the law excludes women from holding official posts.

Having set out the aforesaid reasons, he goes on to speak of the evils women bring their husbands. He asks: What woman marries without demanding the most magnificent clothes that can be found? What new bride spends two days in her husband's house without wanting to create a new order? Does she not criticize everything she finds, speak badly of her mother- and father-in-law, and cause discord between her husband and his brothers? Does she not dispute with her sisters-in-law, abuse her menservants, and cuff her maids? Does she not despoil what she ought to conserve by continually shouting at her husband and poisoning his existence? In conclusion, man can do nothing to please woman, who continually points out her neighbors' comforts to him and thus, passing from one taunt to another, concludes that he is not worthy of her, especially if she is richer, nobler, or younger than he. The same applies if she is adorned with exquisite beauty or else skilled and well read, and because women are not moderate in their actions it follows that they are either covetous or prodigal.

Man should not believe, he says, that he can escape these things if he takes a wife who is ugly, poor, ignoble, or stupid, for she will still bring him a thousand burdens to bear, especially if she has a mother, who then will always be haunting him and never cease to yelp and bawl at him, using words such as "My daughter is not prospering, I don't know why. You can't love her." "One shouldn't do that." "I had better take her back home with me." She goes on saying: "If he wants one thing, you do another, if he says yes you say no, if he swears, you curse and in short never allow him to win, for I myself have tried this out." If a man finds a good woman he will still not obtain peace and quiet, because good women become wicked, and to prove this Tasso cites many authorities from the Scriptures and holy men.

We can give a variety of replies to these different authorities that he cites of wise and literate men. The first is that since their minds were entirely taken up with speculation, they fled from women, as they did from household tasks and management, retiring into solitude as did the Egyptian philosophers in order to philosophize better. We can also say that they had a strange and false attitude toward divine laws and popular opinion, or that they were timid and cowardly of spirit and thought themselves unfit to serve such a noble creature as woman, or indeed that disdain, envy, or their natural tendency to slander induced them to speak badly of her. In addition we can say that in different times and situations and for different reasons they alternatively praised and scolded women. Cato, for example, gave higher praise to a man who treated his wife well than he did to one who governed the republic excellently. He also took two wives, the first not being sufficient for him.[46] Ultimately I can say that for those few great men of letters who scorned marriage and women, there were many others who praised them, such as Theophrastus, who forbade the sharing of women and praised marriage, as did Aristotle and Pittacus.[47]

And how many wise men were married? Infinite numbers of them, including Pythagoras, Socrates, Crates, and Solon. In conclusion, I believe that the whole world is bound by the sweet ties of matrimony. Consider all the lands subject to the most holy laws of Christ, those where the false Mohammed is worshiped, and the New World, where you will clearly see that marriage is upheld, as it would not have been had it been harmful and damaging.

I now pass on to rebutt Tasso's accusations. First, I deny that man has his being from what is good and that he is like the form. Second, I say that woman's proper purpose is not to gratify man, but to understand, govern, generate, and adorn the world. Third, I deny that woman does not possess her own being, given her by God and nature, though I concede that man's rib was the material for it, as mud was for man's. Fourth, I concede that things which are born against the intention of nature are flawed and monsters, but I deny that woman was born in that way, first because monsters are seen rarely, and second because women are in fact generated by nature. Therefore since more women are born than men I would say that man is the monster, since

---

46. Plutarch, *Life of Cato the Elder* 20.3: "He thought it more praiseworthy to be a good husband than a great senator." And 24.1: "He married a second wife when long past marrying age."
47. See below, note 49.

nature always generates a greater abundance of the better creature and a lesser of the worse. Furthermore, if nature wishes to perpetuate the human species, she must intend the generation of the female as much as that of the male, since both are needed in order to procreate. To the fifth reason it is not taught that woman is born because of a defect in the workings of nature.[48] To the sixth, I say it is false that every woman would wish to be a man, and that if she did wish it, it would only be in order to free her neck from the yoke of men's tyrannical dominion and make her rare virtues, which lie hidden within the walls of houses, better known. Going on to the seventh, I deny that woman is influenced by the moon, since astrologers place her under the influence of Venus because of her beauty and pleasing habits. To the eighth, I reply that woman is habitually warm and moist, as the wisest doctor states, and as is shown by the pink and white of her delicate countenance and the moistness and softness of her flesh, which are not so because of overabundant cold and moisture, for this would make them languid, not delicate and soft. To the last, I reply that men make the laws, and thus, like tyrants, exclude women from official posts, even though they know that they would be good and perfectly capable of governing.

One wonders, having listed the above arguments, why he goes on to speak of the evils that wicked women bring on their husbands. To my mind these accusations are either untrue or of little importance, and assume many things to be true that are not. It is rare to find it written in stories that women have killed some man or desired the death of their father in order to inherit his possessions, such as cruel men have done. If women are by nature quiet and peaceful, as everyone asserts, why should they cause so much discord at home?

If some woman laments the fact that her husband is indiscreet and unwise she is not wrong to do so, because many men consume all they have in drinking, dishonesty, gaming, or other vanities, leaving these wretched women to fast even on nonfasting days. This would be nothing if husbands did not beat their honest and prudent wives when full of wine, infuriated by losing money, or with their intellects impaired by the vapors of wine. How many men have gambled away the dowries of their wives and sisters? Let those who maintain the contrary speak out!

Does it seem to you that a husband should marvel if his wife complains about him when she is younger, richer, nobler, wiser, and more adorned

---

48. In the 1601 version this sentence actually reads: "To the fifth reason it is taught that woman is born because of a defect in the workings of nature," which does not make sense. I have therefore followed the 1621 version, which reads: "To the fifth reason it is not taught etc. etc."

with divine beauty than he? How strange and unreasonable! Tell me, would a noblewoman suit a porter? An heiress a beggar? A discreet and prudent woman a boor and ignoramus? A merry and pleasing young woman a monster, a satyr, or a complete wreck? A young woman an old man without teeth and with watery eyes and a runny nose? Certainly not, for she would always be conscious of the lack of equality and proportion between husband and wife, in age, rank, and all the qualities I have listed. As for the beauty and deformity of women that agitates him so much, I follow the opinion of Pittacus, one of the seven wise men of Greece, who said that if you take a beautiful wife it will not be a hardship for you, and if you take an ugly one you will not have to share her.[49]

Alas, the valiant Ercole Tasso could not finish the declamation without truth lifting the veil of darkness from the eyes of his mind so that, repenting, he said: "The truth is that sometimes, contained within this form of woman, superhuman and angelic natures descend to us that are not only far from possessing any of the defects mentioned above, but of such perfection, excellence, goodness, and value that they bring similar comfort, now and for the future, to those whom they are gracious enough to marry."

Since there is little difference beween the opinion of Ercole Tasso and that of Monsignor Arrigo, I will spare myself the effort of replying to him.

2. SPERONE'S OPINION NARRATED AND DESTROYED

Sperone, in a dialogue entitled *The Dignity or Nobility of Women*, in which the speakers are Michele Barrozzi and Daniele Barbaro, says that women are imperfect and impotent, and he endeavors to prove that they are born to serve men and generated by nature for this purpose.[50]

He attempts to show (oh what inventiveness!) that this is the verdict of women themselves. Observe what he has Signora Obiza say to an interlocutor in this dialogue of his: "This happens to her because she is a wife, that is to say servant, to her husband, whose wishes this wife, contrary to her own pleasure, is obliged to obey and to whom she is subject." And then he adds: "Man is to woman as reason is to sentiment." He puts this forward as his own opinion, then narrates Signora Obiza's verdict, which is that: "Woman is not woman unless she serves her husband, for it is woman's natural condition to serve."

In order to demolish this opinion, I deny that woman is her husband's servant. If we wish to adhere to the principles of Aristotle, we will see that

---

49. Pittacus was an ancient thinker said to have lived about 600 B.C.E.

50. Sperone Speroni, *Dialogo della dignita delle donne*, 1542; in *Trattatisti del Cinquecento*, ed. Mario Pozzi (Milan-Naples: Ricciardi, 1978).

in *Economics*, chapter 3, he refers to her everywhere as the partner, and not just the partner but the revered partner of her husband:

> Nothing is more natural than the partnership between man and woman.[51]

Does it not seem to you that he is saying partner by nature, not servant by nature? He adds:

> Rather than these, in nature we see examples of mutual help, goodwill and cooperation,[52]

from which we clearly understand a loving partnership with interchangeable roles. In book II, chapter 2, does he not say openly that a man—a husband—must honor his wife? Here are his words:

> A wise man should not ignore the honors that are due a wife.[53]

He says the same in book I on the care of the family, where he states that man must honor woman and love her respectfully. He also showed this when he quoted Homer saying that woman must at the same time honor man, using the examples of Helen and Ulysses. These are Helen's words to Priam:

> Beloved father-in-law, I must fear and dread and revere you.[54]

Ulysses's words to the Lady Nausicaa are:

> Lady, you fill me with reverence and fear.[55]

He then adds:

> For Homer believes that this is how a husband and wife ought to feel toward one another, for no one ever loves or admires or fears someone inferior to them.[56]

---

51. Aristotle, *Economics* 1.3 (1344a): "Societas enim est maxime fecundum naturam mari et feminae." At the beginning of this passage, a wife is said to be the most important part of a man's household.

52. Ibid. (1343b17), writing of civilized and intelligent animals, including humans: "Apparent enim his magis natura auxilia, dilectiones, et cooperationes."

53. Ibid. 3.2: "Prudentem ignorare non debet qui honores conveniant uxori."

54. Ibid. 3.3 (not book 1 as Marinella says). Marinella's quotation: "O metuende mihi semper, sempero; tremende clare socer" differs slightly from the Latin text that we possess. The *Economics* reads: "Metuendus et reverendus es mihi et terribilis, amatissime socer." The quotation is from Homer, *Iliad* 3.172.

55. Homer, *Odyssey* 6.168: "Te mulier valde equidem admiror, et metuo."

56. Marinella's text is a paraphrase of *Economics* 3.3. Her Latin reads: "Censer autem Homerus virum, et uxore sic se invice debere habere: nam nemo deteriorem se admiratur, ac veretur."

Thus Aristotle concludes, with Homer, that there must be a genuine partnership and unanimous concord accompanied by a certain reverence between husband and wife—something that is not seen between servants and masters. At the same time he proposes in *Ethics*, book VII, chapter 5, that there should be friendship between husband and wife but not between master and servant.[57] I should add that in *Politics*, book I, chapter 8, he demonstrates clearly what type of preeminence a husband has over his wife, and what manner of dominion. He proposes two orders of dominion, one civil and the other regal, but excludes that of the master and servant. His words are:

> Of household management we have seen that there are three parts: one is the rule of the master over the slave, which has been discussed already; another is that of the father; and the third is that of a husband. A husband and father, we saw, rules over wife and children, both free, but the rule differs—the rule over his children being a regal rule and that over his wife being a constitutional rule.[58]

With these words he concludes that man has a civil dominion over women and a regal one over his son. A civil rule is one in which a person at times commands and at other times is commanded. Aristotle describes it in the same chapter in these words:

> In most constitutional states the citizens are ruled by terms, for the idea of the constitutional state implies that the natures of the citizens are equal and do not differ.[59]

What more manifest proof and clearer reasoning can be desired from Aristotle?

Thus we see clearly that Sperone's opinion lacks a true and solid basis. Perhaps he was influenced in his opinion by the tyrannical insolence of those many men who make not only their wives serve them but also their mothers and sisters, showing greater obedience and fear than that with which humble servants and slaves serve their lords and masters.

---

57. Aristotle, *Nichomachean Ethics* 8.11 (1161a–b) (not 7.5 in our edition).

58. Aristotle, *Politics* 1.12 (1259a36–1259b1) (not 1.8 in our edition): "Quoniam vero tres erant partes rei domesticae, una dominica, de qua supra diximus, alia paterna, et alia coniugalis: nam precest filiis et uxori tanquam liberis quidem ambobus, sed non codem modo imperii, uxori quidem civiliter, filiis autem regie."

59. Ibid. (1259b5f): "In civilibus igitur principatibus pierunque commutatur is, qui praeest, is qui subest nam equales esse volut." Marinella's Latin is strange here, though this is the sense of the passage she is quoting.

3. TORQUATO TASSO'S OPINION ADDUCED AND REFUTED

According to one of his discourses entitled *Della virtù feminile e donnesca*,[60] which draws on the opinions of Tacitus and Aristotle, Torquato Tasso believed that women are weak and imperfect in comparison to men, similar, in fact, to the left hand.

He goes on to say that strength does not suit them, nor do they seek fame in making their works known to the world, since their desire is for modesty and retirement. He does not deny further down that strength is a feminine virtue, but not absolute strength—rather that which is called obedient strength. He concludes, therefore, that many acts which are called acts of strength in women would not be acts of strength in men. He then makes a distinction between the virtues, a proportion of which—those appertaining to the intellect—he deems unnecessary to women. Similarly he affirms that prudence is not a female virtue, since women only need enough of it to enable them to obey masculine prudence, which is something Aristotle had said when speaking of women's fortitude.

Having said this, he then goes on to speak of ladylike [*donnesca*] virtue, pretending that he has invented something new, which is that there is a great difference between female virtue and that which he calls ladylike. From this he imagines that the title of lady [*donna*] belongs only to queens, princesses, and those whom he calls heroic ladies, to whom he claims that modesty is no more suitable than it would be to gentlemen. His words are: "Modesty and prudery do not suit heroic ladies any more than they would gentlemen, because they possess their own virtues that cannot be shared by the majority, nor can any immodest act of theirs be called infamous. These ladies resemble both the right and left hands."

These are the essential points that Torquato Tasso makes in his discourse, to which I reply that if he is of the same opinion as Tacitus and Aristotle he must support it with some good and solid grounding, if he would refute that very true answer made by Plato on the subject of the hand, which was that there is no difference between the right and the left, as can be frequently observed in everyday use.[61] When he adds, incited by Aristotle's authority, that women have no need of fortitude, I say that we do not accept Aristotle's opinion as true, having produced a thousand examples of strong women, and not just of queens, in our book. Nor are these examples merely

---

60. Tasso, *Della virtù feminile e donnesca* (Venice, 1582).

61. See Plato's declaration in the *Republic* that it was certain that there would be women as well as men capable of achieving the virtue necessary for a philosopher king. Marinella's Introduction, note 2.

of obedient fortitude—something that belongs to servants—but of lordly fortitude, because in fortitude, as defined by Aristotle, there is a constancy of spirit in the face of things that are frightening, provided they lead to an honest and praiseworthy end.

Who will deny that many women have been adorned with such a virtue? Nor were they spurred on by any man, as can be seen from the infinite examples in the section on strong women, whose acts of fortitude would have been deemed most marvellous in men. But we would find thousands more if women practiced and exercised them in public affairs as men do, according to the distinction between virtues made by Tasso, the speculative part of which he says are not of service to women. I do not admit this supposition of his. If women are of the same species as men and have the same soul and the same powers as all the Peripatetics confirm, and which was also recognized by Xenophon in his *Economics*, where he writes:

> [God] made men more courageous than women, but he gave them equal capacity for memory and intelligence,[62]

I would say that speculation is as much of service to women as it is to men. But man does not permit woman to apply herself to such studies, fearing, with reason, that she will surpass him in them.

I also deny that a woman's prudence is obedient to that of her husband, because Aristotle considers a person to be prudent who is able to advise and recommend what is best in future matters. Who will deny that there have been many very prudent women in both military and peacetime administration? Let them read my section on prudent women. And who will deny that women demonstrate great prudence in managing their households? Nobody, in my opinion. Moreover, this management belongs solely to woman, and not to her husband, as we read in [Aristotle's] *Economics*.

Furthermore, if he who governs and rules is adorned with superior prudence, it would follow that all his subjects possessed obedient prudence. And would they be prudent, according to this opinion, out of respect to their prince, as women are out of respect to their husbands? A great inconvenience, since the highest prudence is not measured in terms of domination but in the use of mature intelligence in order to foresee and act.

Adducing the authority of Tacitus, Tasso also affirms that woman's reputation should not be known outside her home. I, in accordance with the

---

62. Xenophon, *Economics* 7.25–26: "Virum fecit audaciorem muliere, memoriam vero, et intelligentiam dedit fratrem." This is a paraphrase of Xenophon. the word *aequem* (equal) needs to be substituted for Marinella's *fratrem* (brother).

opinions of Gorgias of Leontini and Plutarch, say that the fame of women's achievements in the sciences and in virtuous actions should resound, not only in their own cities but in diverse and varying provinces. Plutarch, in his book on the dignity of women, writes these words: "I esteem as excellent and reasonable that Roman law which permits that good women may be praised in public speeches by their relations, just as men are. We have imitated this custom recently when, after the death of the excellent Lady Leonidas, we praised her deeds in a very lengthy discourse."[63] Let me add to all this that Euripides, that learned and remarkable man, wrote that to praise women's virtues was the act of a wise man.[64]

As for Tasso's new distinction between females and ladies—I say new because Boccaccio, Petrarch, and others have given the name lady to every one of our sex—I will spare myself the effort of demolishing and reviling it.

4. BOCCACCIO'S OPINION ADDUCED HERE AND DESTROYED

Boccaccio, too, reviled the female sex with indecent words full of poison and envy rather than true or apparent reasoning, and thus presumed many things that required actual proof. He presumed therefore that woman was an imperfect animal, afflicted by a thousand disagreeable passions that are abominable to recall, let alone to discuss. He said that women are aware that they are born servants, and that by using humility and obedience they beg all manner of clothes and ornaments from their husbands and then strive to dominate them. Thus they are like ravening wolves who come to usurp their husbands' property and riches.

He followed this by saying that they are timid in matters that can bring benefit to their husbands, but possess an animal strength in dishonest ones. All women's thoughts, all their care and all their work is toward no other end than that of stealing, dominating, and deceiving their husbands, and for this they visit and consult witches and soothsayers. Women possess less humanity than tigers, lions, and serpents. When they are angry they invoke fire, poison, and steel and are prepared to confound and waste the world, the sky, God, and everything that lies above and beneath Him. As well as this, they are extremely avaricious with all types of people and persons but extravagant

---

63. Plutarch, *Bravery of Women*, Introduction (242f). In this passage Plutarch is endorsing the attitudes of Gorgias and the Romans toward the public praising of women.

64. Plutarch next goes on to quote Euripides on the Muses and the Graces, which might explain why Marinella associates Euripides with this sentiment.

in flattery and show. They are fickle—wanting and not wanting the same thing a thousand times an hour. They are presumptuous, and believe that everything is necessary to them and that they are worthy of every honor and every grandeur. They are bashful and disobedient, performing their duties when they please, but in fact their bashfulness is merely a poor artifice that allows them to look down on the richest man in the world.

They profess to be scientific and learned, so they go to mass one morning and instantly understand how the firmament revolves, how many stars there are in the sky, and how the sea ebbs and flows. They know what the Spanish and Indians do and what the Trojans, Greeks, and Romans never did. In conclusion nobody does anything in the city without their talking about it.

They are obstinate. Thus if they say they have seen an ass fly everyone has to concede it; otherwise they will wage mortal enmity, deceit, and hatred for evermore. Since the world was created, out of multitudes of women, we find only ten who have been serious and wise. Women are universally greedy and voracious.

As well as the above, he adds that women are vain, envious, scornful, and filthy. If they were seen when they got out of bed in the mornings with their green and yellow faces, painted badly, the color of smoke from a quagmire, covered in lumps like moulting birds, and completely flabby, they would sicken those who looked at them. Even more so if they were seen brooding shoddily over the fire with livid eyes, coughing and spitting out fatuities, or if it were possible to smell the fetid, goatlike stench that emanates from their bodies when they are hot or tired.

In summing up he concludes that women are the cause and origin of every vice in the world and adds that men would have been happy if they had never been born. Women, however, in their presumption, believe that men would be worth nothing without them and could not survive, and insist tiresomely and imperiously on being served accordingly.

In order to destroy this false opinion of his, starting from the beginning, let us say that women are not imperfect animals, nor are they afflicted by a thousand passions unless they are those that their men's perverse natures force them to listen to and see each day. Women are not aware that they are born servants, because he who is born a natural servant does not aspire to dominion but lives in the servitude to which he is born. Thus one can say that if they aspire, as he says they do, to dominion, it is because they are born not as servants but as mistresses—which is shown by the name "lady" that they bear.

I do not see that discreet, benign women usurp their husbands' patrimonies. When they embark on their task of perfecting men they bring large dowries with them, which they spend not only on necessary expenses for themselves but also on their husbands. Are there not a great number of men whose honor has been restored by dowries, and who go walking around in public all swelled up with pride when they would otherwise be rotting dishonorably in prison? Furthermore, you will never find a woman who dissipates her husband's assets the way husbands do their wives', so much so that there are many women who have never in their lives owned a single penny. Fortune-tellers get little from them, as is shown by the fact that they are always beggars. Women's natures are pleasing and compassionate, far removed from treachery, poison, murder, and such matters. Aristotle states the truth of this, even though he was their enemy, in *History of Animals*:

Women are gentler by nature and swifter to compassion.[65]

There are several reasons why women cannot be called avaricious in my opinion. The first is because men unjustly usurp all that they have, so they cannot spend it on anything, however small. The second is because of the great love they bear their husbands and children, which makes them anxious not to consume or waste their patrimonies but instead, like ants, naturally gifted with prudence and wifely and motherly care, continually to accumulate them. Aristotle, recognizing this, states in his book on family care: "And women conserve things."[66]

Certainly no firmer stability than theirs can be found, as is revealed by the great patience they show in bringing up, feeding, and teaching the impatient male, which is something to marvel at. I would add that diligence, which requires a firm stability, is the special gift of the female sex. Aristotle demonstrates this when he states in *Economics*:

Woman has more application and man less.[67]

Women show themselves to be most prompt and obedient to the smallest sign from their fathers, mothers, brothers, and husbands, unlike men, who are by nature harsher and ruder.

Boccaccio intends to criticize women by saying that if they go to a mass they are able to talk on infinite matters relating to anything from state

65. "Sunt feminae moribus molliores mites sunt. Celerius et magis misericordes sunt." Cf. Aristotle, *History of Animals* 9.1 (608b), although this is not a direct quotation. (See note 9 of chapter 4, part I, above, where she refers to the same quotation but in a slightly different form.)

66. Aristotle, *Economics* 1.3 (1344a3): "Et foemina conservat ea." Cf. part I, chapter 4, note 6.

67. Aristotle, *Economics* 1.3. This line is a mistranslation from 1344a: "Mulier ad sedulitatem optima, et vir deterior." See above, chapter 4, note 4, for details.

government to the subtleties of science.[68] I truly believe this to be a proof of their subtlety of intellect and excellent memory. God grant that he, who after all his studies made himself out to be a great master, had been able in four years to give as detailed an account of them as any little girl could do in a quarter of an hour. There have been and are infinite numbers of women gifted in the noble sciences, as I have shown in my many examples. As well as this, he calls women voracious, gluttonous, and greedy—something that goes against all visible experience, since they are most moderate in their eating habits. He attributes to them innumerable vices, such as envy, scorn, slander, and other similar ones. This supposition is completely false, since their behavior is universally polite and reasonable, unlike men's, as we read in *Ethics*, and as Boccaccio himself states in his stories. Men cannot live without women, though women, such as the Amazons, have ruled and governed not just cities but entire provinces without men.[69]

Lastly, perhaps moved by rage, Boccaccio dares to affirm that women are deformed, ugly, dirty, and stinking.[70] This is an extremely odd thing to say, since beauty is God's and nature's special gift to women, so much so that Xenophon, in his *Economics*, wrote these words:

God formed wives as an object of beauty,[71]

something that we have already demonstrated in our opening chapters.

Cannot the greatest cleanliness and polish in this world of ours be observed in women? They are disgusted by filth, since it makes their graceful bodies unsightly, and by all things that emit a vile smell. But men, being coarser and born to serve, are noticeably less decorative and often filthy and dirty. Some have more dirt and sweat round their ugly faces and necks than a

68. Boccaccio, *Laberinto d'amore o Il Corbaccio*, p. 50 (Venice, Gabriel Giolito de'Ferrari, 1563); *Corbaccio or The Labyrinth of Love*, trans. and ed. Anthony Cassell (Binghamton, N.Y., rev. ed., 1993), 30–31.

69. Stories of the Amazon women have been handed down from Greek mythology, but are also written of as existing historically in many ancient ethnographers. They are said to have been a race entirely of women living around the Caucasus area who invaded many surrounding lands, including those of Greece, Arabia, Syria, and Egypt. They reproduced by making annual visits to the Gargareans, a race of men over the mountains, and handing any male children born to them back to these men. The female children were brought up and trained as warriors.

70. Boccaccio, *Laberinto d'amore*, pp. 84–88; *Corbaccio or The Labyrinth of Love*, p. 65.

71. Xenophon, "Deus uxorem pulcriorem condidit." I do not find this passage in the *Economics*. In 7.23–28 qualities distributed by God to men and women are discussed, but beauty is not mentioned as one of them. The only passage in which the beauty of women is mentioned is 10.9–12, and the closest to the passage cited by Marinella is 10.12: "When a wife's looks outshine a maid's, and she is fresher and more becomingly dressed, they're a ravishing sight." (The translation is by E. C. Marchant (Loeb Classical Library, 1923).)

cook's cauldron, and give off such a displeasing smell that of necessity, under the circumstances, women hold their noses. I do not deny, however, that some women are not very clean and give off an unpleasing smell. The woman loved by the wicked Boccaccio was one of these. Her eyes did not shine brightly because of her advanced age and she was troubled by a perpetual cough and possessed many other defects of old age. In truth she was a woman worthy of him.

Boccaccio (may God have mercy on his soul) composed this book called *The Labyrinth*, as he himself relates, out of spite and a bitter affliction that ultimately led him to desire death. His words are:

> And moved by such affliction both for my own bestiality and for the neglectful cruelty of she whom I loved much more than life, I began to desire death.[72]

He was frequently mocked by this woman, who did not love him at all, which often caused him to grieve and lament that he who was so learned and full of erudition should be so scorned and derided. The poor man was wrong to grieve over the fact that the widow he loved did not love him because she was not obliged to love him, as he himself states at the beginning of his book, any more than he was her, according to his reasoning.

---

72. *Laberinto d'amore*, p. 7. The actual words are: "E in tanta d'afflizione trascorsi, ora della mia bestialità dolendomi, e ora della crudeltà trascurata di colei, che aggiungendo, estimai che molto men grave dovesse essere la morte che cotal vita." *Corbaccio or The Labyrinth of Love*, p. 2.

PART II

THE DEFECTS AND
VICES OF MEN

IV

OF WRATHFUL, ECCENTRIC, AND BRUTAL MEN

The vice of proud and precipitate wrath is hateful and disgraceful to everyone and always worthy of reproof and often of punishment. It obscures the light of reason from those who commit incontinent acts to such an extent that some people refer to wrath as incontinence. Oh how many homicides it has caused, wrath being, as Speusippus states, "a challenge to the wrathful soul to take revenge."[1] Wrath frequently drives angry men to these excesses in order to avenge themselves. Often, for the smallest offense, they take the dear life of another. This happens because reason is blinded by anger as we read in *Politics*, book V, chapter 10,[2] and it is certain that anger obscures the intellect—as when we occasionally see a dear friend or obedient son transported in an instant by such rage that he offends his friend or his dear father and then cries afterward over the mistake he has committed. Ariosto, observing this, writes in *Orlando furioso*:

> When from impetuosity, and from anger you allow your reason to be mastered, nor put up any defense against it, and leave blind rage to force your hand or tongue into offending your friends, then well may you weep, and sigh, the wrong cannot be righted for this; alas, I regret

---

1. "Provocatio irascibilis animae partis ad ulciscendum." Diogenes Laertius begins his account of Speusippus, who took charge of Plato's school after the latter's death, by commenting that he was unlike Plato in character, being prone to anger. There is one story, says Diogenes, that in a fit of anger he threw his favorite dog into a well (4.1.1). His anger, therefore, seems well attested, but I have been unable to locate the source of this particular statement. See chapter 5, note 95 above.

2. Aristotle, *Politics* 5.10 (1312b28): "The angry . . . do not follow the rational principle."

in vain and curse myself for what I said in anger at the end of the last canto.[3]

For the most part the wrathful are angered by those who should least anger them or by light and trivial matters more than by serious ones. They proceed to deafen the world with their oaths and horrible cries and generally behave most unworthily. Of this one can say with Ovid:

Accusations are made, the air resounds with shouts, each one calls the angry gods to his aid. . . . It is the task of good looks to hold crazy behavior in check; fair peace suits men, fierce anger beasts. The face swells with anger, the veins grow dark with blood, the eyes flash more savagely than the Gorgon's snake.[4]

Alexander the Great of Macedonia would deserve the highest praise had he not been so inflamed by anger. He was so extremely agitated by this infernal fury that he did not know how to control his own nature and, as Plutarch relates, committed many unworthy acts such as the murder of Clitus and of other famous and powerful men.[5] Petrarch said of him: "Alexander the conqueror was conquered by anger."[6] What should I say of the Roman Emperor Valentian, a Hungarian by birth? He was so angry with certain of his legions that he broke a vein in his chest shouting at them and died full of wrath, pouring out his blood and soul.[7] What of Cato, who went into such a rage that he could not calm himself down either by prayer or other means?[8] Perses, King of Persia, was so full of cruel and ardent wrath that he killed

3. Ariosto, *Orlando furioso* 30:1: "Quando vincer da l'impeto, e da l'ira / Si lascia la ragion, né si difende, / E che'l cieco furor si inanzi tira, / O mano, o lingua, che gli amici offende, / Se ben dipoi si piange, e si sospira, / Non è per questo, che l'error s'emende; / Lasso io mi dolgo, e affligo in van di quanto / Dissi per ira al fin dell'altro canto."

4. Ovid, *Ars amatoria* (*Art of Love*) 3:375–76 and 501–4: "Crimina dicuntur, resonat clamoribus ether, / Invocat iratos est sibi quisque deos. . . . Pertinet ad faciem rabidos compescere mores: / Candida pax homines, trux decet ira feras: / Ora tument ira, nigrescunt sanguine venae; / Lumina Gorgoneo saevius igne micant."

5. Plutarch, *Life of Alexander* 51. Alexander the Great was renowned in ancient literature for being a man prone to fits of anger. Plutarch relates that in one such fit he threw a spear and killed his companion Clitus. Plutarch also mentions Alexander's anger elsewhere, for example at 4.3.

6. Petrarch, *Canzoniere* 232:1: "Vincitor Alessandro l'ira vinse."

7. Valentian I was emperor of Rome, 364–75. One source for his life is Ammianus Marcellinus, 25–30. See 30.6.1–6.

8. Cato is Marcus Porcius Cato (234–149 B.C.E.), Roman patrician, soldier, and statesman. He is the father of Latin prose, having written extensively, but all that has come down to us whole is his treatise on agriculture. For the rest he is often referred to by Pliny, Quintilian, Cicero, and other writers, but none of these sources yields the sentiment expressed here, whose possible origin I have not been able to locate.

two people who were attempting to console him in a friendly manner.[9] Can there be an uglier example than this, a man who took the life of those who, with gentle words, sought to lighten his melancholy soul? What should I say of Cambyses, also King of Persia, who, not being able to possess the King of Egypt's daughter alive, had her torn from her tomb and cut and beaten with swords and then burned, as Battista Fulgosio relates.[10] This truly was irrational anger, to show cruelty to a lifeless corpose.

When Herod, King of the Jews, the son of Antipater, was told that his wife wished to give him a poisoned love philtre, without inquiring further he flew into such a rage that he had her unjustly murdered. Afterward, when he had discovered the truth and his irrational fury had cooled, he called for her, weeping.[11] Petrarch writes of him:

See how he burns and then consumes himself, repenting too late of his crimes, calling on Mariamne, who hears him not.[12]

Let us not forget Ezzelino, who committed many atrocities out of wrath. I will gladly pass over what he did to others and describe only what he did to himself. He was wounded in battle and taken prisoner, whereupon he was treated and comforted. In spite of this he was incapable of stifling his anger and, not having arms with which to wound himself, he kept his eyes fixed to the ground in obstinate wrath, unbound his wound, tore at it, and thus ended his life, as Sabellico writes.[13] This is what Ariosto says of him in *Orlando furioso*: "Ezzelino, a most atrocious tyrant, shall be reputed the son of a demon."[14]

Valerianus Publius renounced all his honored ranks out of temper.[15] The French, as Livy relates, are wrathful by nature.[16] Tydeus possessed

---

9. Battista Fulgosio, *Dictorum factorumque memorabilium: Exempla virtutum et vitiorum* (Basel, 1555), book 9, chapter 3, p. 623, for the story of Perses, king of Persia.

10. Ibid. 9.3, p. 1018, for the story of Cambyses and the king of Egypt's daughter. Battista Fulgosio or Fregoso, born ca. 1463, was an archbishop, cardinal, and historian.

11. Boccaccio, *Concerning Famous Women* 85, for the story of Queen Mariamne and King Herod. Edition translated by Guido A. Guarino (New Brunswick, N.J.: Rutgers University Press, 1963).

12. Petrarch, *Triumphs*, Love, 2:70: "Vedi com'arde prima, e poi si rode, / Tardi pentito di sua feritate / Mariamne chiamando, che non l'ode."

13. Marcantonio Sabellicus (1436–1506), the official historian for Venice. The story of Ezzelino is to be found in Fulgosio, *Dictorum factorumque*, a selection of the writings of M. A. Sabellicus, book 9, chapter 3, p. 622. Ezzelino is Ezzelino III da Romano.

14. Ariosto, *Orlando furioso* 3:33: "Ezzelino immanissimo Tiranno / Che sia creduto figlio del demonio."

15. Valerianus Publius was emperor 253–60 C.E. See Trebellius Pollio, *Life of Valerian*, in the Scriptores Historiae Augustae.

16. Livy characterizes the French (Gauls) in a number of ways, but never as full of wrath. The passage intended may be a misreading of Livy, *History of Rome* 45.30.

enormous anger, as Statius relates in his *Thebaid*. Having made an alliance with Polincelindus and other kings against the Thebans, he met with Menalippus, an ally of the Thebans, in battle, and was seriously wounded by him. Tydeus, full of fury, killed him, and then seeing that his own wound was mortal, had Menalippus's head brought to him and died biting on it in a great rage.[17] Petrarch, writing on anger, says this of him: "Anger drove Tydeus to such fury that, dying, he gnawed on Menalippus."[18]

Solyman also was full of irrational anger, as Torquato Tasso relates. After having killed Argillan he made war on his dead body:

And not content with that, dismounted from his steed onto the dead body, he still wages war, like an enraged mastiff that seizes the stone that has caused him a heavy blow.[19]

Marganor flew ino a rage against Dursilla, as Ariosto relates: "This Marganor wreaked greater cruelty than any mastiff or snake on the lifeless body."[20] Grandonio, from what Ariosto says, was most choleric: "So that incapable of verbal reply he turned his steed in rage and ill-humor."[21] Ajax, the son of Telamon, was so angry and full of spite that when the Greeks judged Ulysses to be worthy of Achilles's arms and took them away from him, he became mad with fury and ended up killing himself. Hear what Ovid says of him:

Then he who had opposed Hector in single combat and had so often withstood fire and the sword, and even Jove, found anger the one thing he could not withstand. Grief and rage conquered the unconquered Ajax. He snatched out his sword and cried: "This at any rate, is mine! Or does Ulysses demand to have it too? This is what I must use against myself. The blade so often steeped in Trojan blood will now stream with its master's own, that none may conquer Ajax save himself!" So he spoke and, where there was a vulnerable spot, buried the deadly sword in his breast, till then unwounded.[22]

17. Statius, *Thebaid* 8.716–66.

18. Petrarch, *Canzoniere* 323:5: "L'ira Tideo e tal rabbia sospise / Che morendo ci si rose Menalippo."

19. Tasso, *Gerusalemme liberata* 9:88: "Né di ciò ben contento, al corpo morto / Smontato dal destriero, anco fa guerra, / Quasi mastin, che l'sasso; ond'a lui porto / Fu duro colpo, infellonito, afferra." From edition by Claudio Varese and Guido Arbizzoni (Milan, 1972).

20. Ariosto, *Orlando furioso* 37:78: "Tal Marganor d'ogni mastin, d'ogni angue / Via più crudel fa contro il corpo esangue."

21. Ariosto, *Orlando furioso* 35:71: "Sì che senza poter replicar verbo / Volta il destrier con colera, e con stizza."

22. Ovid, *Metamorphoses* 13:384–92: "Hectora qui solus, qui ferrum ignesque Iovemque / Sustinuit toties, unam non sustinet iram: / Invictumque virum vicit dolor arripit ensem, / Et meus hic certe

Just think if this was playful anger!

But what should we say of Achilles, who, when Agamemnon told him he was taking Brises's daughter[23] from him, was so full of rage and fury that he flared up, as Homer relates in the *Iliad:*

> Here the king stops speaking and sits down. But a mad rage inflames the son of Thetis to such an extent that the blood round his heart ignites and boils and an overpowering pain lodges in his heart.[24]

Even after seeing Minerva and being to some extent placated, he continued to insult Agamemnon in the following words:

> Achilles of wrath retained in his heart some portion toward the arrogant king; he railed against him in a harsh and bitter voice: "O lord of the Greeks and servant of wine, of foolish and proud mind, King with the face of a dog and the heart of a doe, this great camp has as its leader elected a man more cowardly than a rabbit."[25]

Reflect for a moment whether his anger was noble, when he had no more respect for King Agamemnon than he would have had for the humblest of his servants.

But what should we say of Gyas, who, seeing Cloanthus close behind him in the race at sea, burned with such anger that, forgetting all decorum, he took Menoetes, the pilot who was steering his ship, and threw him into the sea? Virgil describes this in the *Aeneid:*

> Then indeed anger burned deep in the young man's frame; tears sprang to his cheeks, and heedless alike of his own safety and his crew's safety,

---

est: an et hunc sibi poscit Ulixes? / Hoc ait utendum est in me mihi: quique; cruore / Saepe Phrygum maduit: domini nunc caede madebit / Ne quisquam Aiacem poscit superare, nisi Aia / Dixit et in pectus tum demum vulnera passum / Qua patuit ferro, letalem condidit ensem." The translation is by Mary Innes (Harmondsworth: Eng.: Penguin, 1955), 295–96.

23. I. e., the slave girl Briseis.

24. *Iliad* 1:188–89. Marinella provides a very loose translation in *ottava rima* by Luigi Grotto in *Il primo libro della Iliade* (Venice, 1570), which reads thus: "Qui tace, e siede il Re. Ma un furor folle / Tanto il figlio di Theti in questo avampa, / Che'l sangue intorno al cor, s'accende, e bolle / E un fortissimo duol nel sen s'accampa." In Latin the passage reads, "Sic dixit. Pelide autem dolor factus est; intus autem sibi cor / In pectoribus hirsutis bifariam cogitavit / An ipsemet ensem acutum extrahens a femore / Hos; quidem fugaret: ipse autem interficeret / An iram sedaret compescereque furorem."

25. Ibid. 1:223–28: "Achille che de l'ira riserva / Nel cor qualche reliqua al Re protervo, / Converso grida in voce acra e acerba; / O de Greci signor del vino servo, / Di mente puerissima, e superba / Re, c'hai faccia di cane e cor di cervo, / Come per guida sua questo bel campo, / Elesse un'huom più timido, che un tampo."

he hurled timid Menoetes from the high stern headlong into the sea. Himself steersman and captain, he attended to the helm.[26]

Thus we can say that wrath is the destroyer of virtue, or, as Trissino says: "But if you allow yourself to be dominated by anger, will you not spoil whatever excellence you possess?"[27]

26. Virgil, *Aeneid* 5:172–76: "Tum vero exarsit iuveni dolor ossibus ingens / Nec lacrimis caruere genae, segnemque Menoeten, / Oblitus, decorisque sui sociumque salutis, / In mare praecipitem puppi deturbat ab alta: / Ipse gubernaculo rector subit: ipse magister." Marinella also supplies an Italian translation by Annibale Caro, *L'Eneide* (Venice, 1581), which reads thus: "Grand'ira, gran dolore e gran vergogna / Ne senti il fiero giovine: e piangendo / Di stizza non mirando il suo decoro; / Ne che Menete del suo legno seco / Fosse guida e salute in mezzo il prese, / E da la poppa in mar lungo avventollo, / Poscia ei nocchiero, e capitano insieme, / Diedi piglio al timone."

27. Giangiorgio Trissino, *La Italia liberata dai Goti* 14 (lines 277–78): "Ma se tu lasci dominarti a l'ira, / Quale eccellenza havrai, che non ti guasti?"

XII

OF OBSTINATE AND
PERTINACIOUS MEN

Obstinacy is a firm perseverance in one's own opinion even when it is false and irrational. Cicero says of it in *Academica*:

Many people prefer to go wrong and to defend most vehemently the path that they love, rather than to seek without obstinacy the path that is most consistent.[1]

This is undoubtedly the sign of an unhealthy mind since nothing could be more foolish than to hold uncertain things as certain, false as true, and unknown as known and familiar. These are precisely the admirable effects of obstinacy.

What should I say of Emperor Justinian who, having had his empire taken away from him and then been told it would be easy for him to recuperate it, boarded ship and having sailed north of Necropolis, hit a fierce and dangerous storm at sea. Maiace, a servant of Justinian, said: "Behold sire, we are near death. Make some vow to God for your safety. Let this be your vow, that if you regain your empire you will not revenge yourself on any of your enemies." Then Justinian replied in great fury: "If I pardon a single one of them, let God drown me this instant."[2] He was so obstinate in his desire for vengeance that even if he had been certain of sinking, he would rather have drowned holding to his own obstinate opinion than save himself and pardon a single one of his enemies.

---

1. Cicero, *Academica* 2.3.9: "Plerique errare malunt, eamque sententiam, quam ad adamaverunt pugnacissime defendere, quam sine pertinacia, quod constantissime dicatur, exquirere."

2. Justinian was Emperor of Rome and Constantinople (527–65) and never had his empire taken away from him. I have been unable to trace this story.

XIII

OF UNGRATEFUL AND
DISCOURTEOUS MEN

Ingratitude is the neglect or forgetfulness, often simulated, to render gratitude or some other form of recognition for benefits received. In book IX of the *Ethics*, Aristotle wrote that an ingrate is someone who receives benefit but does not render it:

> He who desires to receive good but not do good is ungrateful.[1]

This is something inhuman, proud, and cruel, as Cicero says, in the *Defense of Gnaeus Plancius*:

> Oh how many people there are who have received assistance not only from other people's abilities but also from their lives and honors who do not, when the occasion arises, wish to render any favor to those who have benefitted them. Often they deny that they have received assistance, pretending that they never had it or forgetting it.[2]

Plautus, speaking of his citizens, writes:

> Here are our citizens: if you are good to them, their favor is lighter than a feather; if you do wrong, their anger weighs like lead.[3]

They are speaking particularly of men rather than women, which is quite obvious. This masculine vice is the cause of infinite evils, as Trissino states in his *Italia liberata*:

---

1. Aristotle, *Nicomachean Ethics* 9.1 (1164a27–29): "Ingratus est, qui suscipere appetit, et non bene facere." This sentiment permeates the book, but I do not find this precise quotation there.

2. Marinella paraphrases Cicero, *Defense of Gnaeus Plancius*, 33.81.

3. Plautus, *Poenulus* 811–13: "Ita sunt isti nostri Cives, / Si quid benefacias, Levior pluma gratia est, / Si quid peccatum est, plumbeas iras gerunt." The word *cives* (citizens) in line 811 appears as *divites* (riches) in the Latin version.

It is wicked ingratitude that is the only cause and root of infinite evils.[4]

This claim can be confirmed with examples. The Athenians were extremely ungrateful, as Sabellico writes, in giving poison to the innocent Socrates.[5] The Syracusans were most ungrateful to Dion, who liberated their country. Once in possession of this benefit, they banished him, as the same author writes, and later recalled him and put him to death.[6] Did this not show the greatest ingratitude? Were not the Thebans ungrateful to Epaminondas and Pelopidas?[7] Were not the Athenians negligent towards Solon, who gave them laws and who was the sole cause of the country remaining free from the tyranny of Pisistratus? They subsequently banished him, as Valerius Maximus writes.[8] The same author writes that the Athenians imprisoned Miltiades, who had conquered the Persians, and when he died, forbade his body to be buried until they had put his son, Cimon, in prison.[9]

What should we say of Themistocles?[10] What of King Demetrius, who

---

4. Giangiorgio Trissino, *La Italia liberata dai Goti* 9 (lines 283–84): "E l'empia ingratitudine, ch'è sola / Causa, e radice d'infiniti mali."

5. Fulgosio, *Dictorum factorumque memorabilium: Exempla virtutum et vitiorem* (Basel, 1555), book 7, chapter 2, a selection of the writings of M. A. Sabellicus, on the ingratitude of different nations; p. 590 on the Athenians' ingratitude to Socrates. See part II, chapter 4, note 13 above.

6. Ibid., p. 590, on the Syracusans' ingratitude to Dion. Dion (ca. 408–353) was a wealthy disciple of Plato who brought Plato to Syracuse to try to convert its tyrant Dionysius. Dion was banished from Syracuse but in 357 took the island by force. Forced to retire because of quarrels with other leaders, he was recalled and became master of the whole city. He alienated his supporters, however, and was assassinated.

7. Epaminondas was a famous Theban celebrated for his private virtues and military accomplishments. He defeated the Spartans in the battle of Leuctra about 371 B.C.E., but on his return to Thebes he was seized as a traitor for neglecting the law which forbade any citizen to retain supreme power for more than a month. Pelopidas was a celebrated general of Thebes who, with other friends of liberty and national independence, was banished from the city when the Spartan interest prevailed. He is best known for his friendship with Epaminondas. On both, see M. G. Tarcagnota, *Delle istorie del mondo* (Venice, 1585), 1.17, p. 567; Fulgosio, *Dictorum factorumque*, p. 590; and Plutarch's *Lives*, *Pelopidas*.

8. Valerius Maximus, *Memorable Deeds and Words* 5.3, ext. 3. The real story of Solon is not quite as Marinella tells it.

9. Ibid. 5.3, ext. 3.

10. Themistocles (ca. 524–459 B.C.E.) was an esteemed Athenian leader who began the development of the Athenian harbor at Piraeus, was behind the decision (483–82) to use the surplus from the silver mines to enlarge the Athenian navy from seventy to two hundred ships (instrumental in defeating the Persian navy in 480), and commanded Athenian forces against the invading Persians in 480. After the Persians were defeated, however, he was ostracized from Athens (end of the 470s). Herodotus's (book 2) sources accuse him of corruption, but Thucydides (book 2) admired him for his farsightedness and considered him one of the greatest men of his generation. The source here is probably Valerius Maximus, *Memorable Deeds and Words* 5.3.

was so tormented by these same Athenians?[11] Were not the Romans most ungrateful to drive Camillus into exile? He who had done so very much for them, as Valerius Maximus relates.[12] Caligula was of such a perverse nature that he felt a mortal hatred toward those who loved him.[13] But what can I say of the Spartans, who often hurled stones at Lycurgus, who had given them so many laws and shown such love for his country? In the end they put out his eyes and drove him from the city.[14] Oh what ingrates, oh what thanklessness!

I remember Scipio Africanus, who freed Rome and conquered Carthage. As a result the ungrateful Romans banished him, to which he, moved by just indignation, retorted: "Ungrateful country, you will not have my bones."[15] Emperor Justinian was ungrateful to Bellisarius, who had been such a judicious captain, and deprived him of all his possessions.[16] Philip of Arabia was more ungrateful and thankless than can be imagined toward Gordianus, who had been such a loving emperor to him, as you will hear. After the death of Misitheus, Gordianus's prefect and captain, he selected Philip, who was poor and of a dishonorable and base ancestry, in his place. As soon as the ingrate found himself raised to such a level he began to think how he could steal the empire from Gordianus. First he ensured that there were insufficient provisions for the army, then that the soldiers' pay did not arrive on time. When they became indignant he told them that these matters proceeded from the Emperor's lack of care and provision, and he did everything in his power to make himself Gordianus's equal in the empire.

Once he had achieved this he started openly to pour scorn on the Emperor and to give orders as if he were sole commander. The unfortunate Gordianus, seeing he was powerless, begged Philip at least to have him in place of the Caesar, or failing that, as his prefect, or finally as one of his captains, which Philip conceded. But when he realized how much Gordianus was loved, he had him brutally slain.[17] Oh what an ingrate! Did he not deserve to be struck by lightning, or that the earth should swallow him up?

11. Plutarch, *Life of Demetrius* 23–35.

12. Valerius Maximus, *Memorable Deeds and Words* 5.3.2a.

13. Caligula was Roman emperor from 37–41 C.E. See Suetonius's biography of him in *Lives of the Caesars*.

14. Plutarch, *Life of Lycurgus*.

15. The story of Scipio is told at Livy, *History of Rome* 38.51.9, but this exclamation by Scipio (*Ingrata patria non habebis ossa mea*) is found in Valerius Maximus, *Memorable Deeds and Words* 5.3.2b.

16. Bellisarius was a general in the Gothic wars under the Byzantine emperor Justinian (ruled 527–65 C.E.). For Justinian's ingratitude see Procopius, *History of the Wars against Justinian* 2.1. Books 5–7 deal with the wars against the Goths.

17. M. Antonius Gordianus Pius was emperor from 224–44 C.E. The source for this story is obscure.

And what should we say of the ingratitude of Theseus, whom the courteous Ariadne taught the way to escape from the intricate passages of the blind labyrinth? As a reward for her courtesy he abandoned her and left her alone on a deserted shore, as Ovid relates in *Metamorphoses*, book VIII:

> But then, thanks to the virgin's help he found the door and the difficult way never found by anyone until then. When the thread had been wound up again, Theseus departed immediately and having taken the beloved daughter of Minos, set sail for the island of Dia, where the cruel man abandoned his faithful companion on the shore.[18]

Aeneas was ungrateful to the courteous Dido, who had taken him most lovingly into her house and whom he left desolate and tormented, ignoring her tears and prayers and forgetting what a miserable state he had been in when Dido came to his aid, as he himself said in her presence:

> You alone have felt pity for the unutterable ordeals of Troy; and now you would receive us as partners in your city and home, us, a mere remnant left over by the Greeks, and in desperate need, our strength all drained away by every misfortune of land and sea. To thank you fitly, Dido, is not within our power or the power of any other survivors of the Dardan race who may still exist dispersed in any part of the vast world.[19]

This outcast and wanderer could not abstain from exhibiting his ungrateful nature to the courteous Elisa, who reproved him in these words:

> No goddess was your mother, nor was it Dardanus who founded your line. Traitor, your parent was Mount Caucausas, rugged, rocky and hard, and the tigers of Hyrcania nursed you.[20]

---

18. Ovid, *Metamorphoses* 8:172–76: "Utque ope virginea nullius iterata priorum / Ianua difficilis filo est inventa relicto / Protinus Aegydes rapta Minoide Diam / Vela dedit comitemque suam crudelis in illo / Littore destituit." Marinella also gives an Italian translation by F. Maretti, *Le metamorphosi* (Venice, 1570): "Ma poi, che per verginea aita data / Trovò la porta, e la difficil via / Mai di nissun fino a quel di trovata, / Lasciando il filo, subito s'invia / Theseo, e rapita a Min [Minos] la figlia amata, / Diè le vele ver l'isola di Dia, / Dove il crudel nel lido a la campana / Abbandonò la fida sua compagna." The Italian translation by Maretti is not especially close to the Latin, and indeed he mistranslates it at one point; "filo . . . relicto," which means "when the thread had been wound up again," is translated as "lasciando il filo"—leaving the thread behind.

19. Virgil, *Aeneid* 1:597–602: "O sola infandos Troiae miserata labores / Quae nos reliquias Danaum, terraeque marisque; / Omnibus exhaustos iam casibus, omnium egenos / Urbe domo socias, grates persolvere dignas / Non opis est nostrae, Dido nec quidquid ubique est / Gentis Dardaniae magnum quae sparsa per orbem."

20. Ibid. 4.365–67: "Nec tibi diva parens, generis nec Dardanus auctor / Perfide, sed duris genuit te cautibus horrens / Caucasus, Hircanaeque admorunt ubera tigres."

XIV

OF FICKLE, INCONSTANT MEN

Inconstancy is undoubtedly the sign of an unwise, unshrewd mind. If the mind understood the true nature of the subject that engaged it, it would not go roaming around different things, unable to make up its mind where to apply itself. Nor, when it did attach itself, would it generally show a preference for the worst, inconstancy being the favorite sister of ignorance. Cicero said with great insight that nothing deserves greater condemnation than inconstancy, fickleness, and light-mindedness, which according to him denote a kind of madness.[1]

Emperor Caligula was both inconstant and excessively fickle—sometimes he liked company and sometimes he fled from it as if it were poison. Sometimes he performed with great promptness so that he seemed the shrewdest man in the world, at other times with such slowness and carelessness that he appeared just the opposite. He did not punish many people who had committed great crimes, but killed others who had committed no crime at all. One day he praised something, the next he wanted to hack someone to pieces for praising it. In the end his inconstancy and changeability—in matters of dress as well as everything else—were so great that his subjects did not know what to do or say to him.[2]

The emperor Servius Galba was also unstable and irresolute. He was contrary in everything, first harsh and then mild. He condemned people to death for no reason, then acquitted those who deserved it.[3] This is a

1. Cicero, *Philippics* 7.3.9: "What is there more disgraceful . . . than inconstancy, fickleness and levity? (*quid est inconstantia, levitate, mobilitate . . . turpius?*)"

2. See chapter 2.13, note 13.

3. Servius Sulpicius Galba was emperor of Rome from June 68–January 69 C.E. The source for his life and personality is Suetonius, *Lives of the Caesars* 7 (*Life of Galba*), especially section 9. See also Plutarch's *Life of Galba*.

hideous and blameworthy vice in everyone, but in a prince nothing can be worse.

Ammon was extremely fickle, first full of love, then of hate, as Petrarch says of him:

See he who at the same time loves and does not love.[4]

The tyrant Aladine, according to Torquato Tasso's portrayal of him, was so full of rage against the Christians that he was incapable of anything else:

He was all enraged with hatred against them and burned with anger and an immense uncontrollable rage. He forgets every consideration, he wants to revenge himself, come what may, and calm his burning soul. He said, this anger will not come to nothing, the unknown thief will die in the general slaughter.[5]

See how he immediately shows instability and inconstancy as soon as he sees Sophronia's honest beauty:

At the chaste boldness, at the unexpected dazzle of haughty and saintly beauties, the king, almost confused, almost conquered, restrained his anger and smoothed his fierce expression. If he had been less severe of spirit or she of countenance he would have become her lover.[6]

Rodomont was completely unstable and fickle. He had resolved to hate all women but changed his mind as soon as he saw Isabella, as Ariosto relates in *Orlando furioso*:

The moment the Saracen saw the beautiful lady appear, he suppressed his inclination to constantly revile and hate the gentle sex, which embellishes the world: Isabella seemed to him a most worthy object for his second love, totally eclipsing the first in the manner in which one nail drives out another.[7]

4. Petrarch, *Triumphs*, Love, 2:46: "Vedi quel che'n un tempo ama e disama."

5. Tasso, *Gerusalemme liberata* 2:11: "Tutto in lor d'odio infellonissi, ed arse / D'ira e rabbia immoderata immensa. / Ogni rispetto oblia, vuol vendicarse, / Segua che pote, e sfogar l'alma accensa. / Morrà dicea non andrà l'ira a voto / Ne la strage comune il ladro ignoto." From edition by Claudio Varese and Guido Arbizzoni (Milan, 1972).

6. Ibid. 2:20: "A l'honest baldanza, a l'improviso / Folgorar di bellezze altere, e sante; / Quasi confuso il Re, quasi conquiso: / Frenò lo sdegno, e placò il fer sembiante. / S'egli era d'alma, o se costei di viso / Severa manco diveniane amante."

7. Ariosto, *Orlando furioso* 28:98: "Tosto che il Saracin vide la bella / Donna apparir, mise il pensiero al fondo / Ch'avea di biasmar sempre, e d'odiar quella / Schiera gentil, che pur adorna il mondo: / E ben gli par dignissima Isabella / In cui locar debba il suo amor secondo, / E spegnar totalmente il primo in modo, / Che da l'asse si trae chiodo con chiodo."

For this reason Ariosto, considering the inconstancy of men, goes on to exclaim:

> Oh the weak inconstant minds of men, how ready we are to vacillate.
> We change our ideas so easily, especially those born of amorous spite.
> I had just seen the Saracen so incensed against women that it broke
> all bounds. I never thought he would spend his passion or even that it
> would ever cool.[8]

Many Greeks are unstable. Hear what Iamblichus says of them in his *Book of Mysteries:*

> The Greeks are by nature keen on revolutionary change, and they dart
> about all over the place, like ships that have no ballast; they don't keep
> hold of what they get from others, but let go immediately and remodel
> everything because of their unstable perverse ingenuity.[9]

And what should we say of those good champions who, as soon as they saw Armida, allowed themselves to be made fools of by their vain desires, so much so that Tasso says:

> Godfrey now with shame and now with anger burns at the knights'
> ravings.[10]

And what of Wenceslaus, who was old and unstable, as the same poet shows:

> Wenceslaus, who was formerly grave and wise though white-haired,
> behaves like a child and like an old man in love.[11]

I believe he was not at all dissimilar to those weathercocks that move each time the wind blows.

Bourbon was inconstant, as Paolo Giovio writes. He was constantly suspended between different desires, and his spirit was impulsive, unreasonable,

---

8. Ibid. 29:1: "O degli huomini inferma, e instabil mente, / Come sian presti a variar disegno, / Tutti i pensier mutiamo facilmente, / Più quei, che nascon d'amoroso sdegno, / Io vidi dianzi il Saracin sì ardente / Contra le donne, e passar tanto il segno, / Che non che spegner l'odio, ma pensai, / Che non dovesse intiepidirlo mai."

9. Iamblichus, *Book of Mysteries* 7.5: "Graeci nam natura rerum novarum studiosi sunt ac praecipites usquequaque feruntur instar navis saburra carentis nullam habentes stabilitatem, neque conservant quod ab aliis acceperunt, sed et cito dimittunt, et omnia propter instabilitatem novaeque inventionis elecutionem transformare solent."

10. Tasso, *Gerusalemme liberata* 5:72: "[Goffredo] or di vergogna or d'ira / al vaneggiar de' cavalier s'accende."

11. Ibid. 5:73: "Vincilao, che grave e saggio inante, / Canuto or pargoleggia e vecchio amante."

and unstable in every way.[12] In Plutarch's *Life of Cicero* we read of the instability of Lucius Metellus, a most light-minded and unstable man. He abandoned his post as magistrate of the tribunal in order to join Pompey in Syria. Later he abandoned Pompey and went back to Rome, more light-minded and fickle than ever.[13]

12. Paolo Giovio, *Le vite di dicenove huomini illustri* (Venice, 1561), *La vita del Marchese di Pescara*, book 4, p. 216, for a description of Charles, Duke of Bourbon (1490–1527).

13. The unstable man in question is actually called Metellus Nepos, and his story is told in Plutarch, *Life of Cicero* 26.7. Marinella has confused his name with that of Lucius Metellus, who also appears in the *Life*.

XV

OF EVIL MEN WHO
HATE OTHERS EASILY

A ll the greatest writers confirm that hatred is old anger grown cold
and difficult to erase. They say that the best and most excellent cure
for it—indeed the only one—is death, since hatred is tenacious, enduring,
and mortal. It is worse than anger, because anger is the sudden, immediate
movement of an irrational spirit whereas hatred is a passion and bad effect of
reason.[1] Those who hate deeply do not allow prayers, convenience, or the
passing of time to mitigate or cancel their emotion. Cicero writes:

> Hatred can be softened by appeals, or renounced as an expediency, or
> calmed by the passing of time.[2]

But let us now cease to ponder on the nature of this appalling vice and move
on to the examples.

Hannibal felt such great hatred toward the Romans that he swore always
to be their most cruel enemy.[3] Cambyses, King of Persia, felt bitter hatred for
his brother and, moved by this passion, had him killed.[4] The Genovese felt

1. Diogenes Laertius, 7.114: "Hatred is anger that has long rankled and become malicious."
This is quoted as being part of the Stoic doctrine espoused by men such as Zeno, Chrysippus,
and Hecato. See also Cicero, *Tusculan Disputations* 4.9.21: "Hatred is anger grown old (*odium [est]*
ira inveterata)."

2. Cicero, *Post reditum ad populum* 9.23: "Odium vel precibus mitigari potest, vel utilitate deponi,
vel vetustate sedari." This is a truncated quotation. The full version reads as follows: "Hatred
can be softened by appeals or it can be renounced as an expediency at times of crisis for the
republic or the common good, or restrained by the difficulty of getting revenge or calmed by
the passing of time." It seems to be saying the opposite of what one would expect to support
Marinella's argument.

3. Livy, *History of Rome* 35.19. The well-known story has the nine-year-old Hannibal swearing
eternal hostility to Rome at the altar.

4. M. G. Tarcagnota, *Delle istorie del mondo* (Venice, 1585), 1.1.9, p. 258, on Cambyses. See
Herodotus, 3.28.

tremendous hatred for the Pisans. They stole two galleys from the Pisans, hanged the captains, and sold all the other sailors for the price of an onion each, as Battista Fulgosio relates.[5] In the time of Scipio Africanus two brothers whose father had died hated each other so much that they could not bear to see each other. They decided to fight, and the more obstinate of the two was killed.[6] Catalina, when he heard he must postpone his wedding to Aurelia for one day because of one of her small sons, conceived such hatred for him that he had him poisoned, as Battista Fulgosio narrates.[7] Hamilcar was invited to Rome, where, seeing four young boys, he said they would make a good meal for his lions.[8] Does it not seem to you that he was full of hatred?

5. Battista Fulgosio, *Dictorum factorumque memorabilium: Exempla virtutum et vitiorum* (Basel, 1555), 9.3, p. 1022, on the Genovese and Pisans.

6. Livy, *History of Rome* 28.21.6–10. See also below, chapter 30, note 16.

7. Fulgosio, *Dictorum factorumque* 9.1, p. 328, on Catalina and Aurelia.

8. Valerius Maximus, *Memorable Deeds and Words* 9.3. ext. 2. Hamilcar was a Carthaginian general who fought against Rome in the third century B.C.E.

XXII

OF MEN WHO ARE ORNATE,
POLISHED, PAINTED, AND BLEACHED

For men born to politics and civil life it is becoming, to a certain extent, to be elegant and polished. Everyone knows this, and it has been verified by Della Casa, Guazzo, Sabba, and the *The Book of the Courtier*.[1] If, according to these authors' reasoning, this is right for men, we must believe that it is even more right for women, since beauty shines brighter among the rich and elegantly dressed than among the poor and rude. Tasso demonstrates this in *Torrismondo*, by means of the Queen's speech to Rosmonda:

> Why do you not adorn your pleasing limbs and with pleasing clothes augment that beauty which heaven has given you courteously and generously? Unadorned beauty in humble guise is like a rough, badly polished gem, which in a humble setting shines dully.[2]

Since beauty is woman's special gift from the Supreme Hand, should she not seek to guard it with all diligence? And when she is endowed with but a small amount of that excellent quality, should she not seek to embellish it by every means possible, provided it is not ignoble? I certainly believe that it is so. When man has some special gift such as physical strength, which enables him to perform as a gladiator or swagger around, as is the common usage, does he not seek to conserve it? If he were born courageous, would he not seek to augment his natural courage with the art of defense? But if he were

---

1. Marinella is referring to four famous books of manners: Giovanni Della Casa, *Il galateo* (Milan, 1559); Stefano Guazzo, *La civil conversazione* (Brescia, 1574); Sabba Castiglione, *Ricordi* (Venice, 1554); and Baldassare Castiglione, *The Book of the Courtier* (Venice, 1528).

2. Tasso, *Il re Torrismondo* 2:4.13–21: "Perché non orni tue leggiadre membra / Di pretiosa veste? e non accresci / Con abito gentil quella bellezza, / Che'l Ciel a te donò cortese, e largo? / Bellezza inculta, e chiusa in umil gonna, / È quasi rozza, e mal polita gemma, / Che'n piombo vile ancor poco riluce."

born with little courage would he not practice the martial arts and cover himself with plate and mail and constantly seek out duels and fights in order to demonstrate his courage rather than reveal his true timidity and cowardice?

I have used this example because of the impossibility of finding a man who does not swagger and play the daredevil. If there is such a one people call him effeminate, which is why we always see men dressed up like soldiers with weapons at their belts, bearded and menacing, and walking in a way that they think will frighten everyone. Often they wear gloves of mail and contrive for their weapons to clink under their clothing so people realize they are armed and ready for combat and feel intimidated by them.

What are all these things but artifice and tinsel? Under these trappings of courage and valor hide the cowardly souls of rabbits or hunted hares, and it is the same with all their other artifices. Since men behave in this way, why should not those women who are born less beautiful than the rest hide their less fortunate attributes and seek to augment the little beauty they possess through artifice, provided it is not offensive?

Why should it be a sin if a woman born with considerable beauty washes her delicate face with lemon juice and the water of beanflowers and privets in order to remove her freckles and keep her skin soft and clean? Or if with columbine, white bread, lemon juice, and pearls she creates some other potion to keep her face clean and soft? I believe it to be merely a small one. If roses do not flame within the lily pallor of her face, could she not, with some art, create a similar effect? Certainly she could, without fear of being reproved, because those who possess beauty must conserve it and those who lack it must make themselves as perfect as possible, removing every obstacle that obscures its splendor and grace. And if writers and poets, both ancient and modern, say that her golden hair enhances her beauty, why should she not color it blonde and make ringlets and curls in it so as to embellish it still further?

Let us then say that women who are born beautiful should conserve their beauty and women who lack beauty should improve themselves but not in such a way that they become painted masks, for it is unworthy and repulsive to cover the face with thick coatings of red and white. The Church Fathers do not entirely condemn women for adorning and polishing themselves; they merely condemn this when it becomes excessive and bad in other respects. As the learned Augustine wrote in an Epistle to Possidius, who permitted married women to adorn and polish themselves but only in order to be attractive to their husbands:

It is fitting therefore for women to adorn themselves and for learned fathers to permit them to conserve their beauty, or to make themselves more beautiful than they are as long as they do not fall into error.[3]

But what should we say of men who are not born beautiful and who yet make great efforts to appear handsome and appealing, not only by putting on clothes made of silk and cloth of gold as many do, spending all their money on an item of clothing, but by wearing intricately worked neckbands? What should we say of the medallions they wear in their caps, the gold buttons, the pearls, the pennants and plumes that they call Argironi or Acroni, and the great number of liveries that bring ruin on their houses? They go around with their hair waved, greased, and perfumed so that many of them smell like walking perfumeries. How many are there who go to the barbers every four days in order to appear close-shaven, rosy-cheeked, and like young men even when they are old? How many dye their beards when the dread arrival of old age causes them to turn white? How many use lead combs to tint their white hairs? How many pluck out their white hairs in order to make it appear that they are in the flower of youth? I pass over the earrings that Frenchmen and other foreigners wear and the necklaces, of Gallic invention, which we read of in Livy.[4]

How many spend three or four hours each day combing their hair and washing themselves with those balls of soap sold by mountebanks in the *piazza*? Let us not even mention the time they spend perfuming themselves and putting on their shoes and blaspheming against the saints because their shoes are small and their feet are big, and they want their big feet to get into their small shoes. How ridiculous!

3. Augustine wrote only one letter to Possidius, Epistle 245. See paragraph 1, where he writes: "Let me say . . . in regard to ornaments of gold and costly dress, that I would not have you come to a precipitate decision in the way of forbidding their use, except in the case of those who, neither being married nor intending to marry, are bound to consider only how they may please God. But those who belong to the world have also to consider how they may in these things please their wives if they be husbands, their husbands if they be wives; with this limitation, that it is not becoming even in married women to uncover their hair, since the apostle commands women to keep their heads covered. As to the use of pigments by women in coloring the face, in order to have a ruddier or a fairer complexion, this is a dishonest artifice, by which I am sure that even their own husbands do not wish to be deceived; and it is only for their own husbands that women ought to be permitted to adorn themselves, according to the toleration, not the injunction, of Scripture. For the true adorning, especially of Christian men and women, consists not only in the absence of all deceitful painting of the complexion, but in the possession not of magnificent golden ornaments or rich apparel, but of a blameless life." *Nicene and Post-Nicene Fathers*, ed. Philip Schaff. Series 1, vol. 1, *Confessions and Letters of St. Augustine* (Grand Rapids, Mich.: repr. 1956), p. 588.

4. Livy has no such attribution of the invention of necklaces to the French. There might, however, have been a confusion somewhere between the Gallic race and the Galli, the priests of the goddess Cybele, who wore ritual jewelry. See Livy, *History of Rome* 38.18.9.

But it seems to me that I must give some examples so I do not appear to have told untruths. Hortensius, the famous orator, used to spend the whole day gazing at himself in the mirror, adjusting the folds of his clothing.[5] Demosthenes, the glory of Greek eloquence, used to compose his features in the mirror before speaking in public[6]—a shameful matter indeed, since instead of concentrating on the loftiness of his precepts, he passed his time in foolish vanity. And what of Lisocrates, who spent the whole day bleaching his hair in order to make himself more handsome?[7] What of Aristagoras, who painted and groomed himself to such an extent that he was known as Madonna Aristagoras?[8] What of Maecenas, who hungered so lasciviously for perfumed unguents, makeup, daisies, and all types of ornament?[9] How about Sardanapalus, King of the Assyrians, who caused a famine because of his artifices and other vanities?[10] And the people of Massilia, who applied makeup and bleached their hair?[11] And the Valencians, who live only for pleasures, delights, and lasciviousness. For this reason Ariosto compares Ruggiero, possessor of a thousand vanities, to them in the *Orlando furioso*:

> His every gesture was amorous, as though he were accustomed to waiting on ladies in Valencia.[12]

Botero tells us that Spaniards delight by nature in charm, elegance, and show. As for their opinion on other matters—they have none.[13]

5. Macrobius, *Saturnalia* 3.13.4. See also Valerius Maximus, *Memorable Deeds and Words* 8.10.2, where Hortensius (a famous Roman orator who lived 114–50 B.C.E.) is said to have rated the importance of an orator's appearance and movement as highly as that of his speaking.

6. Plutarch, *Life of Demosthenes* 7. See also Valerius Maximus, *Memorable Deeds and Words* 8.7, ext. 1, and 8.10, ext. 1. On Demosthenes see above, part I, chapter 4, note 13.

7. I cannot trace this figure. His name might possibly be a misprint for Isocrates—another famous Greek orator—who is also mentioned by Macrobius (7.1.4), although not in this context.

8. M. G. Tarcagnota, *Delle istorie del mondo* (Venice, 1585), 1.9, p. 300, mentions Aristagoras, the deputy tyrant of Miletus (ca. 505–496 B.C.E.), who, having fled to Thrace, was shortly afterward ambushed and killed by the Thracians. No mention is made of his vanity.

9. Macaenas (died 8 B.C.E.) was a close associate of Augustus, the first of the Roman emperors, and was the patron of several well-known Roman poets, including Virgil and Horace. He was characterized by ancient writers as leading a particularly luxurious lifestyle.

10. Diodorus Siculus, *The Historical Library* 2.23–27, on Sardanapalus.

11. Plautus, *Casina* 963, refers to "Massilian customs," i.e., luxurious, sexually perverted behavior. As a Greek colony in the Roman world, the city (known to us as Marseilles) must have been renowned for such practices in the ancient world.

12. Ariosto, *Orlando furioso* 7:55: "Tutto ne' gesti era amoroso, come / Fosse in Valenza a servir donne avezzo."

13. Giovanni Botero (1543–1617), educated as a Jesuit, left the order to become a teacher of philosophy and rhetoric. In 1582 he was appointed secretary to the archbishop of Milan

I should not omit Emperor Commodus, who, though cruel and villain-ous, was nevertheless vain, lascivious, and feeble. His greatest preoccupation was to bleach his hair, and he spent his time in baths and other pleasures. In spite of being wicked, he was not ashamed to adopt the name of a man who opposed vice. He took the name Hercules, so that instead of being Commodus Antonius, son of Marcus Aurelius, he styled himself Hercules, son of Jove. Even more marvellous, he wrapped himself in a lion's skin, took a club in his hand, and walked around, night and day, striking heavy blows with it as if he were Hercules. Sometimes he appeared dressed as an Amazon, but adorned with pearls and gold, and thus this valiant emperor passed his time in frivolity.[14]

But what should I say of the Agrigentians, who so delighted in pomp and rich clothing that they spent nearly all they possessed?[15] Heliogabalus was vainer than anyone, and, as historians tell us, stupid and lascivious as well. Through his vanity and frivolity he impoverished the formerly wealthy Roman Empire. He wore pearl necklaces, jewelry, priceless rings, and clothes made of silk and cloth of gold decorated with pearls and other precious gems. He had priceless stones even on his shoes.[16] Let us say no more of him, since he is all vanity, and go back to Hercules, who, as Ovid said in his letter to Deianira, was vain, soft, and a great flatterer. His verses, translated into the vernacular by Remigio Fiorentino, read thus:

> Look at the necklaces round Hercules's neck, to whom when small the sky was already oppressive: does it not seem shameful to you to have pearls and gold round your strong arms? would you still like to decorate your shaggy locks with ribbons and fringes?[17]

In truth there are innumerable men who indulge their vanity and use artifice in order to appear sleek and polished. I would not wish time to

and in 1588 published his first important work, *The Greatness of Cities* (*Delle cause della grandezza e magnificenza delle città*), and in 1589 *The Reason of State* (*Della ragion di stato*). I can find no trace of this specific reference to the Spaniards in his works; however, they are full of exhortations to piety, temperance and industry, and admonitions against degeneracy and over indulgence.

14. Herodian, *History*, book 1, especially section 14.8. Commodus was a Roman emperor who lived 161–92 C.E.

15. Agrigentum, a large and wealthy city in Sicily, was well known in antiquity for its lavish temples. Perhaps in Marinella's day its decline was associated with extravagance and luxury.

16. Scriptores Historiae Augustae, *Antoninus Elagabalus* 23, on Heliogabalus.

17. Remigio Fiorentino, *Epistole d'Ovidio* (Venice, 1555), book 1, Epistle 9: Deianira to Hercules, p. 118, lines 101–4 and 107–8: "Vidi i monili a quello Erculeo collo, / A cui picciola già fu soma il cielo; / Non ti parve vergogna haver d'intorno, / Le perle, e l'oro a le gagliarde braccia, / Ardisti anchor d'ornar l'irsutte chiome, / Di nastri, e frange?"

erase the memory of a charming young man of about eighty, an illustrious, noble gentleman of good fortune from Lombardy, who, at seventy, fell in love with a beautiful noblewoman from his own city. This young man, who was not very elevated intellectually, convinced himself that his noble lady loved him in return, and committed the greatest follies you ever heard of for her sake. At night, clutching his sweet lute, this young man would sing and play serenades and aubades under the window of the house where she slept, according to the custom of the times. He would warble at great length, believing he sang excellently and had the sweetest of voices, when in fact he made everyone laugh because his voice was like a frog's. Very often while he was declaiming his amorous passions he would break into trills, thus making his song prettier.

In order to hide his hair, which was gray because of his age, he would have it tinted every month, but not his beard, because at the time it was not the custom, although he would have it shaved every two days. Certainly it was a beautiful sight, that young mane of hair all gleaming, well-groomed, and waved with curling tongs above a black, wrinkled, and furrowed brow, two hollow, squinting eyes, a dripping nose, sunken cheeks, a toothless mouth, pale, bruised, trembling lips—in short, an angel face that would frighten the devil out of hell.

When he was at home he was always standing in front of the mirror. He would fly into tremendous rages with it, saying it was a traitor and liar that did not give a true reflection but lied through its teeth. Then, full of fury, he would punish it by throwing it on the ground and trampling on it. What can I say of his clothes? All by himself he surpassed the Fair at Crema![18] He wore a rose-colored beret all cut with cords and gold and silver braids. His clothes were all decorated and embroidered in the most bizarre manner you could hope to see, not even suitable for a clown. What should we say of his dancing? The opening dance at each festival in the city belonged to him, even though he could hardly stand up, and he was more eager to play ball than a bear to eat honey. Whenever he met young players he stripped down to his waistcoat, and sometimes to his shirt, so he could show off the beautiful proportions of his body—in every way equal to those of his face. However, he did not linger there since he spent most of his time pursuing his beloved more zealously than a dog chasing a wild beast.

Each day of carnival he wore a costume, changing his clothes and his style every hour. He was far from reciting litanies or orations, but always spoke of love and light matters. This great simpleton was as crazy after

18. The fair at Crema, near Milan, was famous for exhibiting fabrics.

death as in life, for on his deathbed he left instructions that above his tomb the hand of a famous master should inscribe the tale of Pyramus and Thisbe, a love story, as well as a winged Cupid who, with drawn bow, was piercing a heart. Can there be a better example than this? Certainly not.

Hear what Numanus says of ornaments in Virgil's *Aeneid*:

> You with your purple dye and ornaments and sleeved tunics and ribbons on your heads, what are you fit for? Parading around all painted, and indolent as if to go dancing.[19]

Tasso, speaking of the Egyptians in the *Gerusalemme liberata*, writes:

> The Egyptian crowd carried only swords and bows and would not bear the weight of helmet or cuirass rich in regalia, which conveys to others desire of booty rather than fear of death.[20]

Nero was extremely lurid, ostentatious, and ornate, and never wore anything that was not worth a great deal of money. Standing in front of the mirror, he would praise his hair that seemed to be made of gold and his eyes that shone so brightly. Nor should I omit the Emperor Alexius Comnenus, who, as Nicetas Acominatus relates, always paraded himself publicly in most beautiful golden robes worked with priceless pearls.[21] Plutarch tells us that Aristotle delighted in being smart and well-groomed to an unusual degree, wearing beautiful clothes and rings on every finger.[22]

I do not want time to erase the memory of a certain courtier from Ferrara who owned every soap, perfume, toilet water, and vanity that there was in Italy. He spent the whole morning combing, cleaning, and brushing himself, often swearing when he thought he had not attained the degree of perfection he desired. There was no one in Spain or Italy who wore boots better than his, and he loved cleanliness so much that in twenty years he never ate salad without wearing gloves. Does it seem to you that we will ever find anyone more genteel?

In no way inferior to him was Emperor Gallienus, who always wore extremely expensive clothes covered in precious gems. This wretched man

---

19. Virgil, *Aeneid* 9:614–15 (not 2:618 in the Latin text, as in Marinella's citation): "Voi con l'ostro, e co' fregi e co' le giubbe, / Immanicate e coi fiochetti in testa, / A che valete? Gir così dipinti, / Et così neghitto sì a far balletti."

20. Tasso, *Gerusalemme liberata* 17:18: "La turba egizia avea sol archi e spade, / Né sosterria d'elmo, o corazza il pondo, / D'abito è ricca ond'altrui vien, che porte / Desio di preda, e non timor di morte." From edition by Claudio Varese and Guido Arbizzoni (Milan, 1972).

21. Nicetas Acominatus (or Choniatas), *The Rule of Alexius* 605.

22. This reference to Aristotle's vanity in Plutarch's work has not been found.

was so foolish that he powdered his hair with golden dust so it would shine more, washed his face with various liquids in order to make himself beautiful, and would not appear anywhere without first spending an hour preening himself in front of the mirror. He ate off cloth of gold from golden vessels decorated with huge pearls. In spring he had rooms and beds made of roses, and in autumn castles of apples.[23]

Equal to him was Domitian, who, as Tarcagnota writes, swallowed and uttered impassioned sighs when he saw his bald head in the mirror, since he held beauty in great esteem. Nor did he lose any possible opportunity of making himself appear more handsome.[24] What should we say of Theopompus, who, as Strabo Sidonius confirms, surpassed every lascivious whore in sinful delights?[25] What of a certain Philostratus, who was so overadorned that he was known as "Cinalopeca"—a word used to describe a dog, since he was endowed with vanities similar to those of the sort of lapdog people keep at home to amuse their little daughters, as Aristophanes tells us.[26] Several historians write that Agirrius was so weak and lascivious that the only masculine thing about him was his beard.[27]

We must not exclude Myraces from these ranks, who used to spend an unbelievable amount of time dressing his golden hair and covered it with so many perfumed ointments that he could be smelt a mile away. This is why Flaccus calls him a *semivir*, and says that his youth was sterile, that is, lacking in any honorable action.[28] Where does this leave Bacchus? He may have been adored as a God, but he was no more than a charming, weak man. Hear what Seneca writes of him:

> Tender Bacchus does not blush to sprinkle his flowing locks with perfume, nor to shake a slender thyrsus in his soft hand, when, with a gait that is hardly manly, he trails his robe decorated with barbaric gold.[29]

23. Scriptores Historiae Augustae, *The Two Gallieni* 16.1–6. Gallienus was emperor 253–68 C.E.

24. Tarcagnota, *Della istorie del mondo* 2.3, p. 86, on Domitian.

25. Theopompus was a historian in the fourth century B.C.E. He is referred to by Strabo (14.645), but no mention is made of any immoral behavior.

26. Aristophanes, *Knights* 1069. The word *cinalopeca* means a mongrel born of a dog and a fox, and was a nickname given to brothel-keepers.

27. I cannot trace Agirrius.

28. I cannot trace Myraces.

29. Seneca, *Hercules furens* 472–75: "Non erubescit Bacchus effusos tener / sparsisse crines nec manu molli levem / vibrare thyrsum, cum parum forti gradu/auro decorum Syrma barbaricum trahit."

We would wrong Callisthenes if we were to leave him out of this vain company. He, as several authors write, dressed as a woman and painted and groomed himself to a disgraceful extent.[30] But tell me if you please how long that glorious hero Achilles spun, dressed as a woman, among the daughters of King Lycomedes? I believe he spun quite a lot because, if I understand correctly, several writers say that he was there for many years. Ovid, in book I of the *Art of Loving*, writes:

> Disgracefully, had the action not been prompted by piety toward his mother, Achilles disguised his manhood in a long woman's dress.[31]

Tarcagnota writes that in Hadrian's time it was not the custom to wear a beard, but that he wore one nevertheless, in order to hide some marks he had on his face. His desire to appear handsome was so great that he did not care about flouting the custom.[32] The same author narrates that Lucius Verus spent most of the day bleaching his hair in the sun, and cursing nature for not having given him a stronger head, because it gave him a headache. Even though he was blond he still threw a lot of gold dust on his hair so it would shine more brightly.[33]

What of Tisicrates, who passed into legend because of his lasciviousness? When age turned his hair a fine silver he tinted it the color of gold in order to appear young and handsome. This caused many people to laugh at him, according to Martial.[34] The wretched man knew that love, being young, would scorn to live among the pale wrinkles of his aging visage that he gilded and whitened with a thousand different poultices—trying through these tricks to ensure that Cupid, conquered by his beauty, would not be averse to taking shelter there. All was in vain, however, because even as he sought daily to enhance himself with new beauties he was overtaken by death (ah cruel fate!), which, freezing his heart, left him scarlet in the face—just that shade in fact that he had painted himself. An ignominious matter surely that men, even when old, should care about such things.

In confirmation of what I have said, hear what Seneca writes about men in *Naturales quaestiones*:

30. Callisthenes, the philosopher who accompanied Alexander the great on his campaigns, is praised in many sources in ancient literature. I have not found a reference to this particular attribute of his.

31. Ovid, *Ars amatoria* 1:689–90: "Turpe nisi hoc matris precibus tribuisset Achilles / Veste virum longa dissimulatus erat."

32. Tarcagnota, *Della istorie del mondo* 2.3, p. 98, on Hadrian.

33. Ibid. 2.3 (p. 105), on Lucius Verus.

34. The name Tisicrates does not appear in Martial's poems, although there are several epigrams mocking elderly men who try to appear young, e.g., *Epigrams* 3.43 or 4.36.

We go on stifling whatever is left of morality. By the smoothness and polish of our bodies we men have surpassed a woman's refinements. We men have taken over the cosmetics of whores, which would not indeed be worn by decent women. With a delicate soft gait we swing our steps high—we do not walk, we strut. And we wear gems on every finger.[35]

Does it not seem to you that he is speaking of men rather than women? Nor do I wish to omit the words of the Elder Seneca, which can be read in the Book of *Controversiae:*

See how the cleverness of lazy youth turns to stupidity, and they do not engage themselves in studying a single honest subject. Our young men's only occupation is to curl their hair and dress up in filthy finery,[36]

from which words we can deduce that they are all vain, lascivious, and feeble, because he is not speaking of one or two of them, but of all men in general. Nor should I omit the verdict of Monsignor Sabba Castiglione, a Knight of Jerusalem. He says in his memoirs that

men's vanities include more than a thousand different types of frivolity in their clothing, and still more in their shoes and stockings. I do not speak of young men, in whom it would be less shameful, but of bearded, old, white-haired men. In my opinion these things are most shameful and dishonest—not worthy of a noble old man but of a foolish, infantile one.[37]

35. Marinella is using an Italian translation of Seneca, *Natural Questions* 7.31.2. (*On Comets*): "Tutto quello che ci è di buon costume, guastiamo noi con la leggiadria de' corpi, avanzando ne gli ornamenti le infami meretrici, non che le donne honeste con molle, e con vezzosa andatura, teniamo sospeso il passo, tal che non caminiamo, anzi contegnosi passeggiamo, e in ogni dito delle mani habbiamo pretiose gemme." (English translation by Thomas H. Corcoran, Loeb Classical Library, 1972.)

36. Seneca the Elder, *Controversiae* 1, Preface 8: "Ecco che gl'ingegni della pigra gioventù diventano stupidi, né si vigila allo studio di alcuna cosa honesta; ma solamente gli studi degli huomini sono l'incresparsi i capelli, e l'acconciarsi con monditie immondissime."

37. Monsignor Sabba Castiglione, kinsman of Baldassare, a gallant and accomplished knight of St. John of Jerusalem, defended Rhodes against the Turks, then returned to spend a peaceful old age at Faenza and write his famous *Ricordi*. Chapter 13, for example, on dress (*Cerca il vestire*), advises men to avoid all superfluous ostentation and to appear at all times grave, modest, and sincere.

XXX

OF MEN WHO KILL THEIR MOTHERS, FATHERS, BROTHERS, SISTERS, AND GRANDCHILDREN

It is extremely hard for me to imagine a man who is so lacking in pity and love that, having first been given life by his father and mother (his tender parents), and then with much effort, sweat, vigilance, and worry, been fed and taught by them, rewards them with death for the troubles and privations they have suffered. However, horrible as it may seem, there have been not just one or two of these men, but hundreds. This is something that is shunned by wild beasts and abhorred by nature itself.

It is also both wicked and iniquitous to take up arms in order to spill the blood of a brother, sister, or grandchild. All of these killings were known by the ancient Latins simply as parricide. I do not, however, believe it inappropriate here to quote some examples.

In his *Descrizioni d'Italia*, Fra Leandro Alberti of Bologna writes that the Signore Cangrande della Scala had his brother Paolo Alboino thrown into prison on a charge of conspiring against him. He then became gravely ill, and fearing that Paolo his brother was not secure enough in prison, had him condemned to death.[1] Thus an innocent man was killed because of his evil brother's hatred.

Appian of Alexandria relates that after the praetor Annalis was condemned by the triumvirs, he took refuge in a humble cottage in the suburbs of Rome. He armed himself with an axe and allowed nobody to visit him except his son, who was so wicked and cruel that he brought the guards with him and delivered his father into their hands and stood by (something which is unheard of) while they cut off his head. For this the son was made an aedile by the triumvirs. One night a short time later he was found by the

---

1. Leandro Alberti (a theologian and writer, 1479–1552), *Descrizioni d'Italia* (Venice, 1581), p. 463, on the Signore Cangrande della Scala and his brother Paolo Alboino.

guards who had killed his father and was killed by them on account of his mad deeds resulting from the great quantity of wine he had drunk.[2]

Let us now relate something further concerning the harsh and merciless Nero. Wishing to kill his mother Agrippina, he had a boat made with a bottom that opened easily. His plan was for his mother to go aboard and then be drowned when the bottom opened. He invited Agrippina to attend a solemnity that he was organizing in Baia and in the evening, when she wished to return to Bauli where she was staying, her good son had her step into the false boat. The boat had not gone far from land when it detached itself from the poop, killing many people. Agrippina suffered a blow to her shoulder but was saved because she swam to the bank. Getting into a carriage she went to one of her houses. Pretending not to be aware of her son's deception, she immediately sent word to him that she had been in great danger, but that thanks to the Gods there was nothing wrong with her. On hearing this the wicked emperor pretended that his mother was trying to kill him. He craftily dropped a knife and claimed it belonged to Agrippina's messenger, who was put to death with much cruelty. He then sent Anicetus with a large company to find his mother and have her killed. When she saw them coming, she realized that she was going to die and told them they must strike her in the stomach because that was the part of her body which most merited punishment, since it had given birth to such a fierce and pitiless monster. As she was saying this they killed her with many blows. When she was dead, Nero went to see her and examining every part of her body, he praised parts of it and criticized others. Thus with the eyes not of a son but of a cruel executioner, he admired and abused the mother killed by his own wickedness. He then wrote to the Senate and reproached her in a manner that was beyond belief, saying she was cruel and unjust.[3] Not only, therefore, did he take her life, but also her good name. Oh most cruel son who, without any pity, did so much to harm the woman who had given birth to you!

But what of Emperor Bassianus, who, according to Spartianus, came to Rome from Brittany intent on not sharing his administration with anyone? And since he had a brother called Geta he determined to kill him. He sent a company of wicked men to kill him as he sat on his mother's lap (others write that Bassianus himself killed him at the breast of the woman who was his own stepmother). He also killed all those who supported Geta, together

---

2. Appian, *The Civil War* 4.18.

3. See Tacitus, *Annals* 14.3–8, for the most famous ancient account of this story, and also Suetonius, *Nero* 34. Some details of Tacitus's and Suetonius's accounts differ from Marinella's, which was probably drawn from a more recent source amalgamating the two.

with their wives and families.[4] King Pedro of Castille was another pitiless parricide. He had his two innocent brothers dispatched to the next world and then persecuted his bastard brother and stripped him of all the lands that had been left him by his father.[5]

And what of Artaxerxes, who so gloried in having killed his brother that when others claimed to have done it they were painfully deprived of life?[6] Plutarch writes that Timoleon killed his brother.[7] He also writes that Darius entered his father Artaxerxes's room by night, together with the armed Teribazus, in order to kill him, but that Artaxerxes, who had been warned of this betrayal, kept a door open behind his bed which was covered by tapestries. When he saw his evil son armed in his room he jumped from the bed and fled through the door, thus saving himself. Darius, however, was seized immediately and put in prison, and killed shortly afterward.[8]

Nor should I omit Cesare Borgia from these ranks. Giovio wrote of him: "But the dignity of the cardinal's hat seemed a vastly inferior one to Cesare's soul, so one night he sent for his brother Scanare, with whom he had earlier dined merrily, and had him thrown from the steeple into the Tiber." This brother of his was the Duke of Candia, and now that Candia was without a lord, Cesare renounced the cardinal's hat and made himself duke in his place.[9]

Appian of Alexandria writes that Lepidus, the first of the Triumvirs, allowed his own brother to be put to death by them.[10] We read in Acomina-tus's histories of the Emperors of Constantinople that two sons of Necmones,

---

4. Spartianus is one of the six "Scriptores historiae Augustae," attributed authors of a series of imperial biographies from the third and fourth centuries C.E.. This story appears in *Life of Severus*, 21.7–8. Bassianus is the emperor commonly known as Caracalla, and referred to as such later in the text.

5. M. G. Tarcagnota, *Delle istorie del mondo* (Venice, 1585), 2.17, p. 655, on King Pedro of Castile (1334–69).

6. Plutarch, *Life of Artaxerxes* 14. Wanting to claim the glory for the death in battle of his brother and enemy Cyrus, Artaxerxes tried to bribe the real killer to keep quiet. The man was indignant, however, and went about proclaiming that he *was* the killer. Artaxerxes was infuriated, and his mother ordered that the man should be tortured on the rack for ten days, have his eyes gouged out, and then have molten brass poured into his ears until he died. Of course Marinella does not mention that these evil tortures were devised by a woman!

7. Plutarch, *Life of Timoleon* 4. In Plutarch's version Timoleon's brother is actually killed by one of Timoleon's companions, because Timoleon himself is too good and compassionate to kill his tyrannical brother. However, in another version (Diodorus Siculus, *The Historical Library* 16.65.4) it is Timoleon himself who kills his brother.

8. Plutarch, *Life of Artaxerxes* 29.

9. Paolo Giovio, *Le vite di dicenove huomini* (Venice, 1561), *La vita di Consalvo Ferrando Ernandez di Cordova*, known as *Il Gran Capitano*, book 3, p. 304.

10. Appian, *The Civil War* 4.12.

Prince of Traballus, came to talk together and, by reason of their madness and ambition, the older, Valsco, drove the younger, Stefano, out of principality, country, and world.[11] The fame of this parricide spread to other nations and caused brother to take up arms against brother and kinsman against kinsman, each thus depriving the others of existence. In speaking of them we may say, with Lucan:

> I shall sing of how a powerful race turned their victorious right hands against their own vitals.[12]

And all this in order to rule and tyrannize!

Spartianus and other writers relate that Emperor Severus, being old and troubled with gout, wished to die, but that his son, Antoninus Caracalla, wished it even more. He made it clear that if Severus's infirmity did not kill him, he would do it himself with poison. When Severus heard this he died of grief more than of his malady, thus delighting his wicked son.[13] Brother Leandro Alberti writes that Bartolomeo della Scala had his brother Antonio killed in order to rule alone.[14] In Xenophon's description of the Greek wars, the continuation of the history of Thucydides, we read of two brothers, Polydorus and Polyphron, who were elected *tagus*, or prince, and went to Larissa, where the sleeping Polydorus was unjustly killed by his brother Polyphron.[15]

Livy mentions two Spanish brothers, Corbis and Orsua, who contended fiercely together over a city named Ibes. Scipio tried very hard to reconcile them, but in vain. Since they were both most ferocious and desirous to rule, they replied that neither men nor gods could placate them and that only Mars could judge their quarrel. Nobody could turn them from this cruel rage, and, horribly and tragically for those who watched, the younger of the two was killed.[16]

---

11. Nicetas Acominatus, *History of the Greek Emperors* (translated into Italian and published in Venice in 1569), 705–6. Marinella's version alters the names involved. Originally they are Nemannus and Volcus, and the place name is Triballus.

12. Lucan, *The Civil War* (Pharsalia) 1.2–3: "Canimus populum potentem in sua victrici conversum viscera dextra." (NB emended text.)

13. Scriptores Historiae Augustae, *Life of Severus* 19.1, on the death of Severus, although it makes no mention of his son. The emperor Caracalla mentioned here is the same as the Bassianus mentioned above (see note 4).

14. Leandro Alberti, *Descrizioni d'Italia*, p. 463, on Bartolomeo della Scala. See above, note 1.

15. Xenophon, *Hellenica* 6.4.33. *Tagus* was an elective office.

16. Livy, *History of Rome* 28.21.6–10. The two men are described by Livy as *patrueles fratres*, i.e., cousins whose fathers are brothers.

Volterranus writes that Egbert, King of Anglia, slew his brother's children with the utmost cruelty when they were still tender in years.[17] Seneca narrates that Atreus killed his brother's children and served them up to him as food.[18] Livy describes the hatred, rancor, insulting words, and many attempts to kill each other which were made by the two sons of Philip, Perseus and Demetrius.[19] Paulus Orosius writes of Philip of Macedon:

> Then, after the massacres, the torchings and the pillaging that were carried out in the allied towns, he became involved in fratricide; since he feared the coinheritors of his kingdom, the sons of his father by his step-mother, he undertook to murder them.[20]

Romulus, as everyone knows, killed his brother Remus. And what of Cambyses, who had his brother killed merely because he dreamed he sat on the royal throne of Persia? When his sister reproved him for this impiety, he rained so many blows on her that he killed her. The Greeks write that Cambyses placed a puppy and a lion cub within a type of arena. The lion cub was winning, but then another dog ran in to save its brother and together they overcame their adversary the lion. At this Meroe, Cambyses's sister, wept. Her husband asked her why she was crying and she replied: "I am remembering my brother Smerdis, who had nobody to help or revenge him. When this little dog was losing the other little dog came willingly to his aid." When the wicked Cambyses heard this he immediately and most cruelly had her put to death.[21]

Justin writes that the kingdom of Syria fell into ruin because of fraternal hatred.[22] Antipater was extremely cruel to his mother. Without any gratitude for the benefits received from her, he killed (oh what a wicked thing!) his dear and loving mother, who begged him for her life and, baring her breasts,

---

17. This is a reference to the humanist and historian Raphael Volterranus, also known as Raphael Maffeius, who wrote a *Commentarium* that was published in Rome in 1506.

18. Seneca, *Thyestes*, esp. lines 627 ff.

19. Livy, *History of Rome* 40.7–16.3, 20.4–6, and 24.

20. Orosius, *Histories: Against the Pagans* 3.12.19: "Inde post caedes incendia depraedationesque in sociis urbibus gestas parricidia in fratres convertit, quos patri ex noverca genitos cum coheredes regni vereretur interficere adgressus est" (NB text emended). The Philip referred to here is Philip of Macedon, the father of Alexander the Great, and a different man from the one referred to in the previous note.

21. Tarcagnota, *Delle istorie del mondo* 1.1.9, p. 258, on Cambyses.

22. Justin's *Epitome* of Trogus Pompeius's *History of the World* 15.1–17.2. Justin was a late Roman writer who wrote an abridgment of the work of the Roman historian Trogus, who probably wrote under Augustus. Trogus's original work has not survived, so Justin's *Epitome* is our only source. Thus both this and the following reference are to the same work. See above, part I, chapter 5, note 173.

reminded him of the sweet milk he had drunk from them. He, deaf as Aspe and hard as a rock, scorned the maternal entreaties and eliminated her because it seemed to him that she favored his brother Alexander. This is related by Trogus.[23]

Celio tells us that Mithridates killed his mother and one of his brothers.[24] Volterranus writes that Giovanni Maria, Duke of Milan, had his mother walled up within a tower and left to die there.[25] The same author states that Henry, son of Alfonso XI, killed his brother; and that Pierino Fregoso, Prince of Genoa, also killed his brother, who was held in great honor because of his learning and honest ways.[26] Similarly Plutarch relates that Hostius killed his father.[27] Emperor Frederick was, through deception, killed by his son, who showed no pity.[28]

Did not Aristobolus, King of Judea, kill his brother?[29] Did not Antiochus, son of Seleucus, do the same in order to reign alone?[30] Did not Ferdinand, King of Castille, kill his brother Garcia, King of Navarre?[31] Herodian writes that Learchus gave poison to a brother of his who was sick, as a result of which the miserable man was strangled.[32]

What of Haldave, whose desire to rule was so great that he deprived his two young brothers of life and as a result of this parricide was proclaimed king?[33] Seleucus, desiring to reign alone, also killed his brother,[34] as did

---

23. As above, book 16.1.1.

24. It is not clear whether Marinella is referring here to Celio Calcagnini (1479–1541), the author, humanist, and diplomat with an interest in Egyptian history, or to Celio Magno, the poet quoted in part I, chapter 3, notes 21 and 22 above. Mithridates is frequently mentioned by both Tarcagnota and Plutarch.

25. See note 17 above for Volterranus. Giovanni Maria Visconti, duke of Milan (1402–12), appears in Tarcagnota, *Delle istorie del mondo* 2.40, p. 807. There is no mention of his mother.

26. For Volterranus, see above, note 17. Tarcagnota, *Delle istorie del mondo* 3.13, p. 515, also mentions Henry, son of Alphonso XI of Castile, who committed various outrages before dying at the age of eighteen.

27. Plutarch, *Life of Romulus* 22.4. Lucius Hostius was reported to have been the first parricide after the war with Hannibal.

28. Tarcagnota, *Delle istorie del mondo* 2.14, p. 547, on Frederick II, Emperor of Sicily.

29. Josephus, *Jewish War* 1.72–77; and *Antiquities* 13.11.

30. Tarcagnota, *Delle istorie del mondo* 2.27, p. 216, on Antiochus the Great.

31. Ibid. 2.11, p. 418, on Ferdinand of Castille and Garcia of Navarre.

32. The story of Learchus (or Haliarchus) is told by Herodotus, 4.160, but does not appear in Herodian's writings at all. Perhaps Marinella or her source have confused the two authors with similar names.

33. I cannot trace this figure.

34. Several kings named Seleucus are mentioned in the various works of Josephus, but I have not found this particular reference.

King Aristobulus, who killed his brother Antigonus.[35] Volterranus writes that Piro Ordelapho killed his brother Francesco so he could rule alone, and sent Francesco's children far away into exile.[36] Killing his father seemed such a small matter to Ptolemy Philopator that he turned the knife, still steaming with his blood, onto his brother.[37] Henry, King of Anglia, gouged his brother Robert's eyes out and left him to die of hunger and filth in prison.[38] And Jugurtha, according to Sallust, killed his brothers and their children.[39] Learchus, King of the Cyrenes, gave poison to his sick brother, as a result of which he was strangled.[40] Typhon killed his brother out of envy.[41] Orodes, King of Parthia, did the same to his brother Mithridates,[42] not one of them sparing any torment that would end the life of their brothers.

Bela, King of Pannonia, killed his brother Andrea.[43] Herodian writes that Emperor Commodus killed his sister Lucilla.[44] Critolaus did the same.[45] Isacius was deprived of his eyes, empire, and life by his brother Alessius,[46] as was the brother of Dardanus.[47] Maximianus, the son of Diocletian, killed his

---

35. See above, note 29.

36. On Volterranus, see above, note 17.

37. Plutarch, *Cleomenes* 33.

38. Tarcagnota, *Delle istorie del mondo* 2.12, p. 461, on Henry I of England and Robert, Duke of Normandy.

39. Sallust, *The War Against Jugurtha* 6–26.

40. See note 32 above.

41. Typhon is identical to Python, the Greek Seth. Seth is the Egyptian god, brother of Osiris, whom he killed. According to the famous Egyptian myth, Isis restored the dismembered body of Osiris to wholeness, conceiving by him Horus. In the Egyptian royal myth, Osiris represents the (just) dead king, Horus his living son and new king.

42. Orodes was king of Parthia (ca. 58–37 B.C.E.). The throne was contested for a number of years with his brother, Mithradates III, whom he finally captured and executed in 55–54 B.C.E. *Oxford Classical Dictionary*, 3rd ed. (1996), p. 1077, citing Pauly-Wissowa 1.

43. Nicetas Acominatus, *History of the Greek Emperors* 131ff. On Bela of Pannonia.

44. Herodian, *History* 1.8.8.

45. Cicero, *De natura deorum* 3.91. Critolaus was a general in the Achaean League (147–6 B.C.E., whose defeat by Rome led to the fall of Corinth. Here Cicero says that he destroyed Corinth, not that he killed his brother.

46. Tarcagnota, *Delle istorie del mondo* 2.13, p. 517, on Isacius, Emperor of Greece, and his brother Alessius.

47. Dardanus was Zeus's favorite son by a mortal woman, Electra (*Iliad* 20:304–5). Iasius (also Iasion) was his brother. There are conflicting accounts in the Greek mythological tradition. According to one, Iasius was killed by a thunderbolt (i.e., Zeus) because he tried to make love to the goddess Demeter (*Odyssey* 5.125ff.). The other is that either the brothers separated, Dardanus going to Troad and Iasius to Samothrace; or Dardanus killed Iasius. *The Oxford Classical Dictionary*, 3rd ed. (1996), p. 430.

sister.[48] Sextus Aurelius writes that Emperor Aurelianus killed his daughter's son,[49] and many, indeed an infinite number, of others did the same. Orestes killed his mother.[50] Ninyas, according to Celio, killed Semiramis,[51] and King Tropia was killed by his son.[52]

48. Diocletian was emperor (285–305), and on his abdication Maximianus took over. Although the stories surrounding these figures are fairly lurid, there is no record in the earlier sources of either of them killing his sister.

49. Sextus Aurelius Victor (a Roman historian of the mid fourth century), *Book of the Caesars* 35. Aurelian was emperor 270–75.

50. *Odyssey* 1:29ff., 298ff.; 3:303ff. Also Sophocles, *Electra;* and Euripides, *Electra.* Sophocles has Orestes kill his mother by himself (his sister Electra encouraging him from outside the closed door); Euripides makes Electra the dominant figure, urging the weak Orestes to kill their mother and grasping the sword with him when his hand fails.

51. Tarcagnota, *Delle istorie del mondo* 1.1, p. 15. For Celio see above, note 24. See also Valerius Maximus, *Memorable Deeds and Words* 9.3., ext. 4, and Boccaccio, *Concerning Famous Women* 2.

52. I cannot trace this figure.

BIBLIOGRAPHY

PRIMARY SOURCES

Alberti, Leon Battista (1404–72). *The Family in Renaissance Florence.* Trans. Renée Neu Watkins. Columbia, S.C.: University of South Carolina Press, 1969.

Aprosio, Angelico. *La maschera scoperta.* In Emilia Biga, *Una polemica antifemminista del '600,* Quaderno dell' Aprosiana, 4, Pinerolo, Civica Biblioteca Aprosiana, 1989.

Ariosto, Ludovico (1474–1533). *Orlando furioso.* Ed. Marcello Turchi. Milan: Garzanti, 1974; Trans. Guido Waldman. Oxford: Oxford University Press, 1974; Trans. Barbara Reynolds. 2 vols. New York: Penguin Books, 1975, 1977.

Aristotle, *The Complete Works of Aristotle.* Trans. and ed. Jonathan Barnes. Princeton: Princeton University Press, 1984.

Astell, Mary (1666–1731). *The First English Feminist: Reflections on Marriage and Other Writings.* Ed. and Introd. Bridget Hill. New York: St. Martin's Press, 1986.

Barbaro, Francesco (1390–1454). *On Wifely Duties.* Trans. Benjamin Kohl. In *The Earthly Republic.* Eds. Kohl and R. G. Witt. Philadelphia: University of Pennsylvania Press, 1978, 179–228. Translation of the preface and book 2.

Boccaccio, Giovanni (1313–75). *Concerning Famous Women.* Trans. Guido A. Guarino. New Brunswick, N.J.: Rutgers University Press, 1963.

———. *Corbaccio or the Labyrinth of Love.* Trans. Anthony K. Cassell. 2nd rev. ed. Binghamton, N.Y.: Medieval and Renaissance Texts and Studies, 1993.

———. *The Decameron.* Bari: Editori Laterza, 1986.

Bronzino, Cristoforo. *Dialogo della dignità e nobiltà delle donne.* Florence: Zanobi Pignoni, 1624.

Bruni, Leonardo (1370–1444). "On the Study of Literature (1405) to Lady Battista Malatesta of Moltefeltro." In *The Humanism of Leonardo Bruni: Selected Texts.* Trans. and Introd. Gordon Griffiths, James Hankins, and David Thompson. Binghamton, N.Y.: Medieval and Renaissance Texts and Studies, 1987, 240–51.

Castiglione, Baldassare (1478–1529). *The Book of the Courtier.* Trans. George Bull. New York: Penguin, 1967.

Chiesa, F. A. della. *Teatro delle donne letterate.* Mondovì, 1620.

Elyot, Thomas (1490–1546). *Defence of Good Women: The Feminist Controversy of the Renaissance.* Ed. Diane Bornstein. Facsimile Reproductions. New York: Delmar, 1980.

Erasmus, Desiderius (1467–1536). *The Praise of Folly.* Trans. with an introduction and commentary by Clarence H. Miller. New Haven, Conn.: Yale University Press, 1979. Best edition, since it indicates additions to the text between 1511 and 1516.

———. *Erasmus on Women.* Ed. Erika Rummel. Toronto: University of Toronto Press, 1996.

Kempe, Margery (1373–1439). *The Book of Margery Kempe.* Trans. Barry Windeatt. New York: Viking Penguin, 1986.

King, Margaret L., and Albert Rabil, Jr., eds. *Her Immaculate Hand: Selected Works by and about the Women Humanists of Quattrocento Italy.* Binghamton, N.Y.: Medieval and Renaissance Texts and Studies, 1983; 2nd rev. paperback ed., 1991.

Klein, Joan Larsen, ed. *Daughters, Wives, and Widows: Writings by Men about Women and Marriage in England, 1500–1640.* Urbana, Ill.: University of Illinois Press, 1992.

Knox, John (1505–72). *The Political Writings of John Knox: The First Blast of the Trumpet against the Monstrous Regiment of Women and Other Selected Works.* Ed. Marvin A. Breslow. Washington: Folger Shakespeare Library, 1985.

Kors, Alan C., and Edward Peters, eds. *Witchcraft in Europe, 1100–1700: A Documentary History.* Philadelphia: University of Pennsylvania Press, 1972.

Krämer, Heinrich, and Jacob Sprenger. *Malleus maleficarum* (ca. 1487). Trans. Montague Summers. London: Pushkin Press, 1928; repr. New York: Dover, 1971. The "Hammer of Witches," a convenient source for all the misogynistic commonplaces on the eve of the sixteenth century, and an important text in the witch craze of the following centuries.

Lorris, William de, and Jean de Meun. *The Romance of the Rose.* Trans. Charles Dahlbert. Princeton: Princeton University Press, 1971; reprinted University Press of New England, 1983.

Marguerite d'Angoulême, Queen of Navarre (1492–1549). *The Heptameron.* Trans. P. A. Chilton. New York: Viking Penguin, 1984.

Marinella, Lucrezia. *La colomba sacra. Poema eroico.* Venice: Gio. Battista Ciotti, 1595.

———. *Vita del serafico et glorioso San Francesco. Descritto in ottava rima. Ove si spiegano le attioni, le astinenze e i miracoli di esso.* Venice, 1597.

———. *Amore innamorato ed impazzato. Poema di Lucrezia Marinella.* Venice, 1598.

———. *La nobiltà et eccellenza delle donne co' difetti et mancamenti de gli huomini.* Venice, 1600, 1601, 1621.

———. *La vita di Maria Vergine imperatrice dell'universo.* Venice, 1602.

———. *Rime sacre.* Venice, 1603.

———. *Arcadia felice* (1605), critical edition by Françoise Lavocat (Florence: Accademia toscana di scienze e lettere, "La colombaria," vol. 162, 1998).

———. *Vita di Santa Giustina in ottava rima.* Florence, 1606.

———. *De' gesti heroici e della vita meravigliosa della serafica Santa Caterina da Siena. Libri sei.* Venice: Barezzo Barezzi, 1624.

———. *L'Enrico overo Bisantio Acquistato. Poema heroico.* Venice: Ghirardo Imberti, 1635.

———. *Essortationi alle donne et a gli altri se faranno loro a grado.* Venice: Valvasense, 1645.

———. *Le vittorie di Francesco il serafico. Li passi gloriosi della diva Chiara.* Padua: Crivellari, 1647.

———. *Holocausto d'amore della vergine Santa Giustina.* Venice: M. Leni, 1648.

Petrarch, *Petrarch's Lyric Poems.* Trans. and ed. Robert M. Durling. Cambridge: Harvard University Press, 1976.

Pizan, Christine de (1365–1431). *The Book of the City of Ladies.* Trans. Earl Jeffrey Richards. Foreword Marina Warner. New York: Persea Books, 1982.

———. *The Treasure of the City of Ladies.* Trans. Sarah Lawson. New York: Viking Penguin, 1985. Also trans. and Introd. Charity Cannon Willard. Ed. and Introd. Madeleine P. Cosman. New York: Persea Books, 1989.

Sansovino, M. Francesco. *Delle cose notabili della città de Venezia.* Venice, 1592.

———. *Venezia città nobilissima, et singolare descritta già in XIII Libri.* Venice, 1604.

Spenser, Edmund (1552–99). *The Faerie Queene.* Ed. Thomas P. Roche, Jr., with the assistance of C. Patrick O'Donnell, Jr. New Haven: Yale University Press, 1978.

Speroni, Sperone, "Della dignità delle donne," in *Trattatisti del Cinquecento.* Ed. Mario Pozzi. Milan-Naples: Ricciardi, 1978. No English translation.

Tasso, Torquato. *Discorso della virtù femminile e donnesca.* Ed. Maria Luisa Doglio. Palermo: Sellerio Editore, 1997. No English translation.

Tasso, Torquato (1544–1495). *Gerusalemme liberata.* Ed. Claudio Varese and Guido Arbizzoni. Milan: Mursia, 1972; Trans. Ralph Nash (as *Jerusalem Delivered*). Detroit: Wayne State University Press, 1976.

Teresa of Avila, Saint (1515–82). *The Life of Saint Teresa of Avila by Herself.* Trans. J. M. Cohen. New York: Viking Penguin, 1957.

Vives, Juan Luis (1492–1540). *The Instruction of the Christian Woman.* Trans. Rycharde Hyrde. London, 1524, 1557.

Weyer, Johann (1515–88). *Witches, Devils, and Doctors in the Renaissance: Johann Weyer, De praestigiis daemonum.* Ed. George Mora with Benjamin G. Kohl, Erik Midelfort, and Helen Bacon. Trans. John Shea. Binghamton, N.Y.: Medieval and Renaissance Texts and Studies, 1991.

Wilson, Katharina M., ed. *Medieval Women Writers.* Athens, Ga.: University of Georgia Press, 1984.

———, ed. *Women Writers of the Renaissance and Reformation.* Athens, Ga.: University of Georgia Press, 1987.

Wilson, Katharina M., and Frank J. Warnke, eds. *Women Writers of the Seventeenth Century.* Athens, Ga.: University of Georgia Press, 1989.

Women Writers in English 1350–1805: 30 volumes projected, 8 published through 1995. Oxford: Oxford University Press.

SECONDARY SOURCES: THE MISOGYNIST TRADITION

Bloch, R. Howard. *Medieval Misogyny and the Invention of Western Romantic Love.* Chicago: University of Chicago Press, 1991.

Clark, Elizabeth A. *Ascetic Piety and Women's Faith: Essays on Late Ancient Christianity.* Lewiston, N.Y.: Edwin Mellen Press, 1986.

Dixon, Suzanne. *The Roman Family.* Baltimore: Johns Hopkins University Press, 1992.

Gardner, Jane F. *Women in Roman Law and Society.* Bloomington, Ind.: Indiana University Press, 1986.

Horowitz, Maryanne Cline. "Aristotle and Women." *Journal of the History of Biology* 9 (1976): 183–213.

Lerner, Gerda. *The Creation of Patriarchy.* New York: Oxford University Press, 1986.

Lochrie, Karma. *Margery Kempe and Translations of the Flesh*. Philadelphia: University of Pennsylvania Press, 1992.

Maclean, Ian. *The Renaissance Notion of Women: A Study of the Fortunes of Scholasticism and Medical Science in European Intellectual Life*. Cambridge: Cambridge University Press, 1980.

Okin, Susan Moller. *Women in Western Political Thought*. Princeton: Princeton University Press, 1979.

Pagels, Elaine. *Adam, Eve, and the Serpent*. New York: Harper Collins, 1988.

Pomeroy, Sarah B. *Goddesses, Whores, Wives, and Slaves: Women in Classical Antiquity*. New York: Schocken Books, 1976.

Sommerville, Margaret R. *Sex and Subjection: Attitudes to Women in Early-Modern Society*. London: Arnold, 1995.

Tetel, Marcel. *Marguerite de Navarre's Heptameron: Themes, Language, and Structure*. Durham, N.C.: Duke University Press, 1973.

Treggiari, Susan. *Roman Marriage: Iusti Coniuges from the Time of Cicero to the Time of Ulpian*. Oxford: Oxford University Press, 1991.

Walsh, William T. *St. Teresa of Avila: A Biography*. Rockford, Ill.: TAN Books and Publications, 1987.

Warner, Marina. *Alone of All Her Sex: The Myth and Cult of the Virgin Mary*. New York: Knopf, 1976.

SECONDARY SOURCES: THE OTHER VOICE

Beilin, Elaine V. *Redeeming Eve: Women Writers of the English Renaissance*. Princeton: Princeton University Press, 1987.

Bellis, Daniela de. "Arcangela Tarabotti and the Polemic on Luxury in Seventeenth-Century Venice." Trans. Anne Dunhill. In *Women in Italian Renaissance Culture and Society*. Ed. Letizia Panizza. Oxford: European Humanities Research Centre, 1998.

Benson, Pamela Joseph. *The Invention of Renaissance Woman: The Challenge of Female Independence in the Literature and Thought of Italy and England*. University Park, Penn.: Pennsylvania State University Press, 1992.

Brand, Peter, and Lino Pertile, eds. *The Cambridge History of Italian Literature*. Cambridge: Cambridge University Press, 1996.

Chemello, Adriana. "La donna, il modello, l'immaginario: Moderata Fonte e Lucrezia Marinella." In *Nel cerchio della luna*. Venice, 1983, 59–170.

———. "Lucrezia Marinella." In *Le Stanze ritrovate. Antologia di scrittrici venete dal quattrocento al novecento*. Ed. A. Arslan, A. Chemello, and G. Pizzamiglio. Mirano, 1991, 95–108.

———. "Il 'genere femminile' tesse la sua 'tela': Moderata Fonte e Lucrezia Marinelli." In *Miscellanea di studi*. Ed. Renata Cibin and Angiolina Ponziano. Venice, 1993, 85–107.

———. "The Rhetoric of Eulogy in Marinella's *La Nobiltà e l'Eccellenza delle Donne*." Trans. Anne Dunhill. In *Women in Italian Renaissance Culture and Society* (cited above).

Conti Odorisio, Ginevra. *Donna e società nel Seicento*. Rome, 1979.

Cox, Virginia. "The Single Self: Feminist Thought and the Marriage Market in Early Modern Venice." *Renaissance Quarterly* 48 (1995): 513–81.

Davis, Natalie Zemon. *Society and Culture in Early Modern France.* Stanford: Stanford University Press, 1975. Esp. chaps. 3 and 5.

Ferguson, Margaret W., Maureen Quilligan, and Nancy J. Vickers, eds. *Rewriting the Renaissance: The Discourses of Sexual Difference in Early Modern Europe.* Chicago: University of Chicago Press, 1987.

Frigo, Daniela. "Dal caos all' ordine: sulla questione del 'prender moglie' nella trattatistica del sedicesimo secolo," in *Women of Italian Renaissance Culture and Society.* Ed. Letizia Panizza. Oxford: European Humanities Research Centre, 1998.

Herlihy, David. "Did Women Have a Renaissance? A Reconsideration." *Medievalia et Humanistica,* NS 13 (1985): 1–22.

History of Women in the West, A. Vol. I (1992): *From Ancient Goddesses to Christian Saints.* Ed. Pauline Schmitt Pantel. Vol. 2 (1992): *Silences of the Middle Ages.* Ed. Christiane Klapisch-Zuber. Vol. 3 (1993): *Renaissance and Enlightenment Paradoxes.* Ed. Natalie Zemon Davis and Arlette Farge. Cambridge, Mass.: Harvard University Press.

Hull, Suzanne W. *Chaste, Silent, and Obedient: English Books for Women, 1475–1640.* San Marino, Calif.: Huntington Library, 1982.

Jordan, Constance. *Renaissance Feminism: Literary Texts and Political Models.* Ithaca: Cornell University Press, 1990.

Kelly, Joan. "Did Women Have a Renaissance?" In her *Women, History, and Theory.* Chicago: University of Chicago Press, 1984. Also in *Becoming Visible: Women in European History.* Eds. Renate Bridenthal, Claudia Koonz, and Susan M. Stuard. 2nd ed. Boston: Houghton Mifflin, 1987, 175–202.

———. "Early Feminist Theory and the *Querelle des Femmes.*" In her *Women, History, and Theory* (cited above).

Kelso, Ruth. *Doctrine for the Lady of the Renaissance.* Foreword by Katharine M. Rogers. Urbana, Ill.: University of Illinois Press, 1956, 1978.

King, Margaret L. *Women of the Renaissance.* Foreword by Catharine R. Stimpson. Chicago: University of Chicago Press, 1991.

Labalme, Patricia. "Venetian Women on Women; The Early Modern Feminists." *Studi veneziani* 5, no. 197 (1981):81–109.

Labalme, Patrica, ed. *Beyond Their Sex: Learned Women of the European Past.* New York: New York University Press, 1980.

Langlands, Rebecca. "Lucrezia Marinella's Feminism and the Authority of the Classics." M. Phil. Thesis, University of Cambridge, 1995.

Laqueur, Thomas. *Making Sex: Body and Gender from the Greeks to Freud.* Cambridge, Mass.: Harvard University Press, 1990.

Lerner, Gerda. *Creation of Feminist Consciousness, 1000–1870.* New York: Oxford University Press, 1994.

Maclean, Ian. *Woman Triumphant: Feminism in French Literature, 1610–1652.* Oxford: Clarendon Press, 1977.

Malpezzi Price, Paola. "Lucrezia Marinella." In *Italian Women Writers.* Ed. Rinaldina Russell. Westport, Conn., 1994.

Matter, E. Ann, and John Coakley, eds. *Creative Women in Medieval and Early Modern Italy.* Philadelphia: University of Pennsylvania Press, 1994. (Sequel to the Monson collection, immediately below.)

Monson, Craig A., ed. *The Crannied Wall: Women, Religion, and the Arts in Early Modern Europe.* Ann Arbor: University of Michigan Press, 1992.

Rabitti, Giovanna. "Vittoria Colonna as Role-Model of Later Cinquecento Women Poets," in *Women in Italian Renaissance Culture and Society.* Ed. Letizia Panizza. Oxford: European Humanities Research Centre, 1998.

Richardson, Brian. "'Amore maritale': Advice on Love and Marriage in the Second Half of the Cinquecento," in *Women in Italian Renaissance Culture and Society.* Ed. Letizia Panizza. Oxford: European Humanities Research Centre, 1998.

Rose, Mary Beth, ed. *Women in the Middle Ages and the Renaissance: Literary and Historical Perspectives.* Syracuse: Syracuse University Press, 1986.

Stuard, Susan M. "The Dominion of Gender: Women's Fortunes in the High Middle Ages." In *Becoming Visible: Women in European History* (cited above), 153–72.

Tassini, G. *Curiosità veneziane.* Venice, 1915.

Tiraboschi, G. *Biblioteca modenese.* Modena, 1783.

Wiesner, Merry E. *Women and Gender in Early Modern Europe.* Cambridge: Cambridge University Press, 1993.

Willard, Charity Cannon. *Christine de Pizan: Her Life and Works.* New York: Persea Books, 1984.

Wilson, Katharina, ed. *An Encyclopedia of Continental Women Writers.* New York: Garland, 1991.

Zancan, Marina, ed. *Nel cerchio della luna. Figure di donne in alcuni testi del XVI secolo.* Venice: Marsilio Editore, 1983.

Zanette, E. *Suor Angelica monaca del Seicento veneziano.* Venice, 1960.

INDEX